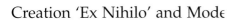

Creation 'Ex Nihilo' and Mode

Directions in Modern Theology Book Series

Born out of the journal *Modern Theology*, the Directions in Modern Theology book series provides issues focused on important theological topics and texts in current debate within that discipline, whilst looking at broader contemporary topics from a theological perspective. It analyses notions and thinkers, as well as examining a wide spectrum of 'modern' theological eras: from late Medieval through to the Enlightenment and up until the present 'postmodern' movements. Attracting distinguished theologians from a worldwide base, the book series develops what is a unique forum for international debate on theological concerns.

Titles in the series include:

Creation 'Ex Nihilo' and Modern Theology

Edited by
Janet Martin Soskice

WILEY Blackwell

Published as Volume 29, Issue 2 of *Modern Theology*
© 2013 Blackwell Publishing Ltd

Blackwell Publishing was acquired by John Wiley & Sons in February 2007. Blackwell's publishing program has been merged with Wiley's global Scientific, Technical, and Medical business to form Wiley-Blackwell.

Registered Office
John Wiley & Sons Ltd, The Atrium, Southern Gate, Chichester, West Sussex, PO19 8SQ, United Kingdom

Editorial Offices
350 Main Street, Malden, MA 02148-5020, USA
9600 Garsington Road, Oxford, OX4 2DQ, UK
The Atrium, Southern Gate, Chichester, West Sussex, PO19 8SQ, UK

For details of our global editorial offices, for customer services, and for information about how to apply for permission to reuse the copyright material in this book please see our website at www.wiley.com/wiley-blackwell.

Library of Congress Cataloging-in-Publication Data has been applied for.

ISBN 9781118705964
ISSN 0266 7177 (Print)
ISSN 1468 0025 (Online)

A catalogue record for this book is available from the British Library.

Cover design by Richard Boxall Design Associates.

Set in 10 on 12 pt Palantino by Toppan Best-set Premedia Limited

Printed in Singapore.

1   2013

Modern Theology

Volume 29 No. 2   April 2013

CONTENTS

Special issue
"Creation 'Ex Nihilo' and Modern Theology"
Guest Editor: Janet Martin Soskice

Articles

Modern Theology 29:2 April 2013
ISSN 0266-7177 (Print)
ISSN 1468-0025 (Online)

INTRODUCTION

JANET MARTIN SOSKICE

Confessing belief in God, "maker of heaven and earth," launches the ancient creeds of the Christian church but, at least in the classical formulation of *creatio ex nihilo*, is today somewhat neglected.

The precipitate cause of this volume was another one, *Creation and the God of Abraham*, edited by Carlo Cogliati, David Burrell, Janet Soskice and William Stoeger (Cambridge: Cambridge University Press, 2010). This was the product of a conference on *creatio ex nihilo* at the Vatican Observatory involving scientists, philosophers and theologians from the three Abrahamic faiths. *Creatio ex nihilo* is a uniting confession for these traditions. It is also a notion that has been ignored or occasionally attacked in recent Christian theology as having little to say to our current circumstances. Yet it undergirds so much of what Christians have wanted to say about prayer, providence, beauty, divine presence, freedom and grace. The purpose of this collection is to re-examine the doctrine with its theological implications in mind. Contributors were told of the 2010 volume but not asked necessarily to respond to it.

David Burrell's article brings us up to date, both with some of the reasons for the current eclipse of the doctrine amongst philosophers of religion and with its historical anchorage. Burrell draws parallels with Islamic and even Hindu thought before returning us, via Aquinas, to Eckhart, John of the Cross and a sense of the wonder and intimacy of God.

Paul Gavrilyuk addresses the murkiness of the biblical origins of *creatio ex nihilo*, before leading us through pressures that resulted in the refinement of teaching, first in the second century CE, with Irenaeus and Gnosticism, and then in the controversies of the fourth century, pointing out that "It could be said that the council of Nicaea indirectly canonized the doctrine of creation out of nothing." Athanasius and others invoked the teaching to clarify the status of the Son, and to make firm the foundations of the doctrine of the Trinity.

Janet Martin Soskice
Jesus College, Cambridge, CB5 8BL UK
Email: jcs16@cam.ac.uk

Virginia Burrus gently delineates a view more critical of *creatio ex nihilo* (and Athanasius), looking to antique discussions of the Many and the One, and then to Franz Rosenzweig's idiosyncratic, but illuminating, discussion of the *nihil* in the *Star of Redemption*. Creation is for Rosenzweig an "ever-renewing present", a "constantly brimming-over newness".

No volume on *creatio ex nihilo* would approach completeness without serious attention paid to Aquinas. The doctrine, informed by Muslim sources and the writings of Moses Maimonides, is the linchpin of Thomas's mature theology. Rudi te Velde takes us into Thomas's sometimes baffling account of primary and secondary causes by means of a question that will be of relevance to most readers: why do we pray? "What I particularly want to show in this article," says te Velde, "is that Thomas's discussion of prayer makes clear that his notion of God is not like the absolute monarch of the *ancien régime*, but "a God of participation, of letting other things share, from His own abundance, in being and in goodness."

Continuing with this theme but moving to the literary register, Vittorio Montegmaggi suggests that an inextricable relationship of contemplation, charity and *creatio ex nihilo* underlies the very form of Dante's *Commedia*. Creation in the *Commedia*, and explained to the Christian Dante by the pagan Virgil, is a work of divine love. It is this which discloses to us the beauty of the world and other people: "Contemplating God does not come at the expense of that which is other than God, with full awareness of how all that exists finds its meaning in God. . . ."

Luther is not usually thought of in connection with *creatio ex nihilo* but in a bold new reading Jon Mackenzie suggests that the teaching is determinative of Luther's last great work, his Genesis commentary. Mackenzie argues that in this work Luther realised the correspondence between his concept of place (important since his early *theologia crucis*), and the doctrine of creation. "Within the pages of the *Genesisvorlesung*," writes Mackenzie, "there is no aspect of God's dealing with creation which takes place outside of the event of *creatio ex nihilo*". This has important implications for Luther's account of the human subject which, "circumscribed by the *nihil* of creation, takes on a different manifestation from the self-subsistent subject of modernity" that Luther is often credited with foisting on the world. Instead Luther's subject bears interesting parallels with the "empty" subject of Žižek, Badiou, and others.

Andreas Nordlander takes us further into the phenomenological tradition and continues with the philosophy of place in an insightful exploration of Merleau-Ponty's "ontology of the flesh". He begins by outlining what is, for most of us in modernity, the keenly felt desire for a philosophy of the concrete and embodied life, here and now—a philosophy of immanence. Merleau-Ponty was amongst those who felt that the price to pay for this was divine transcendence, that "immanence and transcendence stood according to a contrastive logic". Yet Nordlander argues that the philosopher's "enchanted naturalism" was in fact deeply congruent with the Christian understanding of creation, both preserving the wonder of immanence.

"Creation, according to Jews, Christians, and Muslims, should be understood as a *free* intentional act, rather than according to a scheme of necessary emanation", John Hughes suggests. "Yet this leaves the question of how this divine freedom should best be imagined." Hughes explores this question through the lens of Sergei Bulgakov's critique of Aquinas on *creatio ex nihilo* with special attention to the challenging topic of the "divine ideas": "For Aquinas, the divine ideas are clearly not some hangover from Platonic demiurgic or emanationist schemes of creation; but rather, understood according to the logic of the Trinity, are crucial to understanding creation as truly free and personal rather than proceeding from natural necessity, but also as in accordance with the intrinsic order of divine goodness . . ."

A number of the contributors to this volume draw on Kathryn Tanner's illuminating *God and Creation in Christian Theology* (Oxford: Basil Blackwell, 1989), especially her critique of contrastive logic, so it is especially pleasing to have her article on *creatio ex nihilo* as "mixed metaphor". This doctrine is closely linked, she argues, both historically and logically, with divine transcendence. In an elegant and concise survey she takes us, via Spinoza and the early Platonists, through developments in the early church, underscoring the way in which *creatio ex nihilo* means one need not resign oneself to a fixed and disappointing world but rather can "entertain extravagant hopes for a genuinely novel future good for the world as a whole. . . ." It is a loss of a proper sense of transcendence, and one which mixes both natural and personalistic metaphors when speaking of creation, that is in great part responsible for the dualistic alternation, well known in modern theology, "between a deistic, interventionist God and pan(en)theism so common in modern Christian thought."

"Christian teaching about the creation of the world out of nothing" says John Webster "is a cardinal doctrine: on this hinge turn all the elements of the second topic of Christian theology, which treats all things with reference to God their beginning and end, the first topic being God's immanent life." Because of this, *creatio ex nihilo* is also a "distributed doctrine", cropping up in many places across Christian treatments of the divine economy. The doctrine of creation is reflected in what we think of as providence and reconciliation "in which the work of creation has its *terminus ad quem* (a point given its most extensive modern exposition in Barth's ordering of creation to covenant). Equally, however, beliefs about providence and reconciliation only make full sense when we attend to their *terminus a quo*, that is, when we bear in mind that the protagonists in the economy are the creator and his creatures, and that all being and occurrence that is not God is to its very depths *ex nihilo*." After charting some of the main principles of creation out of nothing, he turns to the matter of creaturely worth. "That absolute creatureliness should be such a good thing is no longer self-evident to us", says Webster, but why? At "what point in the history of theological, metaphysical and moral-political thought have exponents or critics of Christian doctrine . . . missed the rhythm of teaching about creation out of nothing, lost heart about its fruitfulness or wholesomenesss . . . ? In what ways and with what results has an evangelical metaphysics of creation been replaced by one owing no allegiance to the gospels?" Webster suggests that the fear that creation out of nothing "entails creaturely ignominy is both a cultural-historical condition and a spiritual malaise. . . ." The idea that must be broken is that of God as a "supremely forceful agent in the same order of being as creatures, acting upon them and so depriving them of movement." Rather, as Aquinas and Barth both suggest, "God's perfection is seen also in bringing into being other agents."

Janet Soskice's article also speaks in praise of the dignity of creatures. Arguing for a foundation of the nascent doctrine of *creatio ex nihilo* in the Psalms and inter-testamental scriptures, she points to the distinctiveness of the Jewish and Christian understanding of the Creator God and its revolutionary entrance into the bloodstream of western metaphysics. She argues for a qualification on the over-emphasis, when speaking of the historical origins of the doctrine, on the creation of matter. Wider principles of divine freedom and transcendence are at work, as can be seen in the writings of Philo of Alexandria. The association, based not on Greek philosophy but on Middle Platonic readings of the book of Exodus, of God as Being itself and the source of all being, underscores the Christian theology of participation. In this creatures are not diminished but made—gloriously—truly themselves.

I hope there will be something of use or even delight for everyone in this volume. It remains for me to thank the contributors and express gratitude for the patient oversight of William Cavanaugh and Jim Fodor. Finally, it happens that this volume will appear just around the 80th birthday of David Burrell, and I would like to express my gratitude to him for his work over the years, a gratitude that will be echoed by Muslim, Jewish and Christian thinkers around the world, as well as by the contributors to this volume.

Modern Theology 29:2 April 2013
ISSN 0266-7177 (Print)
ISSN 1468-0025 (Online)

CREATIO EX NIHILO RECOVERED

DAVID B. BURRELL, C.S.C.

Traditions need always to be recovered, it seems, as fresh perspectives emerge to make traditional inquiries relevant, while critical reflection unveils obstacles that have helped deny us access to those very resources. Modernity found it necessary to render *creatio ex nihilo* obsolete. Kant's strictures reinforced the predilections of scientific inquirers to relegate any discourse about origins of the universe beyond the pale of responsible thought. We shall see, moreover, that the very categories which philosophers of religion used to characterize the relation between a putative creator and created things proved unfit for the task, since they *ipso facto* presumed both creator and creatures to be part of the universe. Let me offer a story to illustrate this oxymoronic situation endemic to modern thought about these matters.

Philosophical Obstacles and Genealogy of Eclipses

Regularly teaching a course in ancient and medieval philosophy has led me to identify the difference between these two periods quite clearly: the presence of a free creator is all important to medievals and almost entirely neglected among the ancients. Jewish, Christian, and Muslim thinkers converged in their efforts to find place for a free creator in the apparently seamless Hellenic philosophy they inherited. (The observation of the distinguished interpreter of Aquinas, Josef Pieper, that "creation is the hidden element in the philosophy of St. Thomas" should have alerted us decades ago to this operative difference from Aristotle, yet many Thomists managed to overlook it in their anxiety to demarcate philosophy from theology.[1]) Yet if we can say, schematically, that the presence of a free creator divides medieval

David B. Burrell, C.S.C.
Hesburgh Professor emeritus of Philosophy and Theology, University of Notre Dame, Notre Dame, IN 46556 USA
Email: David.B.Burrell.1@nd.edu

[1] Josef Pieper, *The Silence of St. Thomas: Three Essays* (New York, NY: Pantheon, 1957). "Negative element in the Philosophy of St. Thomas," pp. 47–67; Title re-issued: South Bend IN: St. Augustine's Press, 2002.

from ancient philosophy, what marks the subsequent transition to modern philosophy? Many things, of course, but to continue speaking schematically, modern philosophy wanted to distinguish itself by eliminating the theological overtones of the "scholastics," so proceeded by avoiding reference to a creator. The creator, however, is a bit large to overlook, so the gradual tendency was to deny its relevance. This was evidenced in Enlightenment fascination with "the Greeks," even though that phrase seemed more a construct than an historical reference. Aristotle, after all, had managed quite well without a creator. Now if that be the case—again, speaking quite schematically—we can characterize modern philosophy as "post-medieval," where the "post-" prefix carries a note of denial—in this case, of a creator, either directly or implicitly. A cursory look at the strategies whereby modern philosophers compensated for the absence of a creator, however, shows them to lead inescapably to foundational grounds, be they "self-evident" propositions or "sense-data" or whatever. Once these proved illusory, we cannot but enter a "post-modern" world. And if our presumptions regarding "philosophy" itself (à la Rorty) are inherently linked to such strategies, then we will inevitably regard a postmodern context as one in which "anything goes." So a singular result of this critique of the limitations endemic to the categories presumed by modern philosophy will suggest a benign and fruitful understanding of the ways "postmodernity" liberates us from the vain search for "foundations". Then we may be pointed towards a more flexible and subtle "foundation" in a free creator. But the very transcendence of a free creator can make modern philosophers nervous, leading them to find ways of eliminating "such an hypothesis". How else explain the paucity of reflection among current philosophers of religion regarding origination of the universe, even when these be Jews, Christians, or Muslims, whose traditions avow a free creator?[2]

Ironically, a movement on the part of the Catholic Church to direct philosophical fascination away from modern philosophy to Thomas Aquinas helped to confirm the modern insouciance regarding free creation. For the encyclical *Aeternae Patris* (1893) the unintended effect to present Aquinas as an alternative to Descartes focused on his philosophical acumen, effectively separating philosophical from theological reflection. Such an ethos was utterly foreign to the world of Aquinas, where a dialectical exchange between faith and reason spiced inquiry at all levels. In this new climate, however, philosophical argument had to "ground" the universe in a creator, thereby sidestepping the inherently theological cast of Aquinas' own treatment of creation in the *Summa Theologiae*, following directly upon his treatment of the triune God. Moreover, if philosophical argument will suffice to "ground" the

---

[2] For current reflections from these traditions, see Carlo Cogliati, Janet M. Soskice, and William R. Stoeger, eds., *Creation and the God of Abraham* (Cambridge: Cambridge University Press, 2010).

universe in a creator, that creator can hardly be free. The argument will have to assume some form of *emanation* modelled on logical deduction, whereby the initial premise cannot adequately be distinguished from what emanates from it. So the source cannot be the free creator espoused by Jews, Christians, and Muslims for their respective revelations. Fortunately, Josef Pieper's insistence that "the hidden element in the *philosophy* of St. Thomas is creation," by which he meant free creation as offered in revelation, leads us away from preoccupation with purely "philosophical" approaches to a dialectical interchange between faith and reason. This directs us to realize the centrality of revelation to Aquinas as well as to his Muslim and Jewish interlocutors, Avicenna and Moses Maimonides.[3]

Paths to Recovering Creatio Ex Nihilo *with Its Implications*

Aquinas' capacity to integrate philosophical with theological demands is displayed in the initial article in the *Summa Theologiae* on creation: "Must everything that is have been caused by God?"[4] Relying on his identification of God as that One whose very essence is to exist, Aquinas shows why one must "necessarily say that whatever in any way *is* is from God". For if "God is sheer existence subsisting of its very nature (*ipsum esse per se subsistens*), [and so] must be unique, . . . then it follows that all things other than God are not their own existence but share in existence".[5] So the Neoplatonic distinction between *essential* and *participated* being is invoked to give everything but the creator the stamp of *created*. Very little, if anything, is said here about causation, but the elements are in place to press for a unique form of it, even though another way of posing the initial question employs Aristotle explicitly: "whether God is the efficient cause of all beings?"

An objection asks about those "natural necessities" which Aristotle presumed simply to be, or always to have been: "since there are many such in reality [—spiritual substances and heavenly bodies which carry no principle of dissolution within themselves—], all beings are not from God." Aquinas deftly diverts this objection by recalling the primacy of existing: "an active cause is required not simply because the effect could not be [i.e., is contingent], but because the effect would not be if the cause were not [existing]."[6] So even "necessary things" will require a cause for their very being. This is a radical revision of Aristotle, depending on the Avicennian distinction of *essence* from *existing*. What it suggests is that Aquinas was seeking a way

---

[3] For a narrative sketch of the interaction among these signal medieval protagonists, see my *Knowing the Unknowable God: Ibn-Sina, Maimonides, Aquinas* (Notre Dame, IN: University of Notre Dame Press, 1986), as well as *Freedom and Creation in Three Traditions* (Notre Dame, IN: University of Notre Dame Press, 1993).

[4] *ST*, I, 44,1.

[5] *ST*, I, 3, 4.

[6] *ST*, I, 44, 1, ad. 2.

of understanding created being using Aristotelian metaphysics, yet the "givens" of that philosophy will have to be transformed to meet the exigency of a free creator. Put another way, which anticipates our elucidation, the *being* which Aristotle took to characterize substance must become (for Aquinas) an *esse ad creatorem* (an existing in relation to the creator). This is another way of saying that "all things other than God are not their own existence", either in the radical sense of distinguishing creatures from the creator, or even in a more attenuated sense in which the being which they *have* cannot be "their own" in the sense of belonging to them "by right" or by virtue of their being the kind of things they are (which was Aristotle's view).

So everything other than God receives its being from the creator as a gift. Nonetheless such derived or participated things are no less real than Aristotle's substances, since for Aquinas there is no other way to be except to participate in the *ipsum esse* of the creator. Indeed, the nature of the creating act depends crucially on our conception of the One from whom all that is comes while the philosophical analogue of the creating act is expressed in the distinction between *essence* and *existing*. Wrangling among philosophical schools regarding the valence of this celebrated distinction is attenuated once we appreciate its effective origin in the interaction between reason and revelation, operative in each of the Abrahamic traditions.

We have suggested how the dialectic internal to faith and reason, evident as they operate together to negotiate an issue so elusive as free creation, can offer some illumination of the ineffable relation of creatures to creator, that must elude causal categories developed to display relations among things in the world. As with creation itself, where the three Abrahamic traditions sought illumination from Hellenic philosophy to articulate an activity at the margin of that philosophy, the ensuing relation of creatures to creator will duly tax our philosophical skills. I have found Sara Grant a fruitful guide into this recondite domain, in the slim volume of Teape lectures: *Towards an Alternative Theology: Confessions of a Non-dualist Christian.*[7] From the perspective of a student of Shankara and animator of an ashram in Pune, India, she reminds us:

> In India as in Greece, the ultimate question must always be that of the relation between the supreme unchanging Reality and the world of coming-to-be and passing away, the eternal Self and what appears as non-Self, and no epistemology can stand secure as long as this question remains unanswered. [It is indeed this startling contention which this essay has been exploring.] . . . A systematic study of Sankara's use of relational terms made it quite clear to me that he agrees with St. Thomas Aquinas in regarding the relation between creation and the ultimate

---

[7] Sara Grant, *Towards an Alternative Theology: Confessions of a Non-dualist Christian* (Notre Dame, IN: University of Notre Dame Press, 2001).

Source of all being as a *non-reciprocal dependence relation*; i.e., a relation in which subsistent effect or 'relative absolute' is *dependent on its cause for its very existence as a subsistent entity*, whereas the cause is *in no way dependent on the effect for its subsistence*.

So the very existence (*esse*) of a creature is an *esse-ad*, an existing which is itself a relation to its source. Nothing could better express the way in which Aquinas' formulation of the essence/existing distinction transforms Aristotle than to point out that what for Aristotle "exists in itself" (substance) is for Aquinas derived from an Other in its very in-itselfness, or substantiality. Yet since the Other is the cause of being, each thing which exists-to the creator also exists in itself. Derived existence is no less substantial when it is derived from the One-who-is, so it would appear that one could succeed in talking of existing things without explicitly referring them to their source. "The distinction", in other words, need not *appear*. But that simply reminds us how unique a non-reciprocal relation of dependence must be: it characterizes one relation only, that of creatures to creator.

If creator and creature were distinct from each other in an ordinary way, the relation—even one of dependence—could not be non-reciprocal. Ordinarily the fact that something depends from an originating agent, as a child from a parent, must mark a difference in that agent itself. Yet the fact that a cause of being, properly speaking, is not affected by causing all-that-is does not imply remoteness or uncaring; indeed, quite the opposite. For such a One must cause in such a way as to be present in each creature as that to which it is oriented in its very existing. In that sense, this One cannot be considered as *other* than what it creates, in an ordinary sense of that term; just as the creature's *esse-ad* assures that it cannot *be* separately from its source. So it will not work simply to contrast creation to emanation, or to picture the creator distinct (in the ordinary sense) from creation by contrast with a more pantheistic image. Indeed, it is to avoid such infelicities of imagination that Sara Grant has recourse to Sankara's sophisticated notion of "non-duality" to call our attention in an arresting way to the utter uniqueness of "the distinction", which Robert Sokolowski shows must hold between creator and creation, yet cannot be pictured in a contrastive manner.[8] Nor does Aquinas feel any compunction at defining creation as the "emanation of all of being from its universal cause (*emanatio totius entis a cause universali*)".[9] Indeed, once he had emptied the emanation scheme of any mediating role, he could find no better way of marking the uniqueness of the causal relation of creation than using

---

[8] See Robert Sokolowski, *God of Faith and Reason* (Washington, DC: Catholic University of America Press, 1995); from a cognate perspective, Kathryn Tanner develops a sense of transcendence that is expressly "non-contrastive", illustrating that suggestive category though the history of some key questions in philosophical theology, in her *God and Creation in Christian Theology* (Oxford: Basil Blackwell, 1988).

[9] *ST*, I, 45, 1.

the term "emanation" to articulate it. For once the scheme has been gutted, that *sui generis* descriptor should serve to divert us from imaging the creator over-against the universe, as an entity exercising causal efficacy on anything-that-is in a manner parallel to causation within the universe. While the all-important "distinction" preserves God's freedom in creating, which the emanation scheme invariably finesses, we must nevertheless be wary of picturing that distinction in a fashion which assimilates the creator to another item within the universe. Harm Goris has shown how close attention to the uniqueness of the creator/creature relation, with its attendant corollary of participation as a way of articulating this *sui generis* causal relation, can neutralize many of the conundrums which can continue to fascinate philosophers of religion.[10]

Faith and Reason in Dialectical Interchange

While invoking Shakara's hybrid term of "non-duality," might seem to have distanced us from Aquinas, we should have realized by now how Aquinas helps himself to various ways of expressing the inexpressible: the "distinction" as well as the "relation" between creatures and their creator. Both prove to be foundational to any attempt to grasp our transcendent origins as gift. Bible and Qur'an conspire to highlight the creator's freedom; philosophy proves helpful in finding ways to think both creature and creator together.

Another mutually illuminating perspective on "the distinction," as well as the "ineffable relation" between creatures and creator, can be found in comparing Meister Eckhart with Ibn 'Arabi, after the penetrating study of Robert Dobie.[11] This inquiry proposes and sustains the thesis that both Ibn 'Arabi and Eckhart were steeped in their respective revelational traditions, and from that vantage point engaged in a mode of philosophical theology using reason to order and clarify the revelational sources. They also used those sources to expand standard philosophical categories to negotiate the known perils of discourse regarding divinity. Each of these thinkers, moreover, while working in disparate traditions, proceeded dialectically to allow reason and revelation to illuminate each other fruitfully. They accomplished this in four areas: revelation itself, existence, intellect, and the ideal human paradigm, in a way that allows each tradition to illuminate the other, yet never eliding difference, especially where difference itself may further illuminate the comparative inquiry.

But let us first position the respective authors. Ibn 'Arabi represents what I like to call the "second phase" of Islamic philosophy, whereby the center of

---

[10] Harm Goris, *Free Creatures of an Eternal God* (Leuven: Peeters, 1996).
[11] Robert J. Dobie, *Logos and Revelation: Ibn Arabi, Meister Eckhart, and Mystical Hermeneutics* (Washington DC: Catholic University America Press, 2010).

gravity returned east from Andalusia, while a fresh set of protagonists sought ways to relate revelation with reason rather than contrasting one to another.[12] That would explain why students of philosophy in the west might not recognize Ibn 'Arabi as a philosopher, habituated as they have become to the story that al-Ghazali's critique of Averroës effectively terminated any hope of philosophical inquiry in Islam. That judgment reflects modernist assessments of properly philosophical inquiry, however, rather than attending to the contours of philosophical theology in the wider Muslim world, comprising Shi'ite as well as Sunni perspectives. On a reading more sensitive to its original context, al-Ghazali's critique represents a dialectical moment in Islamic philosophical inquiry rather than ending it, much as recent scholarship finds Averroës to be less a "rationalist" than one seeking ways to reconcile faith with reason.[13] A trio of eastern thinkers form the vanguard of this "second phase" of Islamic philosophy, introducing a properly philosophical theology: Suhrawardi, Ibn 'Arabi, and Mulla Sadra.[14] The secondary sources cited converge to help readers discover the philosophical acumen of Ibn 'Arabi. Often dubbed a "mystic" (or even a "pantheist"), his work is better appreciated when read as a sustained attempt to articulate what Robert Sokolowski has identified as the crucial "distinction" between creator and creatures in a universe founded on free creation.

Now we begin to suspect why Dobie sought to compare Ibn 'Arabi with Meister Eckhart, who has been saddled with similar incomprehension. Yet applying the Sokolowski test allows us to capture Eckhart's intent as well: to show how a focus on Aquinas' masterful account of creation as "the emanation of all of being from the universal cause of being"—existence itself [*ipsum esse*]—culminates in a "distinction" which eludes proper articulation, since creator and creatures can never be "two" as two creatures are. Let us take their respective treatments of *existence*, which Aquinas introduces as the only "feature" common to creatures and creator, precisely because it cannot properly be a *feature*: "only in so far as things are beings can they be similar to God, as the first and universal principle of all existence [*esse*] (ST 1.4.3), yet ineradicably dissimilar once we recognize that "God alone is being essentially, while all other beings are so by participation" (1.4.3.3). In employing the Platonic

---

[12] See my "Islamic Philosophical Theology and the West," *Islamochristiana*, Vol.33 (2007), pp. 75–90, amplified in "Journey to Mulla Sadra: Islamic Philosophy II," *Journal of Islamic Studies*, Vol. 3 (2010), pp. 44–64.

[13] Avital Wohlman: *Al-Ghazali, Averroes and the Interpretation of the Qur'an: Common Sense and Philosophy in Islam* (London: Routledge, 2009).

[14] For leads to them, see Oliver Leaman and Sayyed Hossain Nasr, eds., *History of Islamic Philosophy* (New York, NY: Routledge, 1996). For Ibn 'Arabi, the most comprehensive treatment can be found William Chittick's trilogy: *The Sufi Path of Knowledge: Ibn al-'Arabī's Metaphysics of Imagination* (1989); *The Self-Disclosure of God: Principles of Ibn al-'Arabī's Cosmology* (1997); and *Imaginal Worlds: Ibn al-'Arabī and the Problem of Religious Diversity* (1995); but see also Salman Bashier, *Ibn al-'Arabī's Barzakh: Concept of the Limit and the Relationship between God and the World* (2004)—all Albany NY: State University of New York Press.

scheme of *essentially/by participation*, Aquinas introduces what Sokolowski will dub "the distinction." As Dobie puts it, comparatively:

> What is important to appreciate in Ibn 'Arabi and Eckhart is the logical rigor or necessity of this understanding of God's nature as dialectical. The absolute transcendence of God necessarily demands his immanence in all things, for what makes God transcendent is God's existence and sustenance of all that is. Likewise, God's true and utter immanence implies transcendence because what is inmost in all things is precisely that which escapes limitation and objectification into a "this" or a "that." Again the logic here is clear: as Ibn 'Arabi puts it, to assert only the transcendence of God without his immanence is, in effect, to limit him, because you are marking him off from creatures. And to assert his immanence without asserting his transcendence is to limit him to the sum of finite creatures. Similarly for Eckhart, God's distinction from creatures, his transcendence, lies precisely in his *indistinction* from all things, i.e., in his immanence in all things as their existence, oneness, truth, and goodness—in short, the transcendental properties that "run through" all the categories of existence and that all creatures have insofar as they exist (p. 95).

This shows why Sokolowski identifies "the distinction" as lying "at the intersection of faith and reason."

Let us explore another of Dobie's four areas, that of revelation. Here especially the very differences will prove illuminating. Ibn 'Arabi's great commentator, Dawud al-Qaysari, notes how, in effect:

> The meaning of revelation is found in the faculty of imagination, the ability to strike similitudes for what transcends reason (p. 27) . . . Thus, in a proper hermeneutics of the Qur'an, understanding is becoming what one ultimately is in the real; . . . uncovering what the divine Word means *for me and my life*, which is to say what it means for me insofar as I exist only in and through God and am what I am in God. It follows that, for Ibn 'Arabi, the imagery of the Qur'an is not a drawback for the rational seeker but an advantage, for through the "imaginal world" (i.e., the interlocking symbolic logic) of the Qur'an and the Prophet (in the *hadith* traditions), the inner meaning of creation manifests itself in and through a creative appropriation of that imaginal world by the believer (p. 28). [Here lies a clear point of contrast between "first" and "second" phases of Islamic philosophy.] To recognize creation as an act of divine imagination, then, is to recognize, to be sure, the ambiguity of creation. But it is also to see all creation as rooted in the divine reality (p. 34). . . . . The Qur'an provides the key: . . . creation as an act of imagination is crucial to understanding the relation between the "book of nature" and the

"divine book of revelation" (p. 40). . . . It is in the Qur'an that the voyage is made that leads man back to his original status, to his divine similitude (p. 54). . . . The goal is the complete assimilation of the self to the Word of God as revealed in the Qur'an (p. 55).

Fascinating for both its similarity and its difference is the way "the birth of the Son in the soul . . ." is central to Eckhart's interpretation of scripture:

all interpretive activity aims at cracking the "outer shell" of the text to reveal its "hidden marrow," which is precisely the process of inner birth. Eckhart thus argues that the Christian life is not one of mere rational assent to the divine Word of Scripture but an actual giving birth to this Word in the innermost ground of the soul, which then bears fruit in a life of detached freedom and love (p. 59).

Yet "human reason is structurally unable to grasp God's oneness or the oneness of creation's source," so

the only way to overcome this alienating effect of reason is to present reason's truths under the cover of parables or myths, so that it will stimulate the hearer to the activity of interpretation and thus to an inward penetration of the divine mystery and the indwelling of transcendent truth (p. 65).

This comparison leads Dobie to delineate "the difference in the ways in which Ibn 'Arabi and Eckhart interpret their respective scriptures," which follows the different contours of their respective religious traditions:

for Eckhart, it is to have the Word of Scripture reborn in the very ground of a fallen and corrupted soul so that the soul may become a true Nobleman [*edele Mensch*]; for Ibn 'Arabi, it is to understand the inner meaning of the Law or *sharî'a* that restores the Muslim to the state of perfect vice-regency as the Universal Man [*al-insân al-kâmîl*], which is itself a return to the pure, original nature of humanity [*fitra*] in which the human being was a perfect mirror of God's essential attributes (p. 88).

These quotations are offered to give a flavor of Dobie's approach to and mastery of each figure. He has a special way of combining interpretive skills with stunning theological and philosophical sophistication, with remarkable clarity of expression. Finally, his manner of comparing Islamic with Christian philosophical theology highlights the crucial parallel between the Qur'an and Jesus: where Christians believe that Jesus is the word of God made human, Muslims believe the Qur'an is the Word of God made book [Arabic]. Since this strictly parallel presentation displays substantial differences as well, it allows him to offer a sustained argument against context-less approaches to "mystical" literature, which he counters in the work itself by grounding each author's substantive philosophical reflection in their respective revelational traditions.

More Specifically Theological and Spiritual Dimensions of Creatio Ex Nihilo

While our focus on the dialectical exchange between faith and reason, notably in the Abrahamic traditions, has primarily featured its philosophical dimensions, recent recovery of Aquinas also reveals a specifically Christian and theological approach. Once we appreciate how radical is the act of faith in a free creator, then it becomes clear that we cannot *be* separate from God. Moreover, we will fail to understand that corollary of free creation—perhaps even mistake it for "pantheism"—if we have not seen how the unique character of the *relation* called "creation" also demands that we learn how to think the creator *not* as an item in the universe, but as its One free creator. Yet engaging in that mode of thinking, which Kathryn Tanner dubs "non-contrastive", will also demand that we appreciate how to employ language analogously. So proficiency in philosophical theology will require poetic sensibility as well, since all analogous speech—whether used of divinity or used to evaluate human situations, as in ethical discourse—will invariably display a touch of metaphor.[15] For employing and grasping metaphors elicits an acute awareness of the tension between our perspective and the one we are endeavoring to elucidate—a tension which God-talk should exacerbate and which is ever in evidence in Aquinas, as Robert Barron's *Thomas Aquinas: Spiritual Master* shows so well, and as Olivier-Thomas Venard, O.P. shows by comparing Aquinas' lapidary forms of expression in the *Summa Theologiae* to Rimbaud's poetry (*Litterature*).[16]

All of this culminates in the realization that "relating to God", as in "praying to God", should take no effort, as there can be no "gap" to be bridged. For if our very being is a "being to the creator", then the interior path to one's own self will lead us invariably to the One who sustains us in existence. There will of course be many obstacles blocking the way to one's own self, as we know very well and as John of the Cross will abundantly delineate, but there can be no "distance" from that created self to its creator. At this point it may help to supplement the theorems we have seen Aquinas employ with those of two distinctive followers of his: Meister Eckhart (1260–1329) and John of the Cross (1542–91). For once Aquinas' task had shown how "sacred teaching" [*sacra doctrina*] could be a mode of knowing [*scientia*], Meister Eckhart felt free to focus on the singularity of the relationship

---

[15] See my *Analogy and Philosophical Language* (New Haven, CT: Yale University Press, 1973).
[16] Robert Barron, *Thomas Aquinas: Spiritual Master* (New York, NY: Crossroad, 1996); Olivier-Thomas Venard, O.P., *Littérature et Théologie: Une saison en enfer* (Genève: Ad Solem, 2002).

between creatures and the creator. And if Aquinas exemplifies the dialectic between faith and reason in appropriating Hellenic philosophy in a manner informed by faith, John of the Cross will amplify Aquinas' suggestive remarks about faith itself to show how it alone can be the proper way by which human beings can activate that *sui generis* relation which is their very "being to the creator".

First to John of the Cross, who is disarmingly forthright in enunciating the goal of the dynamic of faith which activates that grounding relation as: "the union and transformation of the [person] in God".[17] The power leading to that goal is "faith alone, which is the only proximate and proportionate means to union with God" (*Ascent* 2.9.1). He is at pains to distinguish this intentional union from the "union between God and creatures [which] always exists [by which] God sustains every soul and dwells in it substantially.... By it He conserves their being so that if the union would end they would immediately be annihilated and cease to exist" (*Ascent* 2.5.3). In this way, John will presume the unique metaphysical relation of all creatures to their source, which Meister Eckhart elaborates from Aquinas' grounding "distinction", while identifying it as a *union* in persons of faith—indeed, an "essential or substantial union". This grounding fact attends all creatures, hence it is *natural* and found in everything (though displayed differently in animate from inanimate, and in animate, differing from animals to humans, though among humans it can still be found in "the greatest sinner in the world"), while the intentional union is *supernatural* and can only be found "where there is a likeness of love [such that] God's will and the [person's] are in conformity" (*Ascent* 2.5.3). What eliminates any prospect of "heteronomy" between those two wills is precisely this "non-reciprocal relation of dependence" (Sara Grant) as the very being of all creatures.

But let us attend first to the internal connection between *faith* and *union* which John confidently asserts. What makes this sound so startling is our propensity to confine such talk to "mystics" while reducing faith to belief: holding certain propositions to be true. Yet John is simply elaborating some key assertions of Aquinas to cut through the debates which by his time had come to polarize intellect and will in the act of faith. His assertions in the *Living Flame of Love* are bold:

> This flame of love is the Spirit of the Bridegroom, which is the Holy Spirit.
> ... Such is the activity of the Holy Spirit in the soul transformed in love:
> the interior acts He produces shoot up flames for they are acts of
> inflamed love, in which the will of the soul united with that flame, made
> one with it, loves most sublimely.... Thus in this state the soul cannot
> make acts because the Holy Spirit makes them all and moves it towards

---

[17] John of the Cross, *Collected Works*, translated by Kieran Kavanaugh and Otilio Rodriguez (Washington DC: Institute for Carmelite Studies, 1991), Ascent *of Mount Carmel*, 2.5.3.

them. As a result all the acts of the soul are divine, since the movement toward these acts and their execution stems from God. Hence it seems to a person that every time this flame shoots up, making him love with delight and divine quality, it is giving him eternal life, since it raises him up to the activity of God in God (pp. 580–581).[18]

There is no hint of "heteronomy" here, because John presumes that unique metaphysical relation of person ("soul") to its source, which Meister Eckhart had developed from Aquinas, and Sara Grant elaborated from Shankara.

A few texts will suggest how Meister Eckhart underscored the singularity of that relation which Aquinas identifies as constituting creatures' very existence: being related to their creator. These reflections of Meister Eckhart amplify Aquinas' characteristically lapidary expressions regarding the creator/creature relation, the valence of which has often been overlooked by commentators insufficiently sensitive to Aquinas' transformations of Aristotle to which we have called attention.

> Every created being is analogically ordered to God in existence, truth, and goodness. [But] analogates have nothing of the form, according to which they are analogically rooted in positive fashion, in themselves. Therefore every created being radically and positively possesses existence, life, and wisdom from and in God, not in itself as a created being. And thus, [commenting on Sirach 24:29], it always 'eats' as something produced and created, but it always hungers because it is always from another and not from itself. . . . According to our understanding of the truth of analogy, . . . the text "They that eat me shall yet hunger" is perfectly fitted to signify the truth of the analogy of all things to God himself. They eat because they are; they hunger because they are from another. . . . So he is inside all things in that he is existence, and thus every being feeds on him. He is also on the outside because he is above all and thus outside all. Therefore all things feed on him because he is totally within; they hunger for him because he is totally without.[19]

In a sermon on the Trinity he criticizes the

> crude and false picture [which many have in thinking that] the maker, the form, and the end in creatures along with God are two makers or efficient causes, two forms, two ends. That is crude, first, because no being can be counted alongside God. Existence and being, existence and nothing, and also a form and what informs it make up no number.

---

[18] John of the Cross, *Collected Works: Living Flame of Love.*
[19] *Meister Eckhart: Teacher and Preacher,* edited Bernard McGinn, (New York, NY: Paulist Press, 1986) pp. 178–179.

Existence is more intimate than any form [cf. *ST* 1a q8 a1] and is not a source of number. Second, because every being, every maker, every form, and every end that is conceived of outside or beyond existence, or that is numbered along with existence, is nothing—it is neither a being, nor a maker, nor a form, nor an end. This is because existence, that is, God, is within every being, every form and end, and conversely every being, form, and end is in existence itself. Indeed, every maker works through its existence, form informs through its existence, and every end moves through its existence—through nothing else (*Teacher*, p. 210).

These sample texts can suggest why western theologians might be wary of Meister Eckhart, since his rhetoric raises the spectre of "pantheism". Yet we can also see him underscoring the *sui generis* relation implicit in free creation as Aquinas elaborates it metaphysically, and as Sara Grant helps us to appreciate. A serendipitous corroboration of the intimate relation between the *processions* in the triune God and the emanation of all things from that same God—a final way of marking and celebrating the unique relation between creatures and creator—can already be found in a 1957 study by Per Erik Persson, published in English in 1970: *Sacra doctrina: Reason and Revelation in Aquinas*.[20] Building on the primacy of *existing* in Aquinas' account of creation, he links the ensuing special relation with the unprecedented presence of the triune God in Christ to all of creation:

> In Thomas' view the sovereign freedom of the Creator's act presupposes God's perfect life within the Trinity [which] is not only essential for a true understanding of creation, but indispensable . . . for an understanding of the redemption which is wrought through the incarnation of the Son and the gift of the Spirit (pp. 150–151).

Anticipating by a half century more recent appropriation of Aquinas' theological perspective on creation, this study is all the more remarkable for the prescient way it synthesizes his use of transformed philosophical tools to elucidate the interdependence of faith and reason in Aquinas.[21]

Exploring the Anthropological-Spiritual Fruit of Recovering the Dialectic of Faith and Reason in Creation

We may celebrate the implications of this view of creation for human flourishing by contrasting *trust* in creatures' non-competitive relation to their

---

[20] Per Erik Persson, *Sacra doctrina: Reason and Revelation in Aquinas* (Philadelphia, PA: Fortress Press/Oxford: Basil Blackwell, 1970).

[21] For a prime example of such recovery, see Gilles Emery, O.P., *The Trinity: An Introduction to Catholic Doctrine on the Trinity*, translated by Francesca Murphy (Washington DC: Catholic University of America Press, 2011).

creator with characteristic enlightenment emphasis on *autonomy*, which we have seen was introduced in a period in which *creatio ex nihilo* was nearly totally eclipsed. Joseph Godfrey has extensively explored the central role which *trust* plays in any inquiry, asking: if *trust* is ubiquitous, why is it so little appreciated, often until too late in a person's life? My own suspicion is that we children of the enlightenment have been instructed early on to cut our ties with an enveloping context which might lead us to trust, in order to develop something called 'self-reliance', whatever that might be![22] And linked with that ethos is a potentially competitive picture of the creator/creature relation, exemplified in the touted "free will defence" dear to many current philosophers of religion. Brian Davies contrasts their modernist approach to that of Aquinas in his recent survey of "the problem of evil."[23] Underlying Aquinas' entire system, as that "which matters most to him," is his belief that God is the Creator (pp. 39, 43–44). Aquinas will insist upon "the total and absolute dependence of creatures on God" (p. 44), who is that which "accounts for the existence of the universe as a whole and at all times" (p. 43). The distinction Aquinas makes between God's existing (*esse*) and our existing (*esse-ad*) serves as the pivotal argument in his articulation of God as the Creator, for it rests not on necessity and contingency, but God's subsisting being itself (*ipsum esse subsistens*) (p. 42). The classical argument for God's existence, based upon a necessary existent to whom creatures' existence is contingent, can be traced to Avicenna and later to Suarez' revision of the medieval synthesis. Aquinas, however, considers this relation-to the Creator in a slightly different manner. For him, the distinction of necessary and contingent lies in God's created order of things, so the crucial distinction for Aquinas resides in *essence* and *existence*. For creatures, our essence and existence differ, but God as *ipsum esse subsistens* is the subsisting being itself, whose essence and existence are not distinct, but identical (p. 42). So God's creating *ex nihilo* will clarify Aquinas' position here regarding the relation between God and creatures. This alerts us to the relation between Creator and creatures, which is unlike any causal relation we know since God's causation in creating produces no change or motion or succession in time; rather it is instantaneous, like the burning of fire or the sun lighting up the atmosphere (p. 44 [ST 1.8.1]). What results is a non-competitive (or "non-contrastive") way of speaking of creator with creatures.[24]

Interestingly enough, some current philosophers of religion have found themselves drawn to such a picture, as Marilyn McCord Adams has, in canvassing modes of theodicy in her *Horrendous Evils*. After exposing how a

---

[22] See Joseph Godfrey, *Trust of People, Words, and God: A Route for Philosophy of Religion* (Notre Dame, IN: University of Notre Dame Press, 2012).

[23] Brian Davies, *Thomas Aquinas on God and Evil* (Oxford: Oxford University Press, 2011).

[24] I am indebted to my longtime student and friend, Mary Budde Ragan, for this summary of Davies.

set of strategies prevailing among current analytic philosophers of religion fail to meet their goals, she endeavors to offer an alternative of her own.[25] By showing how purported "solutions" to "the problem" can neatly bypass the fact of "horrendous evils," she displays how inane is their way of proceeding in the face of realities we can name. And once having rendered such discussions irrelevant, she uses richly metaphysical language to articulate the unique relation between the protagonists, creator and creatures, notably intentional creatures. She must do so because her brand of interlocutors invariably omit any such considerations, presuming "God" and "human being" to be two items to be related, each quite intelligible in its own right, rather than two which are already internally related as creator and creature. Indeed, one might speculate whether that fundamental oversight might have helped to spawn the enterprise of "theodicy," marking it as "modern." Yet once we follow the invitation of the scriptures, Bible or Qur'an, to identify God as creator, whatever we say *about* God will have to respect the distinctiveness of the creator/creature relation. In particular, this means that whenever God acts, God acts as creator or conserver, where these two names identify one mode of acting, differing from each other only notionally: the action of conserving presupposes creation, while creating presupposes nothing at all. Invoking this rule at once renders all talk of the creator "intervening" inappropriate, as well as neutralizes debates over "compatibilism" or "determinism," since the first term presumes two agents operating within the same field of force, while the second presumes that the causality in question is intramundane. Yet it must be emphasized that we are directed to this rich metaphysical mode of reflection by the scriptures themselves, thereby reminding all who would explore this domain that they cannot be less than philosophical theologians. McCord Adams concludes her extended essay by reminding us that her "strategy for dealing with horrendous evils carries the corollary consequence of blurring the boundary between philosophy and theology" (p. 206).[26] We have noted how Josef Pieper did the same for Thomists some fifty years ago, by identifying the "hidden element in the philosophy of Aquinas as creation." In the world of Catholic academe, however, neo-Thomist institutional separation of philosophical from theological reflection was so firmly established and enforced that it has taken that same period for studies in Aquinas to celebrate his instinctive and pervasive indifference to the boundaries modernity later imposed. So we should no longer be surprised to find scripture demanding philosophical clarifications to display its own coherence, or philosophers turning to scripture to illuminate their way of proceeding in these arcane arenas. Moreover, once they

---

[25] Marilyn McCord Adams, *Horrendous Evils and the Goodness of God* (Ithaca NY: Cornell Unviersity Press, 1999).

[26] See my "Theology and Philosophy" in Gareth Jones, ed., *Blackwell Companion to Modern Theology* (Oxford: Blackwell, 2004), pp. 34–46.

make that "scriptural turn," they will also be led to deconstruct some other ways of proceeding to which philosophers had become accustomed. That represents the patent subtext of McCord Adams' reflections, as well as the avowed goal of our reflection here.

Paul Griffiths invokes *participation* to exhibit a growing tendency among philosophers of religion, in his *Intellectual Appetite*, to acknowledge the operative sense faith can give us of ourselves.[27]

> A Christian understanding of creatures as *imagines dei*, especially inti-mate participants in divine gift, is different in almost every interesting respect from an understanding of humans as autonomous beings pos-sessed of a rational will capable of universal species-wide legislation. And each is equally though differently different from an understanding of humans as desire-driven congeries of causally connected event-continua (p. 116).

What marks the principal difference from a Kantian morality or a materialist ideology, and the only thing that can, lies in realizing the implications of avowing the universe to be freely created by a loving God. The difference which Griffiths is intent on articulating finds primary expression in our characteristic ways of knowing:

> Thinking and speaking of creation as the gift of being from nothing, and of creatures as recipients of and participants in that gift, suggest some things to say about what it is for creatures to . . . perform the act of knowing. By definition, this act must establish a relation between knower and known, and this relation will inevitably be . . . a relation between one participant in God and another [since] knower and known share a fun-damental likeness and intimacy because each participates in God (p. 129).

He acknowledges that "participation" is not a *category* but a *figure*, the point of which

> is to indicate that it is part of the grammar of the Christian account of things to say that no account of what it is for things to be can be given that does not begin and end with God. This is exactly to reject ontological system and to place ontology where it belongs, which is a part—and always a derived and subsidiary part—of theology (p. 87).

He displays that he knows his "ontology" by showing how those who propose to think

---

[27] Paul J. Griffiths, *Intellectual Appetite: A Theological Grammar* (Washington DC: Catholic University of America Press, 2009).

about God in terms of existential quantification and necessity, . . . when pressed tend exactly in the direction of participation, [maybe even sensing] that [their] thinking does not suggest, and tends to contradict, the intimacy between God and creatures intimated by talk of creaturely participation in God, and along with it, an understanding of the intrinsic goodness of creation (pp. 84, 85).

These illustrations are offered to help us taste how the prose this work exhibits is itself an icon of the *intimacy* associated with a conception of knowing which has deliberately replaced a modern fascination with *representation* with a classical predilection for *participation*. And that move is executed by an exacting analysis of what it means to be *gift*, enabling us to approach gingerly and modestly the daunting task of speaking of the universe as gift. For that is what *creatio ex nihilo* challenges us to learn how to do.

Thinking analogously about God's being is more difficult than any other intellectual enterprise: we grope, we fail, and our failures are magnified by our unwillingness to recognize the depth and scope of what we do not know and of the errors in whose truth we have confidence (p. 69)

Philosophers of religion, take note: this extended essay reads like a meditation of one who has come to appreciate the limits of academic study of religion, and would initiate others into the set of attitudes and practices which can nurture wonder and even intimacy with God. What more fitting summary of the way attention to *creatio ex nihilo* can invite transformations in philosophical approaches to God and to the cosmos?

Modern Theology 29:2 April 2013
ISSN 0266-7177 (Print)
ISSN 1468-0025 (Online)

CREATION IN EARLY CHRISTIAN POLEMICAL LITERATURE: IRENAEUS AGAINST THE GNOSTICS AND ATHANASIUS AGAINST THE ARIANS

PAUL GAVRILYUK

1

One of the earliest statements of the Christian doctrine of creation out of nothing comes from Irenaeus of Lyons (*c*.130–*c*.200): "The rule of truth which we hold, is, that there is one God Almighty, who made all things by His Word, and fashioned and formed, out of that which had no existence, all things that exist."[1] Grounding his position in the church's "rule of truth", Irenaeus went on to reject a cluster of cosmological views that he associated with the Gnostics. One such a view, which also had its champions among the ancient Greek poets and philosophers, was that the divine designer (the Demiurge) fashioned the world out of preexistent matter. For Irenaeus, such a solution left open the origin of matter. Among the Gnostics, the Valentinians explained different forms of matter (substances) as byproducts of the divine aeon, Sophia. They proposed that all moist substance proceeded from the tears of Sophia, while the lucid substance derived from her smile, the solid substance came from her sadness, and the mobile substance originated from her terror.[2] While it would be hopeless to reconstruct with any precision the original motivations of the Valentinian cosmology from

Paul Gavrilyuk
University of St. Thomas, Department of Theology, 2115 Summit Avenue, St. Paul, MN 55105, USA
Email: plgavrilyuk@stthomas.edu

[1] Irenaeus, *Adv. Haer.* I.xxii.1; trans. *ANF* I: 347.
[2] Irenaeus, *Adv. Haer.* II.x.3.

Irenaeus's admittedly garbled presentation of it, the general idea was to derive the primal elements of matter from the primal divine passions.[3]

The strategy of the Gnostics was to explain that which was external to the divine realm—the material cosmos—with reference to that which was internal to the divine realm, namely the trials and tribulations of Sophia. Sophia's heightened psychic state, they explained, had to do with her expulsion from the divine Pleroma, the realm populated by the divine aeons. The reason for her expulsion was her desire to comprehend the incomprehensible divine Father (a desire, one might note, generally shared by those who hoped to join the Gnostics). Thus, the bringing forth of the material universe was preceded by a cataclysm within the divine Pleroma, a fallout among the gods. The Valentinians proceeded to justify their cosmology by a peculiar exegesis of the Prologue to the Gospel of John, where some things are said to be "in" the Logos. For example, they interpreted the verse "in Him was life and the life was the light of men" (John 1: 4) as implying that the divine aeons called "life", "light" and "man" indwell the divine Logos. The broader point was to explain the things outside the divine realm (the material world) with reference to the things "in" the divine realm, be it the affections of Sophia or the divine conflict within the Pleroma. The Gnostics construed the act of creation as a bringing forth of that which was in some sense within the divine realm. They believed that by making the causal chain sufficiently intricate—that is, by claiming that the material substances were produced from Sophia's passions, which were caused by her expulsion, which was caused by her desire to know the Father—they offered a profound explanation.

Irenaeus's general objection to this pattern of explanation is worth quoting in full: "For no question can be solved by means of another which itself awaits solution; nor, in the opinion of those possessed of sense, can an ambiguity be explained by means of another ambiguity, or enigmas by means of another great enigma, but things of such character receive their solution from those which are manifest, and consistent, and clear."[4] To offer an explanation of the origins of the world is to attempt to clarify something that is profoundly obscure. Irenaeus was clearly unimpressed by the Gnostic move to push the explanation back to the divine fall before creation.

The problem which drove most Gnostic cosmological speculations, including the divine fall, was the origin of evil. For the Gnostics, the account of the world's origins had to be at the same time a theodicy, or a cosmodicy, to be more exact. The cosmological account failed if it did not provide a sufficiently comprehensive answer to the problem of evil. The general strategy was to

---

[3] For a different reading of the Valentinian system, emphasizing "ignorance" as a major cosmological intention of the aeons, see M. C. Steenberg, *Irenaeus on Creation: The Cosmic Christ and the Saga of Redemption* (Leiden: Brill, 2008), pp. 22–38.

[4] *Adv. Haer.* II.x.1; trans. ANF I: 370.

remove the perfect God, the ineffable Father, from any direct involvement in the production of the imperfect world. With this strategy in mind, the Gnostics pursued different explanatory trajectories with much ingenuity. One possibility was to locate evil and imperfection in the pre-existent matter. The second possibility was to claim that the perfect God delegated the responsibility for creation to a committee of the lesser gods or a subcommittee of angels.[5] The third possibility was to claim that the world was a result of the cosmic fall from the original harmony and perfection. The fourth and final option was to urge that the material world was a divine mistake or an afterthought. According to an important minority report, which in the Middle Ages was resurrected by the Cathars, the world was produced by the Devil, a being intent on bringing about nothing but evil. Such a cosmology brought the problem of evil to its logical and ontological extreme. Most Gnostics resisted such a move, and some vigorously argued against it.[6]

Plato's dialogues, especially *Timaeus*, provided fertile ground for late antique cosmological speculations. For its ancient readers, *Timaeus* yielded interpretative possibilities one to three and with some eisegetical effort even four. The later Platonists developed a theory of emanation, which accounted for the changeable material world in terms of the eternal intelligible world. They placed all existing things on a graded continuum, locating the source of intelligible forms on one end of the spectrum (the Good), the complete formlessness (matter) on the other end of the spectrum and the mixture of forms and formlessness in between. In this scheme, the act of bringing about a changeable material thing was likened to an act of understanding inasmuch as both involved the casting of an intelligible form upon that which was previously unformed (either in the order of being or in the order of understanding). Gnostics readily helped themselves to this rich cosmological fare. More philosophically rigorous followers of Plato abhorred the Gnostic speculations, perceiving in them the vulgarization of their master's teaching, a kind of *Platon cretinisé*.[7]

It is generally accepted that it is amidst Platonic and Gnostic cosmological explorations, or rather in order to offer an alternative to such explorations, that the early Christian doctrine of creation out of nothing was first proffered.[8] While a few early Christian authors allowed matter as a second principle besides God, the majority reasoned that such an assumption made matter godlike and limited divine power. The idea that God is the creator of matter has been around at least since Philo. According to Gerhard May,

---

[5] Irenaeus, *Adv. Haer.* II.xi.1, reporting on the Gnostic views in general.

[6] See Ptolemy, *Letter to Flora*, in Epiphanius, *Panarion*, XXXIII.3.

[7] See Plotinus, *Enneades*, III. 8; V. 8. See H. C. Puech, "Plotin et les Gnostiques", in *Les sources Plotin, Entretiens sur l'antiquité Classique* (Geneva: Fondation Hardt, 1960), pp. 161–174.

[8] For the foundational study of this issue, see Gerhard May, *Creatio ex nihilo: The Doctrine of "Creation out of Nothing" in Early Christian Thought*, trans. A. S. Worrall, (Edinburgh: T&T Clark, 1994).

mid-second century apologist Tatian was the first known Christian author to reject the eternity of matter explicitly, proposing that God first created matter and then everything else.[9]

The Irenaean version of the doctrine of creation out of nothing was decidedly non-speculative. More precisely, the doctrine of creation out of nothing was designed to cut the spider's web of Gnostic speculations. For Irenaeus and other early Christian heresiologists, this doctrine went hand in hand with monotheism, affirming that there was no other god higher than the God who created the universe. While human creations typically involve something that was already there, the divine act of creation does not require anything. In this respect, creation out of nothing was a divine action sui generis, quite unlike any type of human action.[10]

On what grounds did Irenaeus maintain the doctrine of creation out of nothing? He believed the doctrine to be so foundational as to be contained in the "rule of truth", quoted in the beginning of this article. What Irenaeus intended by the "rule of truth" is less obvious. I have argued elsewhere that the most likely referent of the "rule of truth" is a summary of the apostolic tradition imparted to new converts.[11] In the time of Irenaeus such a summary was transmitted orally and did not acquire a fixed form. Structurally, the "rule of truth" paralleled, more or less consistently, the first articles of the future conciliar creeds. Somewhat simplifying, one could say that the "rule of truth" was a baptismal creed. As such, the "rule of truth" was closely aligned with scripture. Irenaeus writes:

> He who retains unchangeable in his heart the rule of the truth which he received by means of baptism, will doubtless recognize the names, the expressions, and the parables taken from the Scriptures [by the Gnostics], but will by no means acknowledge the blasphemous use which these men [the Gnostics] make of them. For, though he will acknowledge the gems, he will certainly not receive the fox instead of the likeness of the king. But when he has restored every one of the expressions quoted to its

---

[9] Tatian, *Or.* 5.3; see May, *Creatio ex nihilo*, pp. 149–150. For an earlier dating of the doctrine of creation out of nothing, see J. C. O'Neill, "How Early Is the Doctrine of *Creatio ex Nihilo*?", *Journal of Theological Studies*, Vol.53 no. 2 (2002), pp. 449–465. Cf. David Winston, *The Wisdom of Solomon: A New Translation with Introduction and Commentary* (New York, NY: Doubleday, 1979), pp. 39–40: "the concept of creation *ex nihilo* formed no part of Greek philosophical thought or of Jewish Hellenistic or rabbinic thought, and its first explicit formulation appeared in the second-century Christian literature, where (undoubtedly under the impetus of the Gnostic challenge) the argument for a double creation is made on the grounds that creation out of an eternal primordial element would compromise the sovereignty of God (Tatian, *Oratio ad Graecos* 5; Theophilus, *Ad Autolicum*, 2.4, 10)."

[10] Irenaeus, *Adv. Haer.* II.x.4; cf. Athanasius, *De decretis*, 11.

[11] I discuss the evidence for this claim at length in "Scripture and *Regula Fidei*: Two Interlocking Components of the Canonical Heritage", in William J. Abraham et al., eds., *Canonical Theism: A Proposal for Theology and the Church* (Grand Rapids, MI: Wm. B. Eerdmans Publishing Company, 2008), pp. 27–42.

proper position, and has fitted it to the body of the truth, he will lay bare, and prove to be without any foundation, the figment of these heretics.[12]

It is clear that the "rule of truth" was more than simply a summary of the biblical teaching. For Irenaeus, the "rule of truth" provided a crucial hermeneutical key to scripture. This hermeneutical key was ignored by the Gnostics. As a result, they violated "the order and connection of the Scriptures"[13] rearranging the tessarae of the biblical mosaic so as to produce the image of a fox, rather than the likeness of a king. A discerning and faithful mind armed with the "rule of truth" was required to see through their exegetical machinations.

2

It could be asked, in what sense was the doctrine of creation out of nothing "biblical" for Irenaeus? The bishop of Lyons certainly believed that scripture, when interpreted with the help of the "rule of truth", yielded such a doctrine. For example, in *Against Heresies* I.xxii.1, he took the doctrine to be implied in John 1:3: "All things were made by Him [the Logos] and without Him was nothing made." But the debate with the Gnostics also made Irenaeus quite aware of the fact that for his opponents the text had different doctrinal implications.[14] Faced with a serious threat to the integrity of the Christian message, Irenaeus heavily relied on the apostolic tradition enshrined in the "rule of truth" in making his case for the doctrine of creation out of nothing. The additional evidence for the creedal status that the doctrine of creation out of nothing has acquired in some churches of the second century is attested by the following statement from the *Shepherd of Hermas*: "First of all, believe that there is one God who created and finished all things, and made all things out of nothing (ποιήσας ἐκ τοῦ μὴ ὄντος)."[15] When Irenaeus quoted a confession of faith containing a formula that God "fashioned and formed, out of that which had no existence, all things that exist",[16] he relied on a similar creedal statement.

Irenaeus's position aside, one could ask more generally, in what sense is the doctrine of creation out of nothing "biblical"? Before any progress could be made in answering this question, it would be helpful to differentiate between different ways in which any theological claim could be said to be "biblical". In the most literal sense, a theological claim is biblical if it is explicitly made in at least one passage of scripture. Such a definition has the advantage of being straightforward. Unfortunately, this definition also has the disadvantage of

---

[12] Irenaeus, *Adv. Haer.* I.ix.4.
[13] Irenaeus, *Adv. Haer.* I.viii.1.
[14] Irenaeus, *Adv. Haer.* I.viii.5.
[15] *Shepherd of Hermas, Mandates*, I.1; cf. *Visiones* I.1.6.
[16] Irenaeus, *Adv. Haer.* I.xxii.1.

being question-begging, since what appears to be asserted in one biblical passage could be in tension with what is said elsewhere in the Bible. In our example, some biblical passages, such as 2 Macc. 7:28, John 1:3, Rom. 4:17, Col. 1:16, and Heb. 11:3, may be plausibly interpreted as yielding support to *creatio ex nihilo*. Other passages, however, compare creation to forming pots out of clay (e.g. Isa. 64:8) or to taming monsters (e.g. Ps. 74:14–17), or to setting boundaries (Ps. 104:9, Job 26:10, 38:8–11) and thereby mastering the forces of chaos. Reading scripture in a theologically responsible way involves some manner of adjudicating between these accounts. Extra-biblical considerations, such as, for example, exegetical approaches and rational arguments, will have to play a role in such adjudication. Whatever the theological outcome, any biblical fundamentalist is going to have an extremely hard time proving that the doctrine of creation out of nothing is biblical in the sense of being explicitly and incontrovertibly taught in scripture.

The second, less obvious way in which a theological claim could be said to be biblical, is if early Christian exegetes took it to be such. Such a sense of "biblical" no longer relies on scripture alone (conceding for the sake of argument that "scripture alone" is a hermeneutically plausible stance), but draws some part of the Christian tradition into the orbit of theological investigation. It could be said that the doctrine of *creatio ex nihilo* is "biblical" in the sense of being taken as such by most ancient orthodox Christian theologians. But such a sense of "biblical" is again question-begging, since many non-Orthodox Christian theologians, notably the ancient Gnostics, challenged the biblical foundation of this doctrine. It is common knowledge that in defending the doctrine of creation out of nothing against the Gnostics, early orthodox Christian theologians had recourse to the apostolic tradition enshrined in the "rule of truth" and rational arguments (such as Irenaeus's observation regarding the nature of explanation).

The third way in which a theological claim could be said to be "biblical" is if contemporary biblical scholars find it to be such. Now, it might seem that to seek consensus among the biblical scholars is just as hopeless as to look for agreement among the ancient Gnostics or modern philosophical theologians. Most contemporary biblical scholars agree that the rich biblical imagery of creation, whether in Genesis, or in Proverbs, or in Psalms, cannot easily fit into a single doctrinal mold, be it the doctrine of creation out of nothing, or any other philosophically-informed account of the world's origins.[17] To straightjacket the biblical narrative in this fashion is to misunderstand its genre and to ignore other hermeneutical possibilities. Therefore, whether taken in a naively literal fashion or with a measure of historical and hermeneutical sophistication, the Bible should not be read in a self-serving manner as a collection of proof-texts. Present-day analytic

---

[17] See, for example, Joseph Blenkinsopp, *Creation, Uncreation, Re-Creation: A Discursive Commentary on Genesis 1–11* (London: T&T Clark, 2011), p. 31.

theologians should be particularly cautioned against encroaching funda-
mentalism in their ranks.

3

While fundamentalist readings of *creatio ex nihilo* are question-begging, the
opposite extreme of theological agnosticism about scripture, elicited by some
forms of modern biblical scholarship, is equally unsatisfactory. The early
Christian theologians believed that when interpreted within the framework
of the "rule of truth", scripture yielded a doctrine of creation out of nothing.
The statement that gives the strongest biblical backing to the doctrine of
creatio ex nihilo appears in 2 Maccabees, a book of irregular canonical status.
The author of the book places in the mouth of the Jewish mother the following statement of faith, as she encourages her son to face death from the hand
of the persecutors: "I beg you, my child, to look at the heaven and the earth
and see everything that is in them, and recognize that God did not make
them out of things that existed (οὐκ ἐξ ὄντων). And in the same manner the
human race came into being" (2 Macc. 7:28). From the second century CE on,
this confession became a central Christian proof text, in support of the doctrine of creation out of nothing. While the historical setting of this statement
is often treated as incidental by modern Christians, the ancient readers
would have judged otherwise. Beginning with Homer, the ancient writers
used the danger and proximity of death to heighten dramatically the significance of the hero's speech. The fundamental distinction between God who is
the world's creator and pagan deities, whom the true believers refused to
serve, would become a common refrain of early Christian martyr-acts. It
was the faith in this unique creator that the martyrs sealed with their final
confession.

It would be anachronistic, however, to interpret 2 Macc. 7:28 as indicative
of a clearly defined doctrine of *creatio ex nihilo*. Rather, this text should be seen
as supplying raw material for what would later be argued by early Christian
theologians in a more systematic and philosophically rigorous manner. The
literature of the Second Temple Judaism provided a fertile ground for early
Christian reflection on creation, but not a ready-made doctrine. In the New
Testament, 2 Macc. 7:28 is echoed in Romans 4:17, where God is said to "give
life to the dead and call into existence the things that do not exist (τὰ μὴ
ὄντα)." As in 2 Macc. 7, God's special ability to create things that did not
previously exist is paralleled by an equally unique divine prerogative to raise
the dead (cf. 2 Macc. 7:9, 23, 29). In Hebrews 11, a summary of salvation
history is introduced with a statement that faith as the "conviction of things
not seen" (οὐ βλεπομένων) is that which makes the believers "understand
that the worlds were prepared by the word (ῥήματι) of God, so that what is
seen was made from things that are not visible" (τὸ μὴ ἐκ φαινομένων, Heb.
11:3). Such texts, while they did not supply a developed doctrine of creation

out of nothing, nevertheless offered rich interpretative possibilities that were explored by later Christian theologians. When read in light of John 1:3 ("All things were made through him [the Logos], and without him was not any-thing made that was made") and Col. 1:16 ("all things were created by God in Christ"), Genesis 1 as well as Hebrews 11:3 also acquired a more direct Christological reference.

It should be noted, however, that the New Testament books became a part of the biblical canon partly on the grounds that they reflected the apostolic tradition, which included an emerging Christian account of creation. Thus, the second-century Church Fathers had to argue as much from the New Testament texts as they had to argue against the heterodox teachers *for* the inclusion of such texts into the developing New Testament canon. The church's handling of Marcion's case will provide an illustration of this general point. As a cosmologist, Marcion was wary of the Gnostic speculations, although he agreed with the view that the world was created by the inferior god, whom he identified with the God of the Old Testament. He distinguished creator god from the superior God, revealed by Jesus. In accordance with his peculiar cosmology, Marcion rejected the authority of the Old Testament as a production of an inferior God. He also produced a highly idiosyncratic canon, which included the gospel of Luke and some Pauline epistles, which he edited and interpolated in accordance with his theology. The church's rejection of Marcion's biblical canon could not be based solely on scriptural consider-ations, for Marcion would have denied the validity of such a premise. The church's response to Marcion was also based on extra-scriptural consider-ations, such as the apostolic tradition enshrined in the baptismal catechesis as well as the exegetical and liturgical practices of the church. For Irenaeus, the doctrine of creation out of nothing was among the foundational Christian beliefs that were a part of the apostolic tradition. Hence, the relationship between the rudimentary, non-speculative version of this doctrine and the emerging New Testament canon was more dialectical than is commonly emphasized. While the intellectual provocation to develop a doctrine of cre-ation came from the outside, it was catechesis and baptismal initiation that guided early Christian thought and practice in formulating this doctrine.

In the apostolic period, the emerging theology of creation involved the following points: (1) all things were created by one God; (2) as creator, God is different from everything else in creation; (3) the divine Logos plays a central role in creation. It followed that to worship the gods other than the creator was delusion and idolatry. In the New Testament, the question of how God created the world acquired an explicit Christological reference. All things were made "in" and "through" the Logos. As a result of the intellec-tual confrontation with the philosophers and the Gnostics, in the second century the idea of creation out of nothing became more salient in Christian teaching. The next major conceptual breakthrough in the development of *creatio ex nihilo* doctrine was made in the fourth century.

4

Athanasius of Alexandria begins his famous work *On the Incarnation* by briefly considering three rival accounts of the origins of the world. He refutes the first two accounts with rational arguments and the third account by appealing to scripture. First, he mentions the Epicurean view that the world came into existence by chance. Since the prevailing climate of philosophical opinion was strongly against the Epicurean theory of the chance collision of atoms, Athanasius did not feel the need to dwell on refuting this theory at length. He briefly states that mere chance could not account for the variety and order of creation. He subsequently turns to the second view that the world was fashioned out of the pre-existent matter, attributing this view to Plato, among others. Athanasius observes that such a view makes God's ability to create dependent on something outside God, namely the pre-existing matter, thereby diminishing God's creative power. In line with earlier orthodox Christian theologians who preceded him, Athanasius maintains that God is the creator of all things, matter included. According to the third view, which Athanasius attributes to the unnamed "sectarians" (apparently implying the Gnostics), the creator God is different from the God revealed by Jesus. Athanasius refutes this view by noting the passages in which Jesus speaks of his Father as the creator of the world.[18]

Having briefly refuted the erroneous views, Athanasius adumbrates the church's teaching regarding creation. According to this teaching, God created the world that did not previously exist without having recourse to anything outside God. God was under no necessity of external compulsion to create. Creation was an act of God's pure goodness and generosity. Creation was not an accident, for it involved divine forethought. God made all things out of nothing and by his Word. For Athanasius, as for Irenaeus before him, the condition of being created out of nothing entailed that the creatures were ontologically different from God. The creator is unchangeable and eternal; creatures, in contrast, are subject to change, corruption and death. In the present state of separation from God, creatures have a tendency to slide back into nothingness. Athanasius's soteriological vision was worked out to address not only the moral, but also the ontological consequences of sin and death.[19]

This general framework of the doctrine of creation, as it came to be taught by the church towards the beginning of the fourth century, constituted the common ground between Athanasius and his supporters on the one hand and those who opposed the council of Nicaea on the other hand. A new dispute arose with respect to the conflicting ways of correlating the Father-

---

[18] Athanasius, *De incarnatione*, 2.
[19] See Khaled Anatolios, *Athanasius: The Coherence of His Thought* (New York, NY: Routledge, 1998).

Son relationship with the God-world relationship. Those who opposed Nicaea tended to collapse the Father's generation of the Son into God's creation of the world out of nothing. They tended to emphasize the preeminence and transcendence of the Father over all things, including the Son. For example, some early Arians held that "creatures could not endure to be wrought by the absolute hand of the Unoriginate" God.[20] As his first act of creation, the Father brought forth the unique Son in order to prevent the creation's annihilation by the direct hand of God. The generation of the Son, who was ontologically inferior to the Father, made possible the subsequent divine creation of all things out of nothing. The uniqueness of the Son consisted in the fact that he alone was directly brought forth by the Father, whereas all other things came into being through and by the Son.[21] The Son ontologically depends on the Father and mediates all other divine actions vis-à-vis the world.

Arius appears to have equivocated between the status of the Son as a subordinate God and a unique creature. Arius taught more definitively that the Son was created out of nothing in the sense of not being a material emanation from the Father.[22] The Nicaean council anathematized "those who say that there was when he [the Son] was not and that before he was begotten he was not and that he came from the things that were not or from another hypostasis or substance".[23] This anathema implies that extreme defenders of subordinationism taught that the Son was created out of nothing. Although the views of those church leaders who were dissatisfied with the doctrinal outcome of the council of Nicaea ranged widely, the general tendency was to conceive of the generation of the Son along the lines of the creation of the world out of nothing. The primary distinction between the Son and the rest of creation lay in the fact that God willed the Son into being directly, while all other things came into being mediated by the Son.

The central conceptual breakthrough that Athanasius made was to distinguish as sharply as possible between the act of generation of the Son and the act of creation of the world.[24] According to Athanasius, the Son is eternally generated out of the Father's essence. The Son is "begotten, not made" and is in all respects equal to the Father, possessing the same divine essence. The world is created by the will of the Father through the Son. Those who opposed the council of Nicaea reserved for the Son a kind of ontological limbo between the uncreated and ungenerated God and the rest of creation.

---

[20] According to Athanasius, *De decretis*, 8, this view of Asterius was followed by Arius.

[21] As reported by Athanasius, *De decretis*, 7.

[22] Opitz, *Urk* III. 5, discussed in R. P. C. Hanson, *The Search for the Christian Doctrine of God* (Edinburgh: T&T Clark, 1988), pp. 6–7.

[23] Nicene creed, anathemas 1 and 2.

[24] See Georges Florovsky, "St. Athanasius' Concept of Creation" (1962), *CW* IV, pp. 39–62.

Athanasius saw with extraordinary clarity and argued tirelessly that the Son, although he was generated, belonged to the sphere of the uncreated Godhead.

Although the Nicene creed does not state explicitly that God created the world out of nothing, the doctrine of *creatio ex nihilo* is strongly implied by the teaching of the council. For the Nicene creed states that (1) God is almighty; (2) the Son is "begotten, not made"; (3) the Son was not made out of nothing. It could be said that the council of Nicaea indirectly canonized the doctrine of creation out of nothing.

The theological achievement of the council of Nicaea was contested for the next fifty years. In these controversies, as formerly in the debates with the Gnostics, the biblical character of competing views came to the fore. Some of the arguments against the consubstantiality of the Father and the Son were made on the grounds that the term "consubstantial" was nowhere mentioned in the Bible. Athanasius and his supporters argued that the term, while not biblical, nevertheless expressed the equality of the Father and the Son, which expressed the overall purpose of biblical revelation. While biblical exegesis played a considerable role in the arguments pro and contra the Nicene position, the debating theologians also had recourse to non-biblical considerations, such as general metaphysical assumptions (e.g. regarding the transcendence and immateriality of God), the arguments from the fittingness of divine action, the presuppositions regarding the function of religious language, the implications of baptismal and liturgical practices, the theological assumptions of worshipping Christ, and so on. While the accusations that one's opponent was too heavily invested in a particular philosophy, rather than in a careful interpretation of scripture, had much rhetorical power then as they also do today, in reality both sides, the pro-Nicene and the anti-Nicene, deployed a wide array of biblical quotations to build their respective theological cases. The final outcome of the controversy was the vindication of the pro-Nicene position at the council of Constantinople. Henceforth, the distinction between the uncreated triune Godhead and the world created out of nothing became a normative part of the Christian faith.

Modern Theology 29:2 April 2013
ISSN 0266-7177 (Print)
ISSN 1468-0025 (Online)

NOTHING IS NOT ONE: REVISITING THE *EX NIHILO*[1]

VIRGINIA BURRUS

If for much of the pre-modern period it was the Many that seemed to bemuse philosophers and theologians, the One has become suspect in our own day. Yet the challenge, surely, has always been to think the two together, to relate them—the challenge, and also the lure. "We are drawn into relation," as Karmen MacKendrick puts it in *Fragmentation and Memory*: "The One to the Many, the whole to the fragmentary, the single to the multiple, and the slipping to the staying are relations of priority but also (less expectedly) of time. . . ." She notes further, "Multiplicity . . . is as near as we come to a sense of 'origin'—the origin as fragmentation, a fragmentation into multiplicity that is the perfection of unity."[2]

MacKendrick's association of origin with a fragmentation that paradoxically perfects unity resonates with certain mystical traditions with which it shares Neoplatonic roots; it also partakes in more diffused, and frequently ambivalent, affinities for the mystical manifest in some recent Continental philosophy. Such a haunting of philosophy by the mystical evokes another relational dyad, which I would here like to lay alongside, and thereby place in relation to, the One and the Many—namely, the Nothing and the Something. Like the One and the Many, the Nothing and the Something is a relation of time—or, more precisely, a relation of the relation of time to eternity. For Jews and Christians, and most profoundly for their mystical traditions, this dyad frames a doctrine of creation conventionally dubbed the

Virginia Burrus
The Theological School, Drew University, 36 Madison Avenue, Madison, NJ 07940, USA
Email: vburrus@drew.edu

[1] I am grateful to Catherine Keller and Laurel Schneider, who invited me to be part of a 2009 conversation on "the manifold" that provoked this essay; to Rebecca Lyman, who encouraged me to give Athanasius another chance; and to Elliot Wolfson, who reminds me that "about nothing there is no limit to our (un)saying."

[2] Karmen MacKendrick, *Fragmentation and Memory: Meditations on Christian Doctrine* (New York, NY: Fordham University Press, 2008), pp. 20, 24.

ex nihilo, in which, I suggest, origin is associated with the negation of a nothingness that may also be thereby perfected.[3]

In revisiting the doctrine of the *ex nihilo* from this perspective, I am hoping to sidestep and thereby also gently question some of the assumptions that fuel the debates currently surrounding the doctrine.[4] As Mary-Jane Rubenstein puts it in a recent article, "The scholars who engage the *ex nihilo* tend to stake powerful claims either with or against the doctrine." She adds, moreover, that both proponents and opponents of the doctrine agree that it "affirms the absolute sovereignty of the creator"; where they differ is in how they value divine sovereignty.[5] This is scarcely a preposterous statement. Yet I wonder if the *ex nihilo* secures divine sovereignty as successfully as Rubenstein, among others, suggests, and also (to the extent that it does indeed do so) if that is the single most significant or interesting thing that it does. Attempting here to encounter the topic from a fresh angle, I shall back into it, chronologically speaking, beginning with the work of the early twentieth-century philosopher-theologian Franz Rosenzweig and moving from there toward texts more ancient. As I shall try to show, Rosenzweig's idiosyncratic multiplication of the *nihil* and its consequent explicit expansion to encompass theology, cosmology, and anthropology, together with his appropriation of

---

[3] A prime instance is found in the version of kabbalah carried forth in the philosophical mysticism of Habad Hasidism, as explicated by Elliot R. Wolfson, "Revisioning the Body Apophatically: Incarnation and the Acosmic Naturalism of Habad Hasidism," in *Apophatic Bodies: Negative Theology, Incarnation, and Relationality*, edited by Christopher Boesel and Catherine Keller, (New York, NY: Fordham University Press, 2009); for a fuller version, see chapter 2 of Elliot Wolfson's *Open Secret: Postmessianic Messianism and the Mystical Revision of Menahem Mendel Schneerson* (New York, NY: Columbia University Press, 2009). The *ex nihilo* concept is so crucially and pervasively generative within Habad cosmology that it is said to be "impossible for something to come to be from something."

[4] Critique of the doctrine of creation out of nothing is the fertile starting point of Catherine Keller, *The Face of the Deep: A Theology of Becoming* (London: Routledge, 2003), a work that has been particularly influential. I confess that it also features strongly in the treatment of Athanasius in chapter 1 of my own *"Begotten, not Made": Conceiving Manhood in Late Antiquity*, Figurae: Reading Medieval Culture (Stanford, CA: Stanford University Press, 2000), and, more fleetingly, in my *Saving Shame: Martyrs, Saints, and Other Abject Subjects*, Divinations: Rereading Late Ancient Religion (Philadelphia, PA: University of Pennsylvania Press, 2008), pp. 72–78. I attempt to locate in Logos theology an alternative to the *ex nihilo* as it is usually interpreted in my *"Creatio ex libidine*: Reading Ancient Logos Differantly," in *Derrida and Religion: Other Testaments*, edited by Kevin Hart and Yvonne Sherwood, (London: Routledge, 2005), pp. 141–156. Positive engagement of Augustine's invocation of the "nothing-something" in his exegesis of Genesis 1 in *Confessions* can be found in my "Carnal Excess: Flesh at the Limits of Imagination," *Journal of Early Christian Studies*, Vol. 17, no. 2 (2009), pp. 247–265, and (more extensively) in chapter 4 of Virginia Burrus, Mark D. Jordan, and Karmen MacKendrick, *Seducing Augustine: Bodies, Desires, Confessions* (New York, NY: Fordham University Press, 2010). "Seeing God in Bodies: Wolfson, Rosenzweig, Augustine," in *Reading the Church Fathers*, edited by Scot Douglass and Morwenna Ludlow (London: T&T Clark, 2011), pp. 44–59, engages the relation of Augustine's thought to Rosenzweig's on this and other topics.

[5] Mary-Jane Rubenstein, "Cosmic Singularities: On the Nothing and the Sovereign," *Journal of the American Academy of Religion*, Vol. 80 no. 2 (2012), p. 488. Rubenstein herself is not above the fray; the burden of her essay is to argue that "even the most atheistic appeals to the *ex nihilo* end up enshrining a figure of absolute power" (p. 488).

the mathematical concept of the infinitesimal that is neither something nor nothing, opens productive avenues for engaging the *ex nihilo* doctrine at the point of its own beginnings—here exemplified by Athanasius of Alexandria's *On the Incarnation* and the midrashic collection known as Genesis Rabbah.

As Luca Bertolino notes, Rosenzweig's distinctive concept of creation *ex nihilo* offers a hermeneutical key to his tripartite *Star of Redemption*; initially encountered in the challenging philosophical exposition of nothingness in Part I, it provides a thread of continuity for the work as a whole.[6] In an opening salvo, Rosenzweig charges philosophical idealism with recoiling from the fear of death by concluding that death is *nothing*. In contrast, he insists that "actually this is not an ultimate conclusion, but a first beginning." The nothing that philosophy has attempted to render both empty and universal—a "yawning abyss"—becomes fecund with mortality's particularity, in Rosenzweig's theologically-mediated revision. "In the dark background of the world there rise up, as its inexhaustible presupposition, a thousand deaths; *instead of the one nothing that would really be nothing, a thousand nothings rise up, which are something just because they are multiple.* . . . [I]t is this that makes a lie of the basic thought of philosophy, the thought of the one and universal cognition of the all" (SR, pp. 10–11; emphasis added).[7] If mortality proves to be the hallmark of humanity's distinctness as well as its multiplicity ("The human is ephemeral, being ephemeral is his essence" [SR, p. 72]), there is a still more fundamental multiplicity of thought and being that interests Rosenzweig, namely, "God-world-humanity." However, he does not initially attempt to define positively these "three separate pieces which are mutually opposed to each other in different ways that cannot yet be stated more precisely" (SR, p. 26). Opting for the *via negativa*, he locates their distinctness in the distinctness of their "nothings."

Less disconcerting is the epistemological dimension: "From the nothings of knowledge, our explorers' journey reaches the something of knowledge. . . . Of what may lie beyond the something, we can as yet have no idea at all from where we are now, that is to say, starting from the nothing." However, Rosenzweig's complex apophasis does not exclude me/ontological implications:[8] "But wherever an existing element of the all rests in itself, indissoluble

---

[6] Luca Bertolino, " 'Schöpfung aus Nichts' in Franz Rosenzweig's *Stern der Erlösung*," *Jewish Studies Quarterly*, Vol. 13 (2006), pp. 247–264, citation at p. 247.

[7] Franz Rosenzweig, *The Star of Redemption*, trans. Barbara Galli, (Madison, WI: University of Wisconsin Press, 2005) (hereafter SR). The German edition consulted is Franz Rosenzweig, *Der Stern der Erlösung*, third edition, (Heidelberg: Verlag Lambert Schneider, 1954; original, 1921).

[8] The priority of the me/ontological becomes explicit in the following passage: "When to the nothing of our knowledge there corresponds a 'true nothing' (as we must probably admit), secret forces beyond all reality ever visible to us, dark forces which are at work inside of God, the world and man, before God, the world and man—are revealed. . . . And even if we preferred to see the nothing only as a nothing of knowledge, and if we climb in this way by carefully holding onto the cable which is the consciousness of cognition, here, too, reality only begins with the end result, and here, too, facing the real, this result becomes the beginning" (SR, p. 98).

and permanent, the main thing is to presuppose a nothing for this being, *its nothing*" (SR, pp. 26–27, emphasis added). Following philosopher Hermann Cohen's turn to the mathematics of calculus, he invokes the concept of the differential to explicate a theory of origin and beginning: "It is a nothing that refers to a something, to its something, and at the same time a something that still slumbers in the womb of a nothing. . . . It thus determines two paths that go from the nothing to the something, the path of the affirmation of that which is not nothing, and the path of the negation of the nothing" (SR, p. 28). The two paths, as Rosenzweig dubs them, yield the twin results of infinitude ("the entire plenitude of all that is—not nothing") and delimitation. "Endlessly, then, the essence (*Wesen*) springs up from the nothing; in a sharp delimitation the action (*Tat*) separates from it. For the essence one asks about the origin, and for action about the beginning" (SR, p. 32). Thus the *via negativa* proves to be twice doubled (despite Rosenzweig's rendering of the initial double negative as an affirmative), encompassing the "not nothing" (*Nichtnichts*) of infinite potentiality and the "not that but this" of delimiting action (SR, p 33). Through such a trifold process of negation, effecting the infinitesimal shift from (a particular) "nothing" to (a particular) "something"—or, perhaps better, *as* such a trifold process—God, world, and humanity sustain their separate and distinctive factuality (*Tatsächlichkeit*).

Having established, however ambiguously and provisionally, the everlasting factuality of this primordial triad ("mythical God," "configured world," "tragic humanity") in Part I of his *Star*, Rosenzweig acknowledges that he may appear to have thereby undercut the doctrine of creation *ex nihilo*. "It seems paradoxical, at first glance, again to assert a creation of the world 'after' its completion as configuration," he notes. "In any case, at least it seems that we have moved irrevocably away from the concept of creation 'out of nothing' which we had received from the tradition" (SR, pp. 129–130). But perhaps Rosenzweig has not so much "moved away" from the concept as moved the concept itself to different ground, both tripling the *ex nihilo* and projecting it back onto the *Vorwelt*, where its multiplicity stands guard over the elemental distinctness of God, world, and humanity. Thus he does seem to begin anew—and not quite from nothing—when, gazing into the abyss of the second verse of the Bible, he observes (once again?) the infinitesimal "something that slumbers in the womb of the nothing" (SR, p. 28): "There, the darkness of the waste-and-void, here the obscurity of brooding; both thing (*Ding*) and act (*Tat*) appear in the form of attributes, and of attributes situated at the lowest limit, where thing and act constantly emerge out of that which is not yet in any manner thing nor in any manner act" (SR, pp. 165–166).

In a later work, Rosenzweig acknowledges that the dauntingly abstract concept of nothingness offered in Part I of the *Star* "appears to be only a methodological heuristic concept." However, he advises his readers to press ahead without delay; so doing, they will discover that the nothing "reveals its inner significance only in the short concluding passage of the volume and its ultimate sense not until the concluding book of the whole."[9] The "inner significance" is glimpsed as Rosenzweig approaches the brink of revelation, where "that which is purely factuality changes into the source of the real movement" (SR, p. 98). From this perspective, the apparent doubling or repetition in the account of creation in Part II manifests as an effect of Rosenzweig's complex treatment of temporality: what was first observed as a series of still photographs is now viewed as a moving picture. That is to say, whereas in Part I the three elements of God, world, and humanity appear (misleadingly) to be separate and static, in Part II they emerge in and as their mutual relationality in "a path of flowing movement" (SR, p. 97). The flow of time brings the three into relation and consequently defines their difference in their relationality, "their reciprocal effect on each other" (SR, p. 414), discernible via the kaleidoscopic shifts of perspective offered by the threefold process of creation, revelation and redemption. Creation places God in an immemorial past, signifying the world in its primordial potentiality via the agency of its creator: "God created the world." Yet for the world itself, creation occurs in the ever-renewing present that opens within time's back-flow, signifying the ongoing actualization, or revelation, of this always-already-granted potentiality in the world's "constantly brimming-over newness" (SR, p. 145). It is, finally, from the perspective of future hindsight that the world may seem complete and thus "necessarily, and absolutely, be 'creation out of nothing' " (SR, p. 131), its providential promise exhausted through the process of redemption mediated by the overflow of divine love for the human and the responsive overflow of love in the human for the divinely created world.

With regard to creation from nothing, Rosenzweig concludes: "Facing this world created at the end, but really facing it," the primordial potentiality of the configured world described in Part I "would really have to be 'nothing,' that is to say, something absolutely incomparable with the created world, something unbound, something which has disappeared along with its inter-ests (*Lust*)" (SR, p. 131). Having been drained of desire, the womb of the configured world will no longer be "insatiable in conceiving, inexhaustible in giving birth" (SR, p. 53); having attained its destined wholeness, the world itself will no longer be bound to the promise of its own potentiality—the umbilical cord having finally been cut, one might say. Thus, only the end of the world enables an arrival at a beginning truly from nothing, and this nothing (the world's nothing) *both is and is not* a different nothing on the second encounter. What may formerly have appeared merely as a "heuristic concept" is now seen to be *really nothing*, but what does that mean? The initial infinitesimal of the "nothing/something" ("a something that still slumbers in the womb of the nothing" [SR, p. 28]) marked the passage from nothing to

---

[9] *Franz Rosenzweig's "The New Thinking,"* ed. and trans. Alan Udoff and Barbara E. Galli, (Syracuse, NY: Syracuse University Press, 1999), p. 73.

something and also (just barely) preserved their difference; on the rebound, however, the difference between affirmation (the chaotic plenitude of "all that is—not nothing") and negation (the fragmenting delimitation that actualizes "all that is" in and as a multiplicity) both widens and seems to collapse, and with it the difference between nothing and something. Have we here reached the "ultimate sense" of the nothing that Rosenzweig has predicted?

Perhaps. Yet to discover that the end (the "ultimate") is a return to the beginning is also to *begin again*—and to find oneself still, or even more than ever, "in the center of life," as Rosenzweig discloses at the very end of the *Star* (SR, p. 446). Precisely as end and beginning, nothingness is enfolded in the center of time. Just as "every moment must be ready to receive the plenitude of eternity" for Rosenzweig (SR, p. 245), so too every "something" of creation must be ready to receive the plenitude of its "nothing," which is to say, of its death—a nothing that is at once *really nothing* and also (an infinitesimal) something, cutting back into time with the opening of new possibility. Death is "the silent and permanent prediction of the miracle of its renewal," notes Rosenzweig (SR, p. 168). Death is also, he suggests, the temporal opening for the gratuitous and unpredictable advent of love, in which creation is not merely completed and renewed but further exceeded and redeemed, as time first orients itself and then opens into the full potency of presence. "The creation which death finishes and completes cannot resist it [love]; it must surrender to it at every moment and thus also ultimately in the plenitude of all moments, in eternity" (SR, p. 178). The riveting particularity of mortality—"a thousand deaths"—thus gives rise, in Rosenzweig's account, not merely to the promised renewal of all creation but, beyond that, to the infinite, overflowing relationality of all creatures.

When this relationality is brought to eschatological perfection in and as divine love, the posited difference between world, humanity, and God would seem to disappear; at the very least, the difference becomes infinitesimal. In redemption, the line between the beloved human and the created world dissolves, and the God who is revealed in and as the temporal processes of creating and loving is liberated from being God: "For him it is the eternal act in which he frees himself from contrasting with something that he himself is not" (SR, p. 406). Now every creature is rendered beloved and loving, and dialogue becomes a liturgical song of praise for the beauty of the multiple, entangled "all-of-us," a song giving way in turn to the mystic's wondrous, wordless gaze upon a "countenance that looks upon me and from out of which I look" (SR, p. 446). In other words, and to be still more explicit, to the extent that Rosenzweig succeeds in arguing for the multiplicity, mobility, and self-exceeding relationality of all that was, is, and will be, he explodes his own (merely) triadic framing. This is accomplished, as we have seen, through a complex and expansive reworking of the concept of creation from nothing, in which a "negative cosmology" is implicated in a "negative theology" and a "negative psychology" (SR, pp. 49, 31, 41). If he does indeed deliver on his promise to draw theology into the service of challenging philosophy's particular monism, he does so, as Elliot Wolfson has argued, only by also delivering a theology that finally eludes theism even as it ceases to resist the "fall into the formless night of the nothing" dreamed of by mystics (SR, p. 33).[10]

"Monisms are tempting, but beneath that temptation, they are disquieting as well," observes MacKendrick.[11] Rosenzweig urges that it is the fear of death that drives idealism to "abandon the body to the power of the abyss," freeing the soul to fly high while obscuring the particularity of the earthly with "the idea of the all." He would have his readers share his disquiet at this falsely imposed tyranny of the philosopher's all; he would have the human being face the nothing, not denying the frightfulness or the pain of mortality, but remembering—disquietingly?—that "the earth wants him back" (SR, pp. 9–10). Life and death, something and nothing, are, finally, not at odds, in his view—dualities only in the most reversible and fluid sense. "What is nothing? . . . [I]t is merely a fact, the awaiting of a something, it is not anything yet" (SR, p. 412). If the nothing is not one, this is not only because it is not anything yet but also because it is not anything anymore: in the nothing, the flux of life ceases to yield to (empties itself of) the determinacy of . . . any . . . thing; and from that . . . any . . . thing may yet arise. But if the nothing is not one, is it many? The most one can say, perhaps, is that in the end it will have been many—a thousand deaths, all the nothings of all the somethings, shadows cast by memories of what was once awaited. If this is so, it will also in the end have been one, for fragmentation cannot ultimately be disentangled from gathering; as Rosenzweig discovers, "now the all, once shattered, has grown together again" (SR, p. 413).

* * *

Rosenzweig remarks that the doctrine of "creation from nothing" is received "from tradition"—but what tradition, exactly? In late antiquity the question of whether the world was eternal or created, and if created, whether from pre-existing matter or from nothing, was much debated. Between the second and the fourth centuries, creation *ex nihilo* gradually became the Christian position, lodged in polemics against gnostic heresy and/or pagan philosophy. For their part, pagan philosophers such as the emperor Julian mocked the Christian doctrine as lacking even biblical foundations. As Maren Niehoff notes, Julian's critique (*Against the Galileans* 49d-e) seems to reflect accurately the assumptions of Jewish exegetical tradition, which prior to the fifth century evidences no explicitly formulated theology of creation from nothing. Philo, for example, was apparently happy to read the *Timaeus* alongside Genesis, unperturbed by the presence of the pre-existent matter that

---

[10] Elliot R. Wolfson, "Light Does not Talk but Shines: Apophasis and Vision in Rosenzweig's Theopoetic Temporality," in *New Directions in Jewish Philosophy*, edited by Aaron W. Hughes and Elliot R. Wolfson, (Bloomington, IN: Indiana University Press, 2010), pp. 87–148.

[11] MacKendrick, *Fragmentation and Memory*, p. 11.

readers of his day discovered in the Platonic text, while also experiencing no conflict with the biblical version (e.g., *On the creation* 5.20–22).[12] Nor does the earliest rabbinic literature betray significant interest in the *ex nihilo*. Niehoff thus suggests that the affirmation of the doctrine attributed to Gamaliel in the fifth-century midrashic compilation known as *Genesis Rabbah* is the result of Christian influence. She points out particular affinities with Tertullian's *Against Hermogenes*, which may have drawn from a lost treatise of Theophilos that was still in circulation in the eastern Mediterranean around the time that the Genesis midrashim were being redacted. Not only the affirmation of the *ex nihilo* but also its framing in *Genesis Rabbah* as a contest between true, scriptural dogma and false, philosophical teaching reflects a degree of rabbinic acculturation to an increasingly Christianized empire, in Niehoff's view.[13]

Niehoff's argument regarding cultural influence and accommodation I find largely persuasive, though I do not have the textual expertise to confirm or challenge her claims for Second Temple or rabbinic literature. Pressing further, nonetheless, I would ask whether late ancient exegetical texts might not also provide evidence of shared shifts in cosmological sensibilities extending beyond what can be accounted for by knowable lines of influence. In a comparative study of Augustine's *City of God* and *Genesis Rabbah* that focuses on closely parallel tendencies to avoid references to angels found in traditional interpretations of Genesis 6:1–4, Annette Yoshiko Reed reflects on the phenomenon of hermeneutical convergences that "cannot be explained in terms of direct contact" yet also cannot be satisfyingly accounted for culturally

---

[12] Here David T. Runia's extensive scholarship deserves special mention; see especially his *Philo of Alexandria and the Timaeus of Plato* (Leiden: Brill, 1986) and *Philo of Alexandria: On the Creation of the Cosmos according to Moses. Introduction, Translation, and Commentary* (Leiden: Brill, 2001).

[13] Maren Niehoff, "*Creatio ex Nihilo* Theology in Genesis Rabbah in Light of Christian Exegesis," *Harvard Theological Review*, Vol. 99, no. 1 (2005), pp. 37–64. See Hans-Friedrich Weiß, *Untersuchungen zur Kosmologie des hellenistischen und palästinischen Judentums* (Berlin: Academie-Verlag, 1966), pp. 9–180, for a more detailed evaluation of the *ex nihilo* with respect to "hellenistic Jewish," "Palestinian Jewish," and "early Christian" literature. For Weiß, the *ex nihilo* is a distinctly Christian and also distinctly theological conceptual development, arising out of a sharply anti-dualist (because anti-gnostic and anti-Manichaean) context of thought; in his view, its later application to cosmology constitutes "ein Mißverständnis" (pp. 178–179). Accepting the conclusions of Weiß and others, Gerhard May sets out to probe more deeply into the early history of the *ex nihilo* in his *Schöpfung aus dem Nichts: Die Entstehung der Lehre von der Creatio ex Nihilo* (Berlin: Walter De Gruyter, 1978). May sees the doctrine emerging in the late second century as part of the debate of Christianity with philosophy, in resistance to the concept of creation from unoriginate matter; more locally, it emerges as part of the platform of nascent "orthodoxy," in response to the accounts of creation arising in gnostic circles, where a version of *ex nihilo* thought seems to have preceded the "orthodox" articulation of the doctrine. Note that due to the extensiveness, inconsistency, and ambiguity of his writings on creation, the place of Philo in the history of the *ex nihilo* continues to be debated, as does that of 2 Maccabees 7:28, and there is still significant scholarly support in some quarters for the pre-Christian Jewish origin of the teaching; see, e.g., J. C. O'Neill, "How Early is the Doctrine of *Creatio ex nihilo*?," *Journal of Theological Studies*, n.s. Vol. 53 (2002), pp. 449–465.

with reference to a lowest common denominator, so to speak.[14] Within the (to us, mostly invisible) domain of hermeneutical commonality and exchange in late antiquity, acts of interpretive differentiation as well as assimilation between Jews, Christians, and pagans are no doubt constantly at play.

Against such a backdrop, there emerges a concept of creation from nothing that is eventually shared by Christians and Jews. As Rubenstein has noted, it is commonly acknowledged that this concept foregrounds the omnipotence of the creator as well as the goodness of the created world. Emphasis falls heavily on the oneness of God and the untrammeled freedom of the divine will; at the same time, the world is endowed with a consequent (albeit contingent) unity, reality, and purposefulness. Such theological concerns are blatantly manifest in the work of pre-Constantinian Christian apologists and heresiologists like Tertullian, and they continue to be expressed by later proponents of the *ex nihilo*, Jewish as well as Christian. However, beginning in the fourth century, I would suggest, there are hints of something new as well—namely, a preoccupation *with the nothing itself* (alternately, with the infinitesimal nothing-something). What comes increasingly to the fore in these articulations of the *ex nihilo* is not mastery but mystery, not power but fragility, not separation but intimacy—and paradoxically so, given that the gap between creator and created has never before seemed to yawn so widely. This shift is manifest in the relevant passages of *Genesis Rabbah*, I would suggest, and distinguishes that text from the otherwise exegetically similar treatise of Tertullian. It is also evident in the *locus classicus* of post-Constantinian Christian *ex nihilo* doctrine, namely Athanasius's *On the Incarnation of the Word of God*.

* * *

Athanasius's exegetical moves are fairly simple and can be swiftly recounted. The broader context of the treatise is, however, crucial. His aim, as he states from the start, is to demonstrate that the apparently novel claim that the divine Word has become incarnate is in fact grounded in, and is continuous with, the biblical account of creation. That account, properly understood, is to be distinguished from other, competing doctrines—the Epicurean claim that "everything (*ta panta*) has had its beginning from itself, and independently of purpose (*khōris pronoias*)"; the Platonic teaching that "God has made the world (*ta 'ola*) out of matter previously existing and without beginning (*ek proupokeimenēs kai agenētou 'ulēs*)"; and the heretical assertion that "the maker of all" (*dēmiourgon tōn pantōn*) is different from the Father of Jesus Christ (Inc. 2).[15] Countering all of these views,

---

[14] Annette Yoshiko Reed, "Reading Augustine and/as Midrash: Genesis 6 in Genesis Rabbah and *The City of God*," in *Midrash and Context*, edited by Lieve M. Teugels and Rivka Ulmer, (Piscataway, NJ: Gorgias Press, 2007), pp. 61–110, citation at p. 107.

[15] Athanasius, *On the Incarnation of the Word*, trans. and ed. Robert W. Thomson, (Oxford: Clarendon Press, 1971) (hereafter Inc.).

Athanasius insists that "out of what was not (*ex ouk ontōn*) God brought into being the world (*ta 'ola*), which was by no means and in no way existing (*mēdamē mēdamōs 'uparkhonta*)." He adduces three scriptural (or parascriptural) passages as proof of the truth of his position, the first of which seems to stand in metonymically for the whole of Genesis 1 (and more): "In the beginning God created the heavens and the earth." The other two citations, swiftly dispensed with, are from *Shepherd of Hermas*, mand. 1, and Hebrews 11:13 (Inc. 3). Athanasius will go on to offer a selective paraphrase of the narrative of Genesis 1–3. However, by ending his direct citation after the first verse of the first chapter, he is able to avoid any mention of the troubling elements introduced in verse 2 and taken by readers like Hermogenes as indicators of the pre-existence and uncreatedness of matter: "but the earth was invisible and unformed, and darkness was over the abyss, and a divine wind was being carried along over the water" (New English Translation of the Septuagint).

Athanasius thus secures an austerely apophatic cosmology both through his explicit and hyperbolic negations ("out of what was not," "by no means and in no way existing") and through his implicit *unsaying* of the very verse in scripture that might seem to introduce ambiguity. The non-unitive nature of creation—its instability, frailty, fragmentation—remains axiomatic for him. The bare existence of "the all" (*ta 'ola, ta panta*—a plurality) is the gift of an inherently generous God whose creative and sustaining beneficence, manifest as Logos, staves off an otherwise inevitable return "through corruption to non-existence." Humanity is granted a "special mercy"—reason (the image of the Logos), commandment, and a place in paradise (Inc. 3). Yet these gifts too prove unstable, finally impossible to retain, due to the inherent insubstantiality of the human will, which appears to be haunted by *its* nothing, just as the flesh is (Inc. 4–5).[16] As a result, a renewal of creation through the incarnation of the divine Logos itself is required, asserts Athanasius: all things will ultimately be redeemed through this intimate reunion of the loving God with humankind (Inc. 8).

Here an apophatic cosmology and psychology do indeed seem to come at the expense of an all-too-affirmative theology. I would, nonetheless, call attention to the weakness that haunts Athanasius's famously strong God (Inc. 3). Rebecca Lyman observes that, "curiously, at the same time as divine will became primary in creation, it lost power."[17] As I myself phrased it, perhaps too facetiously, in an earlier work: "Athanasius's all-powerful God—boasting, in essence, that only weaklings use preexistent matter—can

---

[16] As Rebecca Lyman puts it, for Athanasius, "the innate weakness and instability of the creation . . . overshadow salvation history" and "will was not an important faculty, but was rather a largely negative expression of changeable nature" (*Christology and Cosmology: Models of Divine Activity in Origen, Eusebius, and Athanasius* [Oxford: Clarendon Press, 1993], pp. 139, 144).

[17] Lyman, *Christology and Cosmology*, p. 138.

barely keep his handiwork from unraveling, and the good cosmos seems destined for a bad end."[18] I would here frame the same matter somewhat differently, noting that Athanasius's theological assertions are sustained through a delicate dance with the nothing—the nothing of the world and of humanity, but also (and virtually indistinguishably, I would suggest) the nothing of the God, though this is presumably not a suggestion that Athanasius himself would have welcomed. A craftier, handier deity, given even imperfect materials to work with, might have achieved a level of relative mastery, but *his* God is Lord of *nothing*, giver of *all*. Creation is only fully redeemed when God has submitted Godself to the frailty of flesh and then sacrificed that very flesh: if at the beginning there is creation from nothing, at the end there is the humiliating death on the cross (Inc. 20–26). Of course, Athanasius attempts mightily to uphold the difference between the something of God and the nothing of creation, not least via his Christological dualism; I am suggesting, however, that the difference does not hold.[19]

* * *

The artisan God is also rejected explicitly in favor of a creator from nothing in the above-mentioned passage from *Genesis Rabbah*, to which I would now like to turn. Embedded in chapter 1 of that text, which deals with the first verse of Genesis, is an exchange between a philosopher and Rabban Gamaliel.

A philosopher asked Rabban Gamaliel, saying to him, "Your God was indeed a great artist, but he had good materials to help him." He said to him, "What are they?" He said to him, "The unformed, void, darkness, water, wind, and the deep." He said to him, "May the spirit of that man burst! All of them are explicitly described as having been created by him. The unformed and void: 'I make peace and create evil' (Is. 45:7). Darkness: 'I form light and create darkness' (Is. 45:7). Water: 'Praise him, you heavens of heavens, and you waters that are above the heavens' (Ps. 148:4). Why? 'For he commanded and they were created' (Ps. 148:5).

---

[18] Virginia Burrus, *"Begotten, not Made": Conceiving Manhood in Late Antiquity. Figurae: Reading Medieval Culture*, (Stanford, CA: Stanford University Press, 2000), p. 44.

[19] On the concept of a "weak" God, cf. John D. Caputo, *The Weakness of God: A Theology of the Event* (Bloomington, IN: Indiana University Press, 2006). Caputo astutely follows Keller in aligning the *ex nihilo* with assertions of divine omnipotence. His (rhetorically hyperbolic) claim that the doctrine reflects "an excess of metaphysical zeal" or "an overzealous extension of the concept of God's power to an 'omnipotence' that had a tin ear for life's contingencies and would thereafter have the effect of laying the horrors of this life squarely at the feet of God" does not, however, seem to capture the poignancy of Athanasius's position, nor indeed does it quite communicate the gist (even in the form of an exposé) of any ancient theological text with which I am familiar. Nonetheless, such an uncompromising position does (I acknowledge) seem to place the burden on me to demonstrate that the *ex nihilo* not only *can* but perhaps even ultimately *must* yield a weak God!

Wind: 'for lo, he who forms the mountains creates the wind' (Amos 4:13). The depths: 'When there were no depths, I was brought forth' (Prov. 8:24)." (GR I.IX.1)[20]

As Niehoff demonstrates, both the exegetical challenge issued and the rejoinder provided have striking parallels in Christian sources, as does the notable violence of the anathematization of the contrary doctrine. Here the rabbis are apparently happy, in her view, to make common cause with the Christians in refuting pagan philosophical teachings; in so doing, they take up the *ex nihilo* with an explicitness and passion unprecedented in Jewish exegetical tradition. Niehoff instructively emphasizes the singularity of the passage, and Jacob Neusner comments in the annotation that accompanies his translation that "the point stands autonomous of the context established by the redactors."[21] Yet whatever the original history of this literary unit might be, the redactional context is highly suggestive with regard to the interpretation of the exchange between Gamaliel and the philosopher.[22]

Hiddenness is one of the leitmotifs of the first chapter of this midrashic compilation. Proverbs 8:30–31 ("Then I was beside him like a little child . . .) is initially introduced to interpret Genesis 1:1 ("In the beginning God created") via triangulation with Proverbs 8:22 ("The Lord made me as the beginning of his way"). The rabbinic commentators point out that the letters for "child" (and by extension, for "beginning") can also mean "teacher," "great," "covered over," "hidden," or "worker" (GR I:I.1–2). Thus, suggests David Aaron, a multiplication of exegetical possibilities facilitates the transfer of images of Wisdom current in gnostic (and/or Christian?) thought to the personified Torah, indicating not preexisting matter but a preexisting plan or ideas.[23] The particular possibilities of "hiddenness" are not yet explicitly elaborated, but they will be. Indeed, the next set of discussions revolves around Psalm 31:19 and other passages that relate to the themes of muteness, silence, the importance of keeping a secret—in particular the secret, or mysteries, of creation. Two striking comments end this sequence, touching back upon the text of Genesis 1:1–2:

> Rab said, . . . "Will not whoever comes and says, 'This world was created out of chaos, emptiness, and darkness' give offense?" R. Huna in the

---

[20] Citations from Genesis Rabbah follow Jacob Neusner, *Genesis Rabbah, the Judaic Commentary to the Book of Genesis: A New American Translation, Volume I* (Atlanta, GA: Scholars Press, 1985) (hereafter GR).

[21] Neusner, *Genesis Rabbah*, p. 13.

[22] Here I am attracted to the literary critical approach and hermeneutical assumptions of David Howard Aaron, "Polemics and Mythology: A Commentary on Chapters 1 and 8 of 'Bereshit Rabba'," PhD Dissertation (Brandeis University, 1992).

[23] Aaron, "Polemics and Mythology," pp. 88–89. Note that Niehoff, "Creatio ex Nihilo," pp. 61–64, suggests that the opponent or competitor might be not a gnostic but a Christian like Origen.

name of Bar Qappara: "Were the matter not explicitly written in Scripture, it would not be possible to state it at all: 'God created heaven and earth'—from what? From the following: 'And the earth was chaos.'" (GR I:V:1)

Here we learn that the creation of the world from chaos, emptiness, and darkness—precisely the topic that Gamaliel will be forced to take up with the blasphemous philosopher—is a secret best kept from outsiders or non-experts, only speakable at all because it has already been written in scripture. As Aaron notes, the rabbis are presented as caught in an awkward position, so that the most they can do is "seek to expose the motivation one might have for bringing attention to it. . . . The irony of this unit lies in the fact that after having argued for the silencing of unauthorized exegetes, the rabbis must admit that the world was created from the very material that their sardonic adversaries criticized."[24]

The theme of secrecy continues in the next section, as R. Judah bar Simon applies Daniel 2:22 ("He reveals deep and secret things") to Genesis 1:1 ("In the beginning God created the heaven"), noting that "the matter was not spelled out" in the first verse of the Bible: the hermeneutical mysteries must be teased out of other passages (GR I:VI:4). Such emphasis on silence and secrecy leading up to Gamaliel's exchange with the philosopher intensifies the transgressiveness of both the philosopher's challenge and Gamaliel's unavoidable discussion of the mysteries of creation with a non-Jew, rendering Gamaliel's eruptive curse—"May that one's spirit burst!"—more understandable. Moreover, it has already been professed that "six things came before the creation of the world," a fact that seems (like the more ambivalent discussion of chaos, emptiness, and darkness) to render Gamaliel's position both more vulnerable and more duplicitous—the "six things" there being identified as Torah and the throne of glory (actually created before the creation of the world), as well as the patriarchs, Israel, the temple, the name of the Messiah, and possibly the power of repentance (contemplated by the divine before the creation of the world) (GR I.IV.I). Which "six things" were in fact created (and/or contemplated) by God prior to the creation of the world, and how much has Gamaliel really divulged to the philosopher?[25] Immediately following the exchange between the philosopher and Gamaliel is a discussion of why Scripture begins with the Hebrew letter *bet* rather than

---

[24] Aaron, "Polemics and Mythology," pp. 101, 107–108. Note that Niehoff, "*Creatio ex Nihilo*," p. 59, sees the passage (in its final form) as explicitly pro-*ex nihilo*; it seems to me decidedly more ambiguous as well as ambivalent.

[25] I should acknowledge, with regard to Aaron's commentary, that by this point my own reading has become more strictly (and locally) "literary" as well as theological, and less concerned with the historical reconstruction of "polemics and mythology" than his is. Note, too, that Niehoff's more recent positioning of this passage as an accommodation to the doctrinal hegemony of the Christian *ex nihilo* is not embraced by Aaron's earlier thesis, which views the *ex nihilo* as an anachronistic imposition on this text (Aaron, "Polemics and Mythology," p. 184).

alef, the conclusion of which seems to reseal the secret underlying and also covering up such impending revelation: "Just as the letter B[ב] is closed [at the back and sides but] open in front, so you have no right to expound concerning what is above or below, before or afterward" (GR I.X.1).

Like Tertullian and unlike Athanasius, chapter 1 of *Genesis Rabbah* thus directly engages the problems potentially introduced by the second verse of Genesis for the doctrine of creation. Unlike Tertullian, however, the rabbinic text proposes that beginnings—or rather, what is already underway when beginnings begin—must remain shrouded in mystery. Though there are no strong exegetical parallels, this mystery may nonetheless share more with Athanasius's austere *nihil* than is apparent at first glance. We have seen that Gamaliel's curse performatively negates the philosopher's interpretation of the second verse of scripture as implying creation out of uncreated matter—a verse that Athanasius simply passes over. Gamaliel's own counter-exegesis, however, does not displace this ambiguous verse with a disambiguating interpretation but rather displaces the one verse with many, in a move that arguably intensifies ambiguity. Moreover, the literary context of the midrash encourages the reader to consider the possibility that Gamaliel is hiding more than he is revealing.

Before the first letter of scripture, *bet*, the beginning of "beginning," *bereshit*, there is . . . nothing. Put otherwise, before the second letter of beginning there is the first letter of cursing—a negation that must itself be negated. Why was the world created with *bet* rather than *alef*? Having already been answered with respect to the form of the letter, the commentator repeats the query, so as to multiply answers. "Because this is the first letter of the Hebrew word for curse." Were the text to begin with the curse of *alef*, heretics might ask, "But how can the world endure when it has been created with a word meaning curse?" (GR I.X.3–4). An earlier question echoes through this one: How can the world endure when it has been built on the equivalent of "sewers, garbage, and junk"? (GR I.V.1).[26] This question would be met with a curse, had Scripture itself not suggested it, for surely the image of a world built on a cesspool is potentially far more compromising than the proposal that God is a skilled artist working with superior pigments. Encrypted in the first chapter of *Genesis Rabbah*, then, is the ambivalent and unsettling suggestion that before the beginning there is a curse and a negation; there is "chaos, emptiness, and darkness"; there is exposure to the contempt of the world, the blasphemy of heretics. How, indeed, does the world endure, grounded in such groundlessness?

Yet we have seen that the text also asserts that in the beginning there are already six things (but not yet the fullness of seven); in the beginning, there are many things (but it is not certain exactly what they are). We are reminded

---

[26] As Niehoff points out, the two passages are linked by the figure of Bar Qappara. See Niehoff, *"Creatio ex Nihilo,"* p. 56.

again that the *nothing is not one*—that it is far less and much more. Far less and much more, not only because the world is (grounded in) both an abyss and a multitude, but also because the same can be inferred of humanity and the divine. This is an inference that later kabbalists will draw explicitly, discovering both a "Divine Naught" and an emanationist doctrine of supramundane creation in the text.[27] Strikingly and unexpectedly, the eighth chapter of Genesis Rabbah[28] pulls Genesis 1:26 ("And God said, 'Let us make humanity in our image") back to the hermeneutically bottomless depth of verse 2, revealing on its shifting surface a divine-human mirroring of glorious monstrosities—androgynous, unformed, unlimited (GR VIII.I). Here, I am tempted to suggest (though, as with Athanasius, I am pushing the text in directions it may not quite want to go), we are also brought back to Rosenzweig's infinitesimal *Nichtnichts*. Is it—*are they*—God-world-human— emerging from or receding into "the formless night of nothing" (SR, p. 33)?

* * *

From Rosenzweig to the Fathers and Rabbis, and back again: in the yawning gap in between, a long history of nothing, including many of its greatest hits, remains untold. Rosenzweig read the Fathers—Tertullian and Augustine, if not Athanasius—before he encountered the Rabbis, but he may have learned more about nothing from the medieval kabbalah than from either of these earlier, and more widely authoritative, bodies of literature.[29] Nonetheless, my goal here has not been to inscribe a linear history of thought. Rather, I have tried to erase a certain history, beginning again with nothing, so as to discover whether it might be possible to think something new. Above all, I have not intended to reinscribe a history of Christian-versus-Jewish thought. In fact, I have tried gently—but only gently, for I don't question its basic insight, only its tendency toward reification—to unsay a history of the Christian origin of the *ex nihilo*, while also resisting relapse into a prior version that

---

[27] See Alexander Altmann, "A Note on the Rabbinic Doctrine of Creation," *The Journal of Jewish Studies*, Vol. 7 (1956), pp. 195–206.

[28] I have engaged this chapter briefly in Virginia Burrus, "Carnal Excess: Flesh at the Limits of Imagination," *Journal of Early Christian Studies*, Vol. 17, no. 2 (2009), pp. 247–265.

[29] Bertolino, " 'Schöpfung aus Nichts' " pp. 247–264, points toward the influence of kabbalah as mediated by Schelling. Wolfson, "Light Does Not Talk" 87–148, demonstrates with greater depth and nuance both Rosenzweig's ambivalence and his attraction to the mystical, and the resulting contradictions of thought that arise. Elsewhere Wolfson brings out Rosenzweig's affinities with kabbalistic thinking implicitly, by drawing the strands of his thought into the weave of his own meditations on mysticism and messianism; see Elliot R. Wolfson, "Postface: In an Instant-Advent of the (Non)event," in *Open Secret: Postmessianic Messianism and the Mystical Revision of Menahem Mendel Schneerson* (New York, NY: Columbia University Press, 2009). Still further affinities of Rosenzweig's thought with Jewish mystical traditions become evident to the reader of Elliot R. Wolfson, "Revisioning the Body Apophatically: Incarnation and the Acosmic Naturalism of Habad Hasidism," in *Apophatic Bodies: Negative Theology, Incarnation, and Relationality*, edited by Christopher Boesel and Catherine Keller, (New York, NY: Fordham University Press, 2009)—e.g., the concept of an infinitesimal point, or a "space-between," where something and nothing coincide, or the assertion of the reversibility of creation from nothing.

would attribute that same origin to Judaism. I have attempted instead to inhabit a dialogue already underway in the beginning and still ongoing to this day, one by no means exclusive to Jews and Christians.[30] Moreover, what I have identified as a certain austerity in Athanasius's text, a contrasting richness of ambiguity in the rabbinic corpus, should not be taken as typical of Christian and Jewish exegetical tactics, respectively. Continuities of that sort can be traced, but just as easily can their reversals, and in the end the mystery of the nothing is such that what seems to be void and empty is already the beginning of everything, and what seems to be something is really . . . nothing at all. Perhaps resistance to both identity and sameness in this conceptual context should not be surprising: nothing is not many, any more than it is one.

---

[30] See Wolfson's comparison of the thought of Habad Hasidism with Mahayana Buddhism, especially the Madhyamika tradition in "Revisioning the Body Apophatically." See also Harold H. Oliver, "Nagarjuna and *creatio ex nihilo*," in *Theology in Global Context: Essays in Honor of Robert Cummings Neville*, edited by Amos Yong and Peter G. Heltzel, (New York, NY: T & T Clark, 2005), pp. 229–240. Mary-Jane Rubenstein, "Cosmic Singularities: On the Nothing and the Sovereign," *Journal of the American Academy of Religion*, Vol. 80 no. 2 (2012), pp. 485–517, argues for the influence of the *ex nihilo* on physicists.

Modern Theology 29:2 April 2013
ISSN 0266-7177 (Print)
ISSN 1468-0025 (Online)

THOMAS AQUINAS'S UNDERSTANDING OF PRAYER IN THE LIGHT OF THE DOCTRINE OF *CREATIO EX NIHILO*

RUDI te VELDE

1. Introduction

The idea of prayer, of why we pray and what we expect to achieve by praying, presents a serious challenge to any theology which conceives of God and his relationship to the world in terms of *creatio ex nihilo*. This doctrine states, among other things, that nothing can exist outside God which is not totally dependent upon God. Everything we are and do—including the act of prayer—has its enabling condition in God's universal active power, outside which nothing can exist at all. The notion of *creatio ex nihilo* emphasizes the encompassing universality of God's creative influence in things: there is nothing in us which is exempt from God, no place from which we can address Him, as it were, from the outside, as if God is not already there, at the very beginning where we start to live, to act, to desire for the good, to pray.

In the metaphysical approach of Thomas Aquinas the universality of God's active power with respect to the whole of reality has the important implication that it is impossible for God to receive from the world. Nothing that happens in the world or in human history can constitute a "new fact" for God, which is not already included in His productive knowledge of things and events. God does not relate in a *reactive* way to His creatures. If we think of God as the universal determining ground of all existing things, the consequence will be a theologically closed universe, being the result of the one-way causality going from God to creatures. The question may be raised

Rudi te Velde
Department of Systematic Theology and Philosophy, Tilburg University, PO Box 90153, 5000 LE
Tilburg, THE NETHERLANDS
Email: r.a.tevelde@tilburguniversity.edu

whether, in such a world, it makes sense for us to pray to God, to expect Him to fulfill our desires, to show us mercy and forgiveness as consequence of our prayers. What is the use of prayer if God's causality with respect to the world is from all eternity fully determined and not liable in any way to change?

The question of prayer and its "utility" (*utilitas*) in view of the immutability of God is addressed by Aquinas in his *Summa contra Gentiles* as part of the extensive treatment here of divine providence (*divina providentia*). The religious practice of prayer and the concept of providence belong intrinsically together in the sense that the act of prayer presupposes a God who takes care of us, who provides us with the good things we need and desire. Prayer, in all its different aspects of petition, supplication, repentance, confession, praise, etc., requires a God who is the principle of a providential (moral) order: a just and merciful God who is leading His creatures to their end and good. But at the same time, providence seems to make prayer superfluous and ineffective, since, according to Thomas, God's will cannot be changed and neither can His providential plan. What, then, do we think to achieve, and in what way, when we pray to God?

The problem of the "utility" of prayer is dealt with by Thomas in terms of his famous distinction between the first cause, which is God, and the order of second causes within the created world, which have their own power and operation. God wants some effects to be realized as a result from the operations of secondary causes, among which are our prayers. These prayers, Thomas argues, are included in God's providential order; they are foreseen as the means by which certain effects are realized. How this is to be understood exactly is not easy to explain. To many, the classical notion of providence is tainted with the implication of determinism. The plan of providence, as it exists in God's mind, must be certain and immutable, which seems to mean that nothing can occur in any other way than it actually does. Nowadays, many would reject this metaphysical conception of all-determining providence as something which reminds us too much of the God of the *ancien régime*, the sovereign deity of absolute power who is in charge of everything, leaving no room for genuine human freedom, not allowing for real interaction between man and God.

What I particularly want to show in this article is that Thomas's discussion of prayer makes clear that his notion of God is not like the absolute monarch of the *ancien régime*; on the contrary, it is a God who grants the secondary causes (nature, human will) their own power and operation, not by "retreating" as it were from the "autonomous" space of the human world, but by being actively present in all things and by positing them in their own being and operation. The God of Aquinas is a God of participation, of letting other things share, from His own abundance, in being and in goodness.[1] The gift of

---

[1] See Rudi te Velde, *Aquinas on God* (Burlington, VT: Ashgate, 2006).

being entails the gift of causality; God makes other things to be a cause in their own right, including the causality of freedom. It is a God who favors, so to speak, a governmental system of "subsidiarism", according to which the secondary causes have their own operation. Thus, Thomas's view of providence must be understood against the background of the participation concept of *creatio*. It is from this perspective that his account of prayer is interesting and worthy to be considered with respect to the actual theological debate.

We will start with the notion of providence, whether and in which way providence, in Thomas's view, will leave sufficient room for contingency and freedom in the human world ("here below"). Next, we will address the problem of prayer and the paradox of providence: without providence, prayer seems to be quite useless, but even with providence, at least in the certain and immutable way in which Thomas understands it, the utility of prayer is questionable. After that, we will look at how Thomas deals with the biblical picture of a merciful God who hears the prayers of those who repent of their sins and is willing to change His former verdict. The biblical way of speaking seems to allow for a sort of interactionism between God and His people, which Thomas thinks to be impossible, being contrary to the logic of *creatio ex nihilo*. Finally, in the last section we will conclude with a few remarks about the place of human freedom within the providential order of the world.

2. Providence and the "Second Causes"

The question of the utility of prayer is discussed in the context of the treatment of the notion of providence.[2] It is only with respect to a providential God that the religious act of prayer can be understood to be meaningful (according to the words of Matthew 7:8: "ask, and it shall be given you"). At the same time, however, the idea of providence, in its classical-metaphysical sense, seems to imply a deterministic view of the world we humans live in.

---

[2] The basic text underlying this article is chapter 95/96 of *Summa Contra Gentiles* III: "That the immutability of divine providence does not suppress the value (*utilitas*) of prayer." I use the translation of Vernon J. Bourke (New York, NY: Hanover House, 1955–57). Other relevant texts about prayer are *S.Th.* I, q.23, a.8; *S.Th.* II-II, q.83. From the extensive literature on the subject of prayer in Aquinas I mention a few studies: Lydia Maidl, *Desiderii interpres. Genese und Grundstruktur der Gebetstheologie des Thomas von Aquin* (Paderborn: F. Schöningh, 1994); Brian Davies, "Prayer", in Brian Davies and Eleonore Stump (eds.), *The Oxford Handbook of Aquinas* (Oxford: Oxford University Press, 2011).

The problem of prayer, of whether it is compatible with God's unchangeable providence, touches on the position of Process Theology, which denies that God can be totally unchangeable, omnipotent, etc. See especially Lewis Ford, "Our Prayers and God's Passions," in H. J. Cargas and B. Lee (eds.), *Religious Experience and Process Theology: The Pastoral Implications of a Major Modern Movement*, (New York, NY: Paulist Press, 1976), pp. 429–430. For the concept of providence in *Summa contra Gentiles* III, see Norman Kretzmann, *The Metaphysics of Providence: Aquinas's Natural Theology in Summa contra Gentiles III*, (Cambridge: Cambridge University Press, 2001).

One especially might wonder whether providence does not do away with contingency, which is an essential feature of our human world. The question is, "What difference prayer can make if providence means that everything in the world is already settled and ordered according to God's plan?" We shall first look at Thomas's understanding of providence, in particular the complex relationship between the first cause (divine agent) and second causes (created agents). This will put us on the right track to understand the effectiveness of prayer as an instance of the secondary causality of the human agent.

Providence means, to begin with, that the world is ruled by divine reason, which orders all things to the good. Thomas distinguishes between "providence" in the strict sense, which is the "rational plan", existing in God's mind, of the order of all things, and "government" (*gubernatio*), which denotes the execution of the divine plan by leading creatures to their end and good.[3] Providence, we may conclude, stands for the "rule of reason". For Thomas, the providential order of the world is essentially an order exhibiting divine reason and wisdom.

The question, then, might be raised why (divine) reason should exclude, or appears to exclude, contingency? Contingency, as Thomas understands it, is characterized by a relative lack of reason: something is contingent inasmuch as it has the possibility to exist or not to exist. The contingent can fail to be or to act in a determined way; hence, it is marked by a certain weakness and deficiency. According to the Greek-Aristotelian view the universe is divided into a higher part, characterized by necessity and perfect rationality, and a lower part, in which contingency reigns. Therefore, the rational order of the universe has its limits in the lower part of nature. But then two possibilities present themselves: either providence is restricted to the higher part of the universe, that is, the perfect and uniform movements of the celestial bodies as opposed to the "messy" sublunary sphere of nature where things happen more or less without reason, or providential reason extends to the whole universe in such a way that there can be, from the point of view of divine reason, no contingency whatsoever. The problem of providence, especially as it is addressed in the *Summa contra Gentiles*, arises at the crossroads of Greek-Arab necessitarianism and Christian thought about freedom, in which providence must be made to fit the moral realm of human free agency.

In order to appreciate how subtly and carefully Thomas deals with this problem in *Summa contra Gentiles*, we shall draw a sketch of the different steps along which he develops his "Christian" understanding of providence. First, the very existence of God's providence is affirmed and argued for: one must say that God governs all things in the world with respect to the good, which is God Himself.[4] Next, if we speak of God governing the world, this

---

[3] Cf. *S.Th.* I, q.22, a.1.
[4] *ScG* III, c.64: "That God governs things by his providence"(*Quod Deus sua providentia gubernat res*).

should not be understood in an external manner as if God governs an already existing world. God is active in the world in the sense that He *gives* being to all things and *preserves* them in being.[5] Providence, it should be stressed, is not really different from the act of creation. By one and the same act God produces all things, preserves them in being and leads them to their end and good. Providence, one might say, is a continuation of the act of creation; the difference is that in providence (or in *gubernatio*) God specifically relates to creatures as constituted in their own specific nature and mode of operation. In the case of providence there are two levels of causality to be accounted for: the first cause, which is God, and the second causality of creatures, who are active in virtue of their own power. Now, the causal activity proper to creatures is said to be totally dependent upon the divine power which is active *in* all things. This is expressed in the thesis taken from the *Liber de causis* that "nothing gives being unless it acts by divine power".[6] The immediate consequence of this is that "God is the cause of operation in all things that operate".[7] God's causality is such that He is active in all things causing them to operate according to their own nature and kind. In no way can God be thought of as standing outside the world; God is everywhere and actively present in all things.[8] There is no operation of whatever kind possible without God operating in it.

However, the omnipresence of God's power in all things should not be understood in the sense that the proper actions of things are suppressed or replaced by that absolute power. For Thomas, an absolute power is not a power which does not tolerate any other power besides itself; "absolute" means that it can cause something else to be and to act by its own power. This is precisely what creation for Thomas entails. God operates, Thomas continues, in the operation of nature in such a way that the effect is both from God and from the natural agent. Not in the sense that the effect is partly from God and partly from nature, but that the whole is done by both (*totus ab utroque*).[9] We see Thomas defending here, against a false understanding of God's omnipotence, the efficacy of the secondary causes. Providence does not imply that God does everything by Himself to the exclusion of nature's own operation (or the operation of human free will).

What characterizes Thomas's understanding of God's providential government is that it includes the operations of all the secondary causes. In the same way as he rejects the view that God does everything by Himself at the

---

[5] *Ibid.*, c.65: "That God preserves things in being" (*Quod Deus conservat res in esse*).

[6] *Ibid.*, c.66: "That nothing gives being except insofar as it acts by divine power" (*Quod nihil dat esse nisi inquantum agit in virtute divina*).

[7] *Ibid.*, c.67: "That God is the cause of operation for all things that operate" (*Quod Deus est causa operandi omnibus operantibus*).

[8] *Ibid.* c.68: "That God is everywhere" (*quod Deus est ubique*).

[9] *Ibid.* c.70: "How the same effect is from God and from a natural agent" (*Quomodo idem effectus sit a Deo et a natura agente*).

cost of nature's own operation, so he rejects the view that some other cause may add something to God's operation from the outside. Both views follow the same model of mutual concurrence, according to which God and creature are two particular entities within a common field: either God is everything and does everything, but then the creature is no more than a puppet, or God leaves something for us to do, but then our free decisions may effect a change in God. For Thomas, both scenarios are equally unacceptable. Divine providence includes the operations of secondary causes. It is carried out by means of both natural (necessary or contingent) and human (rational, free) agency. Thus the exercise of providence, understood correctly, is not exclusively God's doing; the effects of providence are realized by means of secondary causes, thus through natural causes and through human actions (amongst which is prayer). This means that providence, as Thomas points out in full detail, does not entirely exclude the existence of evil (c.71), contingency (c.72), free will (c.73), fortune and chance (c.74). These four are all essential characteristics of the world in which we live; they mark the open and unpredictable character of the human world, open and unpredictable not in spite of God's providence, but rather as the dimension in which God's providence will be fulfilled. Hence, providence, being the rule of reason (wisdom) in all things, does not remove contingency from our world. The world of human life—that is the religiously significant world in which we experience so many reasons for prayer—remains intact in its aspects of contingency and temporal openness. Thomas does not allow a massive presence of the first cause in the order of secondary causes, in such a way that the secondary causes would be suppressed or pushed aside.

3. The Value of Prayer

Why should we pray to God? What is the use of prayer? The answer Thomas gives is simple and straightforward: the purpose of prayer consists in that a person may obtain from God the object which he desires.[10] Prayer is primarily a matter of asking, of expressing one's desires, and presenting them to God, who will provide us with the good things we need. But does it make sense to do this if God's providence is said to be unchangeable? Are the good gifts from God not already programmed as part of His eternal plan, whether we pray for them or not? The hidden presupposition behind these questions is that by means of prayer we intend to effect some change

---

[10] *Ibid.*, c.95 (1): "... that a person may obtain from God the object which he desires." I agree with Brian Davies who underlines this point very well: "His [Thomas's] approach to prayer is, we might say, an attempt to demystify it, to view it as a regular exercise of practical reason, as a matter of asking for something one wants." (*The Oxford Handbook of Aquinas*, Eleonore Stump and Brian Davies (eds.), [Oxford: Oxford University Press, 2011], Chapter 35: Prayer, p. 469).

in God's will; that as result of our prayers something will happen in God's ordering of things, as a consequence of which we may enjoy the desired effect. This magical understanding of prayer is rejected by Thomas: "Prayer is not established for the purpose of changing the eternal disposition of providence, since this is impossible".[11] I call this a "magical" interpretation of prayer because it regards prayer as a means of controlling and manipulating the divine power toward our human needs and ends. The purpose of prayer cannot be to make God do something He otherwise would not have done, thus trying to influence God. For Thomas, this is not how God is; God does not receive from the world. There is no interaction, at least not in this sense, between God and man.

"Ask, and you shall receive". For Thomas, prayers are indeed "efficacious" before God.[12] Prayer and gift are connected with each other in a non-accidental way. That connection, according to Thomas, is founded in the fact that prayer belongs to the order of secondary causes and that God wants to carry out the effect of his providence by means of these secondary causes. "The cause of some things that are done by God is prayers and holy desires"[13], Thomas says. The effectiveness of prayer should not be understood in a causal-instrumental sense as if the gift were the produced effect of our prayer. The connection itself between prayer and its fulfillment by God falls under the order of divine providence. In other words, God wants and foresees a certain connection between our prayers and their fulfillment by His gifts. To say that we should not pray, Thomas remarks, because God's providence is immutable so that prayer does not have a real effect on how things happen, is the same as to say that we should not walk in order to get to a place, or eat in order to be nourished, which is clearly absurd.[14] There is something for us to do, but we should not think that our agency itself falls outside the order of providence, as if it is an additional factor operating independent of that order.

One has to accept, it appears, some intrinsic or intelligible connection between prayer, taken in the sense of a specific articulation of human desire for good things, and its fulfillment by God; not, of course, in the sense that each prayer will automatically and infallibly lead to its fulfillment, but neither is the fulfillment merely a matter of divine lottery. The logic of the connection is rooted in God's goodness, which is the principle of the teleological order of all things. According to this logic, we see Thomas arguing in the following way: "all things naturally desire the good, and since it pertains to the divine goodness to assign being, and well-being (*esse et bene esse*) to all in accord with a definite order, the result is that, in accord

---

[11] *Ibid.*, c.95 (1).
[12] The term "efficacious" (*efficax*) is used in c.96, n.8.
[13] C.96 (8).
[14] C.96 (8).

with his goodness, he fulfills the holy desires which are brought to completion by means of prayer."[15] Thomas speaks here remarkably of "holy desires" of the rational creature, that is, desires ordered by God to Himself as principle and source of all goodness, and as such already "acknowledged" by God, so to say. Perhaps one can interpret the expression "holy desire" as referring to human desires under the aspect of the ultimate desire for God Himself.

It appears that the connection between one's desires, which are presented to God by prayer, and their fulfillment has its ruling principle in God's goodness. It is appropriate for God's goodness "to bring to a fitting conclusion the proper desires that are expressed by our prayers". In another argument Thomas employs the logic of friendship as a means to argue for the non-accidental nature of the connection between prayer and gift. It pertains to the essential meaning of friendship that the lover wills the fulfillment of the desire of the beloved, because he wishes the good for the beloved. When we apply this to the relationship between God and His creatures, we can say that God loves His creatures (as sharing in His goodness), and especially the rational creature (man), and so God wills the desires of a rational creature to be satisfied, for, compared to other (non-rational) creatures, it participates most perfectly in divine goodness.

This very interesting argument raises several questions. First, Thomas speaks here of "friendship", but what he seems to have in mind is not the mutual relationship between friends, but only this aspect that, according the "love of friendship", one wishes the good for one's friend and beloved. Connected to this aspect is the question of the role of prayer as expressing and presenting one's desires to God. Thomas argues that God, because He loves the rational creature in a special way, wants its desires—*presented to Him through prayer*—to be satisfied. But why do the desires need to be explicated by prayer, so that they exist in a conscious manner for the human creature? This aspect of what the specific activity of prayer (articulation, specification, presentation to God) adds to the desires is hardly touched on by Thomas. One might reason that the manifold of our factual desires must be subsumed under the fundamental desire for God, and this is what happens when we explicate our desires and present them to God through prayer.[16] Thomas would probably say that explicating one's desires by means of prayer is something appropriate to a "rational creature".

---

[15] ScG III, c.95, n.1: "*Cum enim omnia naturaliter bonum desiderent, ut supra probatum est; ad supereminentiam autem divinae bonitatis pertinet quod esse, et bene esse, omnibus ordine quodam distribuat: consequens est ut, secundum suam bonitatem, desideria pia, quae per orationem explicantur, adimpleat.*"

[16] Cf. the definition of prayer used in the question on prayer *S.Th.* II-II, q.83: *oratio est interpres desiderii* "Prayer is the interpreter of desire." See the study of Lydia Maidl mentioned in note 2.

4. The Divine Immobilitas *and the Biblical Picture of a Merciful God*

As said before, God cannot receive from the world. No creature can really add something to God. There exists only one-way causation between God and the world. Still, Thomas claims that prayers are efficacious (*efficacies*) before God, surely not in the sense that they may cause some change in God's providential plan, but in the sense that God wants and foresees good gifts for us as result of our prayers, fulfilling the role of "second causes". Thus prayers are said to be helpful, but what must be excluded is efficiency in the practical-technical sense of the word. The aim of prayer should not be understood as an attempt to influence God or to manipulate the divine power.

Thomas clarifies his position by distancing himself from a twofold error concerning prayer.[17] In both errors the underlying assumption is that prayer should effect a change in the order of providence. On the one hand, there are those who have denied the usefulness of prayer, either by claiming that there is no providence altogether (like the Epicureans), or by claiming an all-pervasive necessity in things subjected to providence (like the Stoics). In both cases it follows that prayer is useless, and consequently, that all worship of the Deity is vain and without value. On the other hand, there are those who thought that the divine disposition could be changed by means of prayers. This position is associated by Thomas with the Egyptians, who tried to influence fate by prayers and "by means of certain idols, incensing, or incantations".[18] We have, thus, two errors: according to the first, prayer is useless because it cannot change the order of things, and according to the second, prayer is useful because it can effect a change. The common root of both errors is the assumption that prayer is only then useful when it effects a change in God and His will.

Now, Thomas says, there are several passages in Scripture which, when read superficially, fit the position of the Egyptians, as they suggest a God who may change His will as the consequence of prayers and supplications from our part. There is an apparent contradiction between the principle that God does not receive from the world (the principle of *immobilitas* or *immutabilitas*) and the biblical picture of a God who is merciful and prepared to forgive those who repent of their sins and return to Him. The God of the Bible is *moved* by the prayers of His people; He will eventually reconsider His sentence and show mercy. This seems to imply that, as it is the case with the Egyptians, the disposition of providence is held to be somehow variable.

A ready example of such a passage where God is said to change His will is a text in Jeremiah: "I will suddenly speak against a nation and against a

---

[17] C.96 (9): "a double error concerning prayer."; see also *S.Th.* II-II, q.83, a.2.

[18] C.96, (10). This reference to the "Egyptians", who assumed that the order of fate can be changed by prayers and sacrifices, is taken from Gregory of Nyssa (in fact Nemesius), *De natura hominis* c.36. Cf. *S.Th.* I, q.23, a.8; q.116, a.3.

kingdom to root out and to pull down and to destroy it. If that nation against which I have spoken shall repent of their evil, I will also repent of the evil that I have thought to do to them." (Jer. 18:7–8). Thus, in reply to the repentance shown by His people God Himself will repent the punishments He has in mind for them. This passage suggests that God's will is mutable, and that a certain change in His providential order may occur as the result of what happens in the temporal world of man. Another example is the story of King Hezekiah whose death is announced by the prophet Isaiah at the command of God. After prayers of Hezekiah, his death sentence is postponed for an additional fifteen years: "Go and say to Hezekiah . . . I have heard your prayer . . . behold I will add to your days fifteen years" (Isa. 38:1–5).

These scripture passages, if understood superficially, may lead to the inconvenient conclusion that God's will is mutable and that something which occurs in time will effect a change in God's eternity. How, then, should we interpret these passages in which it is suggested that God is able to change His will? For Thomas, the key to the solution lies in the important difference between a universal and a particular order. In case of a particular order, which depends on a particular cause, we can conceive of something outside that order through which it may be changed, either by prayer or by some other means. Thus nothing prevents a particular order from being changed by some action from outside that order. For Thomas, the order of fate, which follows from the constellation of the stars, is still a *particular order*, which can be changed by God existing outside and above that order. Thus the Egyptians wanted to effect through their prayers a change in the order of the stars by appealing to the higher God above the stars. The order of fate is superseded by a higher and more universal power which is God.

But in case of a universal order, there is no "outside". I think this follows from Thomas's conception of *creatio ex nihilo*: the order stemming from the universal cause, which is God, must embrace all things; it leaves no room for an "outside", thus no possibility to change or cancel the order in name of some higher order.

The "magical" model of the Egyptians can therefore be explained, Thomas says, in this way; namely, that the order of fate, which in their opinion can be changed through prayers, represents a *particular* order, superseded by a higher and more universal power which is God. The Egyptians adhere to an astrological religion, according to which the order of human affairs is ruled by fate, which depends on the movements of the stars. Insofar as human affairs fall under some particular order of inferior causes, that order may be changed through prayers directed to God who transcends all causes. Thus if some biblical passages suggest that God may change his mind as a result of prayers, one should interpret this way of speaking in the sense that some order of inferior causes, established by God, is changed through prayer, not the "eternal disposition" of God himself. Thomas quotes Gregory who had said that "God does not change His plan (*consilium*), though at times he may change His judgment (*sententia*)".[19] "Judgment", Thomas explains, should here be taken in the sense of what expresses the order of inferior causes. God's judgment, not in itself but as expressed in such a particular order, may be changed (postponed, suspended), and such a change may be called metaphorically "God's repentance".

Not everyone shall find this interpretation wholly satisfactory, I would think. However, two aspects of Thomas's view deserve to be underlined. First, God is a universal cause, establishing an order that embraces all things. In the case of such a universal order we cannot conceive of an external position from which that order may be changed. The God of *creatio ex nihilo* thus makes an end to any magical use of religion. Such a God cannot, strictly speaking, *react to* or be *influenced by* something which is not already included in the "eternal disposition" of the first cause. Secondly, we may speak of a "particular order", or an order of "inferior causes" (for instance, the order of nature or of the celestial bodies), which depends on God's free creation and which, therefore, can be changed. The biblical language of a merciful God is justified to the extent to which it can be shown to be reconcilable with the basic principle that the eternal disposition of God does not allow for any change.

5. Human Freedom and the Order of the Good

Thomas's account of the utility of prayer echoes the words of Matthew: "Everyone who asks receives, and he who seeks finds, and to him who knocks it shall be opened." For Thomas, the point of praying consists in that we may obtain from God what we desire (*ut aliquis illud quod desiderat, assequatur a Deo*). At first sight this may seem rather simple, but its deeper meaning becomes evident if we realize that the "desires" we are talking about are fundamentally the desires of a creature which depends for its being and well-being on the Creator. The religious practice of prayer is motivated by the fact that our many daily desires and needs (for food, safety, health, peace, justice, etc.) are rooted in our creaturely desire for God. In prayer we turn to God, presenting our desires to Him, in the hope that He will turn Himself, the goodness itself and the source of all good, to us and bring our desires to fulfillment. We pray to God for good things, but fundamentally we pray to God for God Himself, because we cannot live and live well without God.[20] The fundamental and ultimate desire of man as a *rational creature*, implicit in each prayer, is for God Himself, for personal communion with God in the *visio beatifica*. Our desires, as rooted in our creaturely condition, are already linked to God in a certain way; or

---

[19] C. 96 (15); the reference is to Gregory the Great, *Moralia* 16, c.10: "Omnipotens enim Deus, etsi plerumque mutat sententiam, consilium numquam."

[20] According to the words of Psalm 79:4: "Show us Thy face, and we shall be saved." *Ostende faciem tuam, et salvi erimus*, quoted by Thomas in *S.Th.* II-II, q.83, a.5.

more precisely, our *motus ad bonum* expresses the way in which God draws human creatures towards Himself. Prayer is something we do, a free and personal act, but at the same time the act of prayer brings us to acknowledge God's infallible will in all that happens to us (we pray: "Thy will be done"), as we trust that His infallible will is a will for the good. In prayer God is addressed as the Good, that He, being the principle of our movement towards the good, may fulfill our desires. In prayer we articulate what Thomas calls "our pious desires" (*pia desideria*); desires which are, so to say, already recognized and accepted by God as included in the providential ordering of all things to the good. In the expression, "What 'I' really desire is . . .", Thomas takes the identity of this "I" as that of a creature, thus not of a free-floating subject which relates itself in a free and spontaneous act to God. "I" am already, "from the beginning", related to God, by my being and my desire for the good, by God Himself.

Thomas defends the usefulness of prayer by means of the scheme of first and second causes. Prayer and everything else we can do ("good works") to promote the salvation of ourselves and of others, are included under the universal order of God's providence. There cannot be a neutral (non-creaturely) position for human freedom outside the teleological order of providence, thus outside God. For Thomas, freedom pertains to the *modus operandi* of the "second cause" of the human agent. Human freedom, as proper to the mode of causality of the rational creature, is integrated in God's providential regime, since God's providence does not only concern "effects" but also the (free) way in which these effects are brought about by human action.[21] Freedom, as presupposed by the act of prayer, therefore cannot be conceived of as standing over against God, outside the order of providence, as if our free decisions were to inform God's providential knowledge which in turn would not be sufficiently determined in respect to the actual course of things without this extra information. For Thomas, freedom can never be a matter of the possibility to act outside and independent of the order of providence, or of experiencing the inner realm of freedom to act or not to act (to pray or not to pray) as absolute, and thus as incompatible with the order of providence, in which the outcome of my free decisions is already foreseen. The problem of human freedom and providence (of a sovereign and all-powerful God) is a typically modern problem resulting from the difficulty to reconcile human freedom with our status as a secondary cause. Also typically modern is the tendency to think about freedom in terms of counterfactuals: *what if* I decide to do otherwise, can my free decision be a surprise for God? If not, how can it then be a *free* decision? How can the outcome of the spontaneity of my free will be included under the immutable and certain providence of God? These really

---

[21] Cf. *ScG* III, c.94 (15): "For the effects are foreseen by God, as they are freely produced by us." (*Sic enim sunt a Deo proviso ut per nos libere fiant*).

difficult questions are not yet posed by Thomas. For him there is in the end no real conflict between human freedom and the certainty of God's providence, for freedom pertains to the causal mode of "secondary causes", of rational creatures who are made to operate in their specific way by virtue of the immanence of God's power in them. And what we, as rational creatures, really want is not so much freedom as such, but the free fulfillment of our desires. The exercise of human freedom is therefore embedded in the teleological order of creation.

Modern Theology 29:2 April 2013
ISSN 0266-7177 (Print)
ISSN 1468-0025 (Online)

CONTEMPLATION, CHARITY AND CREATION *EX NIHILO* IN DANTE'S *COMMEDIA*[1]

VITTORIO MONTEMAGGI

I

My aim in this article is to reflect on the importance of creation *ex nihilo* for our understanding of Dante's *Commedia*. I would like to do so, in particular, by reflecting on the inextricable relationship existing in Dante's poem

Vittorio Montemaggi
Department of Romance Languages and Literatures, 343 O'Shaughnessey Hall, University of Notre Dame, Notre Dame, IN 46556, USA
Email: vmontema@nd.edu

[1] The present article has its origins in a paper for the symposium "Dante and the Contemplative Tradition" sponsored by the Devers Program in Dante Studies at the University of Notre Dame in November 2007. I presented a second version in April 2008 at a research seminar of the Department of Italian at the University of Leeds, sponsored by the Leeds Centre for Dante Studies. I am extremely grateful for these opportunities to discuss my work. On both occasions, the papers were prepared in close conversation with Matthew Treherne and his work on "Contemplation and the Created World in the *Commedia*". I am especially grateful to Matthew for his comments. I am also especially grateful to Janet Soskice, whose encouragement to think deeply about the question of creation *ex nihilo* in the *Commedia* opened up fruitful perspectives on Dante's work, from which the article in its present form issues. Most recently, I am extremely grateful to have had the opportunity of presenting and discussing these ideas at the Centre of Theology and Philosophy of the University of Nottingham. I am moreover extremely grateful to Zygmunt Barański, Piero Boitani, Theodore Cachey, Peter Hawkins, Robin Kirkpatrick and Christian Moevs for their detailed advice on earlier versions of this article. I also wish to thank Scott Annett, Ann Astell, Jason Baxter, Eleonora Buonocore, David Burrell, Sarah Coakley, Carlo Cogliati, George Corbett, Andrew Davison, Marco Emerson-Hernandez, David Ford, Ben Fulford, Innocenzo Gargano, Filippo Gianferrari, Manuele Gragnolati, Douglas Hedley, Ronald Herzman, Jacob Holsinger Sherman, Claire Honess, Samuel Kimbriel, Elena Lombardi, John Marenbon, Giuseppe Mazzotta, Philip McCosker, Alison Milbank, John Milbank, Susannah Monta, Edward Morgan, Charles Nejedly, David O'Connor, Simon Oliver, Cyril O'Regan, George Pattison, Catherine Pickstock, Tamara Pollack, Elizabeth Powell, Russell Re Manning, Janet Martin Soskice, Jennifer Spencer Goodyer, Carole Straw, Jonathan Teubner, Alain Tschudin, Denys Turner, Ineke Van 't Spijker, Heather Webb, and Anna Williams for their comments on the ideas this article explores.

between creation *ex nihilo*, contemplation and charity. More specifically, I would like to outline an understanding of how Dante's idea of the relationship between these three can be seen to underlie the very structure and narrative form of the *Commedia*. Through reflection on the relationship between contemplation, charity, and creation *ex nihilo*, I suggest, form and content might be seen, from a theological point of view, to be perfectly at one.

Underlying the reflections that follow are also some broad questions, a proper exploration of which lies beyond the scope of the present article, but which are nonetheless important to raise so as to be able to foreground some of the possible wider implications of the reading proposed here, and of the doctrine of creation *ex nihilo* in general. What is the *Commedia* ultimately about? What is Dante's final end in writing his poem?[2] What bearing does this have on our understanding of the form of Dante's text as a narrative poem? And what, in turn, are the broader theological implications of all this?

This article is written in the context of recent interdisciplinary scholarship on the relationship between theology and poetry in the *Commedia*.[3] Recent years have seen a growing interest in the study of Dante's theology.[4] On the one hand, this has meant that theological modes of thought are increasingly recognized as of primary importance for our understanding of Dante's work. On the other hand, it has meant that Dante is increasingly recognized as an important author for contemporary theologians to engage with. In these respects, it is significant to note that reflection on creation *ex nihilo* is a natural point of convergence between current Dantean and theological scholarship.[5] On the one hand, there is the increasing interest in creation *ex nihilo* in contemporary theology, which finds significant expression in *Creation and the God of Abraham*.[6] On the other hand, we find creation as one of the most

---

[2] For the importance of the teleological in Dante's theology, see Anna N. Williams, "The Theology of the *Comedy*", in *The Cambridge Companion to Dante*, edited by Rachel Jacoff, second edition (Cambridge: Cambridge University Press, 2007).

[3] This article can also be read in the light of broader debates concerning the relationship between literature, religion and theology, on which see the special issue of *Religion & Literature*, Vol. 41 no. 2 (2009), edited by Susannah Monta.

[4] For an overview, and further Dantean and theological bibliography, see Vittorio Montemaggi and Matthew Treherne, "Introduction: Dante, Poetry, Theology" in *Dante's "Commedia": Theology as Poetry*, edited by Vittorio Montemaggi and Matthew Treherne (Notre Dame, IN: University of Notre Dame Press, 2010). The essays in this volume offer a sense of the range of perspectives that interdisciplinary reflection on the theology of Dante's poem can open up. Some of their theological implications are explored in the two afterwords: John Took, "Dante, Conversation and Homecoming" and David F. Ford, "Dante as Inspiration for Twenty-First-Century Theology". For a systematic survey of the implications for Dante scholarship of multi-faceted study of Dante's theology, see *Reviewing Dante's Theology*, edited by Claire Honess and Matthew Treherne (New York, NY: Peter Lang: forthcoming).

[5] See also Montemaggi and Treherne, "Introduction", *Dante's "Commedia": Theology as Poetry*, pp. 5–8.

[6] *Creation and the God of Abraham*, edited by David Burrell, Carlo Cogliati, Janet Soskice and William Stoeger (Cambridge: Cambridge University Press, 2010).

prominent questions being addressed in recent studies of Dante's theology. Two of the studies that stand out in this regard for our present purposes are Piero Boitani's "The Poetry and Poetics of the Creation" and Matthew Treherne's "Liturgical Personhood: Creation, Penitence and Praise in the *Commedia*".[7] The former offers a poetic and theological interpretation of some of the most important references to creation (of the cosmos and of the human soul) in the *Commedia*, showing just how intimately Dante's understanding of creation is tied to his poetic practice; the latter reveals just how central the notion of creation is to the structure of the *Commedia*, characterized by the depiction of a journey of transformation from a distorted to a flourishing relationship between Creator and creation, especially as seen in and through the human self. As will be evident, I am greatly indebted both to Boitani's and to Treherne's essays.

As will also be evident, the greatest debt underlying the present reading is to Christian Moevs' *The Metaphysics of Dante's "Comedy"*,[8] which offers the fullest account available of Dante's understanding of the relationship between Creator and creation. Moevs places creation *ex nihilo* at the centre of Dante's metaphysics and theology,[9] in ways which resonate constructively with the work of theologians such as David Burrell and Sara Grant.[10] As Moevs shows, when Dante refers to creation he is referring, like the other great theologians of the Middle Ages, specifically to creation *ex nihilo*. For Dante, creation does not refer to a discrete action or moment, as much as it does to a relation, that relation with its source whereby anything that is has its being. There is no existence apart from God, creation being the self-giving manifestation of the love which God is. All that is only *is* insofar as it is brought and sustained into existence by God; which is to say that all that is only is insofar as the love which is God freely gives itself in and as creation. To exist is to be constituted, out of nothing, by (or as) divine love. This, for creatures endowed with intellect, means that to be true to one's existence is to respond to one's createdness by freely giving oneself to (or as) divine love. Which, as we shall see, means in turn that for Dante creation *ex nihilo*, contemplation and charity are inextricably connected. Indeed, the story told by the *Commedia* is the story of this interconnection as the defining characteristic of human life properly conceived.[11]

---

[7] Both in *Dante's "Commedia": Theology as Poetry*.

[8] Christian Moevs, *The Metaphysics of Dante's "Comedy"* (New York: Oxford University Press/AAR, 2005).

[9] See in particular Chapter 4, "Creation".

[10] See, for example, David B. Burrell, *Faith and Freedom: An Interfaith Perspective* (Oxford: Blackwell, 2004), and "The Act of Creation with its Theological Consequences", in *Creation and the God of Abraham*; Sara Grant, *Towards an Alternative Theology: Confessions of a Non-Dualist Christian*, with an introduction by Bradley J. Malkovsky (Notre Dame, IN: University of Notre Dame Press, 2002).

[11] For the related question of how the *Commedia* might be read as prayer, see Giuseppe Mazzotta, "The Book of Questions: Prayer and Poetry", *Dante Studies*, Vol. 129 (2011), pp. 25–46.

II

That creation *ex nihilo* in the *Commedia* is tied to contemplation and charity can be gleaned from the two instances in the poem in which the words "Creator" and "creature" are spoken in the same breath. The first of these is found at the centre of the *Purgatorio*, in Virgil's Augustinian disquisition on love,[12] which has been taken by commentators to be the structural heart of the *Commedia* as a whole. As Virgil puts it: "Né creator né creatura mai/[. . .] figliuol, fu sanza amore,/o naturale o d'animo; e tu 'l sai"[13] [Neither creator nor created thing/was ever, dearest son, without . . ./the love of mind or nature. You know that][14] (*Purg.* 17.91–93). Or, in other words, love is the underlying condition of creation, that which governs and defines the relation between all that is and its source. Indeed, the first reference to creation in the *Commedia* tells us that creation is the work of divine love (*Inf.* 1.39), and Dante's journey famously ends at one with "l'amor che move il sole e l'altre stelle" [love that moves the sun and other stars] (*Par.* 33.145). It is in, through and as love that creatures most truthfully reveal their createdness and return to their Creator.

"Creator" and "creature" are also spoken in the same breath in Dante's description, as he and Beatrice reach the Empyrean, of the light in which a creature endowed with intellect can come to see its Creator:

> Lume è là sù che visibile face
> lo creatore a quella creatura
> che solo in lui vedere ha la sua pace. (*Par.* 30.100–102)

[There is, above us there, a light that makes/the All-Creator in creation seen/by those who only seeing Him have peace.]

The final, eternal, end of human (and of angelic) existence is the perfect peace that derives from the heavenly vision of God.[15] It is in seeing God that human beings are most truly themselves. Contemplation is thus presented as the most perfect human activity, the perfection of human createdness.

---

[12] On this, and on the questions addressed below of contemplation and of the relationship between Dante's poem and Scripture, see the essays in Peter S. Hawkins, *Dante's Testaments: Essays in Scriptural Imagination* (Stanford, CA: Stanford University Press, 1999).

[13] The text of the *Commedia* is cited from Dante Alighieri, *Commedia*, ed. and comm. Anna Maria Chiavacci Leonardi, 3 vols (Milan: Mondadori, 1991–97).

[14] Translations are taken from Dante, *The Divine Comedy*, trans. and comm. Robin Kirkpatrick, 3 vols (London: Penguin, 2006–07). Kirkpatrick's commentary stands out for its detailed and sustained attention to the theological dynamics and implications of Dante's poetic narrative, and is as such an indispensable point of reference for theologians wishing to engage with Dante's text.

[15] See Tamara Pollack, "Dante and the Beatific Vision", in *Reviewing Dante's Theology*. See also Steven Botterill, "Mysticism and Meaning in Dante's *Paradiso*", in *Dante for the New Millennium*, edited by Teodolinda Barolini and H. Wayne Storey (New York, NY: Fordham University Press, 2003).

This had already been stated in *Purgatorio*, at the start of Dante's journey up the mountain during the ascent of which penitent human beings learn properly to orient their being towards the beginning and end of their existence. In chastising Virgil, Dante, his friend Casella and the penitents that have lost themselves in the beauty of Casella's music, the guardian of Purgatory, Cato, urges them: "Correte al monte a spogliarvi lo scoglio/ch'esser non lascia a voi Dio manifesto" [Go run towards the mountain. Shed that skin/ Which won't let God be manifest to you]. (*Purg.* 2.122–123). The purpose of Purgatory is that of removing that in human beings which does not allow them properly to contemplate God. But Cato's words ought not to be seen as a call for the penitent to move towards heavenly things simply by leaving behind the worldly. Contemplating God does not come at the expense of that which is other than God, but with full awareness of how all that exists finds its meaning in God, who grounds and sustains all existence. Indeed, as he approaches final contemplation of God at the end of the poem, Dante tells us—with philosophical precision and with an image that meta-textually points to Dante's own book as ultimately wanting to show that all that is is in God—that in the divine depths of eternal light,

> [. . .]vidi che s'interna,
> legato con amore in un volume,
> ciò che per l'universo si squaderna:
>   sustanze e accidenti e lor costume
> quasi conflati insieme, per tal modo
> che ciò ch'i' dico è un semplice lume. (*Par.* 33.85–90)

[I saw, contained,/bound up and gathered in a single book,/the leaves that scatter through the universe/beings and accidents and modes of life,/as though blown all together in a way/that what I say is just a simple light.]

Full vision of God is not possible if the world is taken as the *primary* object of one's thought and desire (this is Cato's point), but it entails proper appreciation of how all that is relates to God.[16]

A similar point is made at the very beginning of the *Commedia*. Having escaped the dark wood, Dante begins to ascend a hill moving towards the sun that gives it light, only for his journey to be impeded by three beasts. So strong is this impediment—especially the she-wolf, the third of the beasts— that Dante loses all hope of ever reaching the top of the hill, or God:

---

[16] See also Zygmunt Barański, "Dante's Signs: An Introduction to Medieval Semiotics and Dante", in *Dante and the Middle Ages*, edited by John C. Barnes and Cormac Ò Cuilleanáin (Dublin: Irish Academic Press, for the Foundation for Italian Studies, University College, Dublin, 1995).

E qual' è quei che volontieri acquista,
e giugne 'l tempo che perder lo face,
che 'n tutti suoi pensier piange e s'attrista;
   tal mi fece la bestia sanza pace,
che, venendomi 'ncontro, a poco a poco
mi ripigneva là dove 'l sol tace. (*Inferno*, I. 55–60)

[We all so willingly record our gains,/until the hour that leads us into loss./Then every single thought is tears and sadness./So, now, with me. That brute which knows no peace/came ever nearer me and, step by step,/drove me back down to where the sun is mute.]

It is no coincidence that in the fruitful ambiguity of line 58, both the she-wolf and Dante are said to be without "pace"—without that delight which can only properly come through vision of God. Of particular interest for our purposes, however, is the simile Dante uses to describe despair. This is as theologically precise and important an image as any other in the poem: Dante is doing nothing less than setting out the central theological principle underlying the exploration of the relationship between human beings and God presented in the *Commedia*. For the image reveals that the reason Dante is unable to go beyond the she-wolf is that he does not properly understand how God relates to God's creation. The pilgrim thinks of the summit of the hill, and the possibility it symbolises of reaching the divine, as one would of a material possession: a thing, object or idea a human being can desire, reach, acquire, possess, and consequently lose. The pilgrim is thinking of God as part of creation, as being merely one of the things that are. This, however, is not what God is. If it were, it would mean God could not have created all there is *ex nihilo*, and this would be a theological contradiction. If one is not thinking of the ground of all existence, itself not existing in any particular way but, as being itself, bringing and sustaining everything into existence, one is simply not referring to God, no matter whatever else one goes on to say about particular aspects of divine being.

Dante, then, is in need of instruction about how to conceive his relationship to God and the possibility of seeing Him. To be so instructed he has, as Virgil says in rescuing him (*Inf.* 1.91–93, 112–123), to be guided through another kind of journey, that will bring him to meet the damned, the penitent and the blessed—in short, to consider how other individual human beings have either failed or succeeded in living a proper relationship to God.[17] This is very

---

[17] For theological reflection on the *Inferno* see Denys Turner, *Julian of Norwich: Theologian* (New Haven and London: Yale University Press, 2011), pp. 88–92 ("Sin as Misperception: Dante"). See also pp. 109–115 ("Dante and the Incompleteness of 'Narrative' ") for reflection on the theological significance of the *Commedia*'s narrative form, and Chapter 6 ("Substance and Sensuality") for a reflection on the relationship in Julian between creation *ex nihilo* and the human self that is illuminating for reflection on the same question in Dante.

significant, since it suggests that, for Dante, there might be an intimate connection between, on the one hand, relating to and contemplating God, and, on the other, encountering other human beings. In other words, we are told in the opening scene of the poem that contemplation is the ultimate goal of human createdness, and that a proper understanding of this requires direct encounter with the particular existence of other human beings as seen in relation to God. It is through this kind of journey that Dante can learn how human beings might come to see and be at one with divine love. It is no coincidence, therefore, that he should choose to do theology precisely in and through a narrative poem telling the story of such a journey.

III

To reflect further on the significance of the interconnections between contemplation, charity and creation *ex nihilo* in the *Commedia*, let us begin from a passage which qualifies the lines from *Paradiso* 30 cited above. These are the words of Piccarda Donati (sister of one of Dante's dearest friends), who in *Paradiso* 3 responds to Dante's amazement at the fact that not all the blessed enjoy the same degree of blessedness by saying:[18]

> Frate, la nostra volontà quïeta
> virtù di carità, che fa volerne
> sol quel ch'avemo, e d'altro non ci asseta.
>   Se disïassimo esser più superne,
> foran discordi li nostri disiri
> dal voler di colui che qui ne cerne;
>   che vedrai non capere in questi giri,
> s'essere in carità è qui *necesse*,
> e se la sua natura ben rimiri.
>   Anzi è formale ad esto beato *esse*
> tenersi dentro a la divina voglia,
> per ch'una fansi nostre voglie stesse;
>   sì che, come noi sem di soglia in soglia
> per questo regno, a tutto il regno piace
> com' a lo re che 'n suo voler ne 'nvoglia.
>   E 'n la sua volontade è nostra pace:

---

[18] For a study of the crucial importance of the figure of Piccarda in the *Commedia*, in relation to the equally crucial significance of the presence in the *Commedia* of the other members of the Donati family referred to by Dante, see Piero Boitani, *Dante's Poetry of the Donati: The Barlow Lectures on Dante, Delivered at University College London, 17–18 March 2005*, edited by John Lindon (Leeds: Maney, for the Society for Italian Studies, 2007). For a theological gloss on Piccarda's words, see Vittorio Montemaggi, " 'E 'n la sua volontade è nostra pace': peace, justice and the Trinity in the *Commedia*", in *War and Peace in Dante*, edited by John C. Barnes (Dublin: Four Courts Press, for the UCD Foundation for Italian Studies, forthcoming).

ell' è quel mare al qual tutto si move
ciò ch'ella crïa o che natura face. (*Par.* 3.70–87)

[Dear brother, we in will are brought to rest/by power of *caritas* that makes us will/no more than what we have, nor thirst for more./Were our desire to be more highly placed,/all our desires would then be out of tune/with His, who knows and wills where we should be./Yet discord in these spheres cannot occur—/as you, if you reflect on this, will see—/since charity is *a priori* here./In formal terms, our being in beatitude/entails in-holding to the will of God,/our own wills thus made one with the divine./In us, therefore, there is, throughout this realm,/a placing, rung to rung, delighting all/—our king as well in-willing us in will./In His volition is the peace we have./That is the sea to which all being moves,/be it what that creates or Nature blends.]

"Pace" is used both in *Paradiso* 3 and in *Paradiso* 30 to denote the final well-being of the human person in God; but in *Paradiso* 3 it is said to lie in conformity to God's will, whereas in *Paradiso* 30 it is said to consist in the vision of God. There would appear to be a slight contradiction here. Indeed, on meeting Piccarda the pilgrim is baffled precisely by the fact that she can be perfectly happy while she could be enjoying a clearer vision of God:

Ma dimmi: voi che siete qui felici,
disiderate voi più alto loco
per più vedere e per più farvi amici? (*Par.* 3.64–66)

[But tell me this: you are so happy here,/have you no wish to gain some higher grade,/to see and be as friends to God still more?]

The answer Piccarda gives, as we have seen, is that the blessed are perfectly happy (literally so!) in seeing just as much as is granted them to see by God; and that this is necessarily the case because the essence of heavenly being is charity, where by "carità" is meant the love by which the will of each blessed is perfectly at one with that of God and that of all the other blessed. With great poetic skill and philosophical precision—note for instance the rhyme on "necesse" and "esse"—Dante thus beautifully articulates the dependence of all being on divine love.

As Piccarda explains, then, to be in perfect peace is not only to see God, but also to be at one with the will of God, in which everything that is has its being; and this means that to be in perfect peace is to be in charity, at one in love both with God and with all the other blessed. What baffles the pilgrim is only baffling if due consideration is not given to the fact that to be in heaven is to be in charity and in conformity to the will of God, one because of the other; and to the fact that this implies—as the pilgrim finds out for himself at the end of his journey—that to see God *is* to be at one with the love which God is.

In other words, the pilgrim's doubt comes from an error in theological perspective—not altogether unlike that characterizing his despair in *Inferno* 1—as a result of which proper attention is not given to the fact that, as the love which is the ground of all existence, God is not simply that *to* which all that exists moves—as we are told in lines 86 and 87 of Piccarda's speech. He is also, as we are told both in lines 79–81 and in line 85, that *in* which human existence can find its most perfect expression (no matter "where" one abides in relation to God).[19] God is not some-thing there for human beings to see. God is that truth in seeing which human beings recognize themselves to be existing as expressions of the love that grounds their being.

For Dante, then, to see God is to be at one with his will, which is to say that to see God is to exist in and as perfect charity, at one not only with God but also with all the other blessed. Contemplation and charity are inextricably linked: perfect contemplation of God entails—as love—perfect unity with God and with other human beings, one through the other. This is the blessed "esse" for which God, out of nothing, brings and sustains us into existence.

IV

The fertile interplay between creation *ex nihilo*, contemplation and charity found in the *Commedia* is one of the defining characteristics of Dante's theological poetics. Indeed, his particular way of foregrounding, through narrative poetry, the inextricable link between creation, contemplation and charity, can also be seen as one of the marks of originality of Dante's theology with respect to his medieval context. In this respect, one might connect reflection on the relationship between creation, contemplation and charity in the *Commedia* to Peter Hawkins' claim that Dante's greatest contribution to the Christian tradition is his exploration of the theological value of the smile.[20] Thus, one of the continual markers of the progress made by Dante in his journey towards and into the divine is the increasing truthfulness, beauty, profundity and inscrutability of Beatrice's smile, itself reflecting the increasing truthfulness, beauty, profundity and inscrutability of the charity between them.[21] Furthermore, the smile as embodied in Beatrice is itself a preparation for the

---

[19] See Cormac Ó Cuilleanáin, "Patterns of Enclosure in the *Commedia*", in *Patterns in Dante: Nine Literary Essays*, edited by Cormac Ó Culleanáin and Jennifer Petrie (Dublin: Four Courts Press, 2005), pp. 119–120.

[20] Peter S. Hawkins, *Dante: A Brief History* (Oxford: Blackwell, 2006), pp. 98–130 and "All Smiles: Poetry and Theology in Dante's *Commedia*", in *Dante's Commedia: Theology as Poetry*.

[21] See also Douglas Hedley, "Neoplatonic Metaphysics and Imagination in Dante's *Commedia*", in *Dante's "Commedia": Theology as Poetry*. On the theological importance of the interpersonal, see Janet Martin Soskice, *The Kindness of God: Metaphor, Gender and Religious Language* (Oxford: Oxford University Press, 2007).

smile which, in referring to the eternal act of divine love and contemplation on which all that is depends, Dante ascribes to the Trinity itself.[22]

So truthful is Beatrice's smile that at one point on the journey through Paradise it has to be purposefully withheld from Dante, lest he be incinerated by its divine excess (*Par.* 21.1–12). We are at the entrance to the Heaven of Saturn, the episode in the *Commedia* dedicated explicitly to contemplation.[23] It is here that Dante sees the blessed who in life stood out for their contemplative activity and meets, as representative of these, Peter Damian and Benedict.[24] As generally recognized, one of the defining theological characteristics of the cantos of the Heaven of Saturn is Dante's wish not simply to present the contemplative life as the form of existence that might bring the human being closest to God, but to do this by foregrounding an inextricable connection between the contemplative and the active lives.[25] One of the ways in which this is done is, once again, through reflection on charity.

Of central importance, in this respect, is Dante's encounter with Peter Damian in *Paradiso* 21. It is Peter Damian who, alone amongst the contemplatives, first comes to greet Dante and Beatrice on their arrival in the Heaven of Saturn. To Dante's request for an explanation regarding this, Peter Damian replies:

> [. . .] l'alta carità, che ci fa serve
> pronte al consiglio che 'l mondo governa,
> sorteggia qui sì come tu osserve. (*Par.* 21.70–72)

[But *caritas* on high that makes us serve/so readily the wisdom of the spheres/allots the places here as you observe.]

The only explanation Peter Damian can give to Dante is the charity which, as in the words of Piccarda, is said to make the blessed move in perfect accordance with the will creating all that is. The pilgrim however is not satisfied

---

[22] *Paradiso* 33.124–126. See Oliver Davies, "Dante's *Commedia* and the Body of Christ", in *Dante's Commedia: Theology as Poetry*; and Christopher Ryan, "*Paradiso* VII: Marking the Difference between Dante and Anselm", in *Dante and the Middle Ages: Literary and Historical Essays*, edited by John C. Barnes and Cormac Ò Cuilleanáin (Dublin: Irish Academic Press, for the UCD Foundation for Italian Studies, 1995).

[23] See Amilcare A. Iannucci, "Saturn in Dante", in *Saturn from Antiquity to the Renaissance*, edited by Massimo Ciavolella and Amilcare A. Iannucci (Ottawa: Dovehouse, 1992).

[24] For fuller theological reflection on Dante's encounter with Peter Damian, see Vittorio Montemaggi, "Esempio di carità tra teologia, contemplazione e giustizia: il Pier Damiani del *Paradiso* di Dante", in *La "Grammatica di Cristo" di Pier Damiani: Un maestro per il nostro tempo*, edited by Guido Innocenzo Gargano and Lorenzo Saraceno (S. Pietro in Cariano (Verona): Il Segno dei Gabrielli, 2009). A full treatment of Dante's idea of contemplation would also have to take into account the significance in the *Commedia* of the figure of Gregory the Great. Further studies are needed in this area. See Vittorio Montemaggi, "Dante and Gregory the Great", in *Reviewing Dante's Theology*.

[25] See also Giuseppe Mazzotta, "Language and Vision (*Paradiso* XXI and XXII)", in *Dante's Vision and the Circle of Knowledge* (Princeton, NJ: Princeton University Press, 1993).

with Peter Damian's answer. He wants to know not only *how* but also *why* it is Peter Damian, and only Peter Damian, who comes to greet himself and Beatrice (*Par.* 21.73–78).[26] In responding to this second question, Peter Damian reveals, once again, an error in theological perspective on the part of the pilgrim.

> Né venni prima a l'ultima parola,
> che del suo mezzo fece il lume centro,
> girando sé come veloce mola;
>   poi rispuose l'amor che v'era dentro:
> «Luce divina sopra me s'appunta,
> penetrando per questa in ch'io m'inventro,
>   la cui virtù, col mio veder congiunta,
> mi leva sopra me tanto, ch'i' veggio
> la somma essenza de la quale è munta.
>   Quinci vien l'allegrezza ond'io fiammeggio;
> per ch'a la vista mia, quant' ella è chiara,
> la chiarità de la fiamma pareggio.
>   Ma quell' alma nel ciel che più si schiara,
> quel serafin che 'n Dio più l'occhio ha fisso,
> a la dimanda tua non satisfara,
>   però che sì s'innoltra ne lo abisso
> de l'etterno statuto quel che tu chiedi,
> che da ogne creata vista è scisso.
>   E al mondo mortal, quando tu riedi,
> questo rapporta, sì che non presumma
> a tanto segno più mover li piedi.
>   La mente, che qui luce, in terra fumma;
> onde riguarda come può là giùe
> quel che non pote perché 'l ciel l'assumma». (*Par.* 21.79–102)

[Nor had I reached the last of all these words/when that light took its centre as a hub,/spinning around itself as grindstones do./The love within it then replied to me:/"Divine light drives its point upon me here./And, penetrating that in which I'm wombed,/its virtue, joined with my own powers of sight,/lifts me so high above myself, I see/on high the essence where that light is milked./Hence comes the brightening joy in which I flame./Equal to what I see in clarity/is this clear flame that I myself display./But still the soul in Heaven that brightens most—/that seraph with its eye fixed most in God—/could never satisfy your last

---

[26] The use of "predestinata" in line 77 enhances the theological significance of Dante's encounter with Peter Damian, as it seems to indicate that it can also be seen as the conclusion of Dante's exchange on predestination with the Eagle of the Heaven of Jupiter.

demand./For what you ask so in-beyonds itself/within the chasm of divine decree,/it is cut off wholly from a creature's sight./And so when you return to mortal things,/bear this with you, so none there may presume/to move their feet to any suchlike aim./Minds that shine here, on earth give off mere smoke./So just consider whether those down there/could do what, raised to Heaven, no mind can do."]

There is no answer to the kind of question Dante asks. While Peter Damian, like all the blessed and the angels, can see the divine essence, this does not mean that he can also comprehend the workings of the divine will. This is simply something a creature cannot do. And *not* because, as often suggested, of a weakness of intellect, but because of its dependence on God. To be able to give an answer to Dante's question would mean being able to place oneself outside such dependence. This is clearly not possible, as it would mean stepping outside existence itself.[27] The workings of the divine are not unknowable on account of a weakness inherent in the creature, but rather on account of the fact that one is *created*, that God is the love from which the creature derives its existence and in which the creature can come, even in its weakness, perfectly to participate.[28]

Such is the nature of Peter Damian's explanation that the pilgrim's error in theological perspective seems, finally, to have been corrected—and the poet gives us one of the most important *terzine* of the *Commedia*:[29]

> Sì mi prescrisser le parole sue,
> ch'io lasciai la quistione e mi ritrassi
> a dimandarla umilmente chi fue. (*Par.* 21.103–105).

[His words so cut and limited my thoughts/that I gave up the question, holding back,/to ask him, very humbly, who he was.]

The pilgrim's journey towards vision of God passes from an individual quest for comprehension of the workings of the divine, to the humility required properly to encounter another human being. Properly to see God is also properly to see human personhood, and vice versa. Contemplation is, indeed, the end and perfection of human existence: seeing God, for human creatures, coincides with seeing the truth of one's own individual and communal being.

---

[27] See also, William Franke, *Dante and the Sense of Transgression: "The Trespass of the Sign"* (London: Continuum, 2012).

[28] This is not the only time in the *Commedia* that Dante refers explicitly to createdness as a way of pointing to the limits and vulnerability of the human intellect before the divine. See, for instance, *Par.* 11.30; 19.89; 20.119; 33.45

[29] I am extremely grateful to the students in my "Between Religion and Literature: Meaning, Vulnerability and Human Existence" class in Fall 2011 for helping me appreciate just how important these lines are.

This *terzina* marks a moment of fundamental importance in the narrative structure of the *Commedia*. It would seem that it is to this moment of recognition that Virgil's explanation in *Inferno* 1 regarding the nature of the journey Dante has to undertake is aimed. Indeed, *Paradiso* 21.103–105 marks the pilgrim's crucial transition from the presumption of aiming to count God as but simply one of one's "possessions", to the recognition that journeying towards God is only possible through dispossession of such a presumption in and through one's encounter, in humility and love, with other human beings. This is the kind of journey required in order to come to see the nature of one's createdness.

Dante's moment of recognition before Peter Damian is also the point of arrival of a narrative and theological progression which explicitly starts with Dante's encounter with Casella at the beginning of *Purgatorio*. As already mentioned, Dante's encounter with his musician friend, and Cato's rebuke, raises the question of the relationship between heavenly truth and earthly existence. As such, they are generally seen as the prelude to the explicit reflection that occurs early in the following canto on the nature of human embodiedness. Soon after Cato's rebuke, Dante is taken aback by not seeing Virgil's shadow on the ground next to his. To which Virgil responds:

Ora, se innanzi a me nulla s'aombra,
non ti maravigliar più che d'i cieli
che l'uno a l'altro raggio non ingombra.
    A sofferir tormenti, caldi e geli
simili corpi la Virtù dispone
che, come fa, non vol ch'a noi si sveli.
    Matto è chi spera che nostra ragione
possa trascorrer la infinita via
che tiene una sustanza in tre persone.
    State contenti, umana gente, al *quia*;
ché, se potuto aveste veder tutto,
mestier non era parturir Maria (*Purg.* 3.28–39)

[If nothing now is shadowed at my feet,/don't wonder any more than when the rays/the heavens project don't block each other out./To suffer torments both of heat and chill,/the Utmost Power gives bodies, fit for that,/not wishing *how* it does to be revealed./It's madness if we hope that rational minds/should ever follow to its end the road/that one true being in three persons takes./Content yourselves with *quia*, human kind./Had you been able to see everything,/Mary need not have laboured to give birth.]

As in *Paradiso* 21, we find here an explicit connection between the unknowability of God and the nature of human personhood—in this case human personhood as constituted by the mysterious union of body and soul.[30] Of particular interest are the references to the Trinity and the Incarnation. The workings of divine "Virtù",[31] we are told, allow the human soul to generate an aerial body upon reaching the afterlife, so as to be true to human hylomorphism even between death and the resurrection. This process is said to be as unknowable as the mystery of the unity of the Trinity.[32] And, in order to allow human beings to confront such unknowability, we are further told, Mary gave birth to Christ. For Dante, the Incarnation does not undermine the unknowability of God; it reveals how an acceptance of such unknowability lies at the basis of a right comprehension of God. By reading *Purgatorio* 3 and *Paradiso* 21 alongside each other—as two ends of the same overarching theological reflection—we are thus presented with the idea that, for Dante, a right comprehension of God does not require or entail full comprehension of the workings of divine life and its creative activity, but *does* require and entail full recognition of the createdness of the human person (body-and-soul) as seen in relation to divine being, as well as a humble intellectual and ethical openness to the encounter with the individual and communal particularity of other human beings.

The words with which Peter Damian describes his contemplative life on earth further enhance the significance of this:

Tra ' due liti d'Italia surgon sassi,
e non molto distanti a la tua patria,
tanto che' tron suonan più bassi,
  e fanno un gibbo che si chiama Catria,
di sotto al quale è consecrato un ermo,
che suole esser disposto a sola latria.
  [. . .] Quivi
al servigio di Dio mi fe' sì fermo,
  che pur con cibi di liquor d'ulivi
lievemente passava caldi e geli,
contento ne' pensier contemplativi. (*Par.* 21.106–117)

[Between the littorals of Italy/not far from your own fatherland, hard rocks/surge up so high the thunder sounds beneath./These form a hunch-back ridge called Catria./Below that lies a consecrated cell/ devoted, once, to God's unending praise'/[. . .] Here I remained/so

---

[30] See Manuele Gragnolati, *Experiencing the Afterlife: Soul and Body in Dante and Medieval Culture* (Notre Dame, IN: University of Notre Dame Press, 2005).

[31] On Dante's understanding of "virtù", see Ruth Chester, "Ethics, Ontology and Representation: The *Virtù*-Dynamic of Dante's *Commedia*" (PhD Thesis, University of Leeds, 2012).

[32] See also Vittorio Montemaggi, " 'La rosa in che il verbo divino carne si fece': human bodies and truth in the poetic narrative of the *Commedia*", in *Dante and the Human Body*, edited by John C. Barnes and Jennifer Petrie (Dublin: Four Courts Press, for the UCD Foundation for Italian Studies, 2007).

steadfast in the service of our Lord—/oil, simply, of the olive dressed my food—/that I lived lightly through both heat and chill,/contented with contemplative intent.]

Peter Damian's "caldi e geli" (116) exactly recalls that in *Purgatorio* 3.31. We move from the "tormenti caldi e geli" spoken of by Virgil to the "caldi e geli" lived gladly by Peter Damian, contented in his contemplation. Through contemplation, and the joy deriving therefrom, the body is no longer presented primarily as source of suffering but as an integral part of the union between human beings and God. Peter Damian's asceticism is presented not as entailing a rejection of the earthly but as one of the ways in which the earthly might be oriented towards contemplation of the divine. At the level of form, further confirmation of this can be found in the intense and theologically pregnant physicality that, as Robin Kirkpatrick has recently foregrounded, characterizes Dante's language and imagery in this canto.[33]

The pilgrim understands the significance of his encounter with Peter Damian, and when he meets Benedict in the following canto, eagerly expresses his desire to see him in all his human appearance.

> [. . .] L'affetto che dimostri
> meco parlando, e la buona sembianza
>   ch'io veggio e noto in tutti li ardor vostri,
>   così m'ha dilatata mia fidanza,
> come 'l sol fa la rosa quando aperta
> tanto divien quant' ell' ha di possanza.
>   Però ti priego, e tu, padre, m'accerta
> s'io posso prender tanta grazia, ch'io
> ti veggia con imagine scoverta. (*Par.* 22.52–60)

[. . . The feeling you display/in speaking thus to me, the looks/I note so well-disposed in you, and all these fires,/have caused in me my trust to open wide/as sun does to the rose when this becomes/as fully open as its power can be./Therefore I pray, do, Father, make me sure/that I may come to take such grace that I/might see your face, uncovered, as you are.]

Benedict replies by explaining that the pilgrim's desire cannot be satisfied now, but will be satisfied in the Empyrean, where he will see all of the blessed in all their human appearance (*Par.* 22.61–72); and where, as we saw above, Dante will see the whole of creation bound together, as love, in God.

Of particular interest is the image of the rose in *Paradiso* 22.56–57. This is famously also the same image that Dante uses to describe the community of

---

[33] Dante, *Paradiso*, trans. and ed. Kirkpatrick, pp. 419–422.

the blessed in the Empyrean (*Par.* 30.117, 124; 31.1; 32.15, 120). In asking Benedict to see his human form, Dante's inner being opens itself up like a rose in the sun, just as the community of the blessed opens itself up like a rose under the light of the divine sun. In and through the image of the rose, individual and community are blended into one another.[34]

The significance of Dante's blending of individual and community into one in and through the image of the rose is further enhanced in Dante's presentation of the Church in *Paradiso* 23.[35] In that canto Dante witnesses the heavenly triumph of the Church, illumined by the light emanating by the resurrected body of Christ. Dante attempts to turn directly to this source of light, but is overwhelmed (*Par.* 23.16–45). Having thus been overwhelmed, however, and having learned important lessons concerning divinity from his encounters with Peter Damian and Benedict, Dante is now strong enough to sustain Beatrice's smile again, and is invited to do so by her (46–48). Beatrice, however, also urges Dante to turn his gaze from its exclusive attention on her and onto the heavenly triumph of the Church:

> Perché la faccia mia sì t'innamora,
> che tu non ti rivolgi al bel giardino
> che sotto i raggi di Cristo s'infiora?
>   Quivi è la rosa in che 'l verbo divino
> carne si fece; quivi son li gigli
> al cui odor si prese il buon cammino. (*Par.* 23.70–75)

[Why is it that my face in-loves you so/that you don't turn to see the garden where,/beneath Christ's rays, such beauty is en-flowered?/The rose, in which the Word of God became/our flesh is here. And here those *fleurs-de-lys*/whose perfume marks the path we rightly tread.]

Particularly significant for our purposes is the ambiguity of 73–74. The rose at 73 is generally taken to be Mary, and the lilies at 74 the apostles who with their example first encouraged the world to follow the right path. Undoubtedly correct, such interpretation does not however preclude the possibility that this may not be the only way to read the lines in question. For it is difficult not to see "rosa", used in such close proximity to the Empyrean, also as a reference to the Church as a whole. On this second reading each lily would be an individual person whose life encourages others to follow the right path. The two readings mutually illuminate each other and, in their

---

[34] One could, furthermore, consider the implications of all this for our understanding of Dante's amazement at the confluence of singular and plural in the speech of the Eagle in the Heaven of Jupiter (*Par.* 19.1–12) and of the reference to the confluence of singular and plural in Dante's profession of belief in the Trinity in his examination before Peter (*Par.* 24.139–141).

[35] For the significance of charity in Dante's understanding of the Church, see Paola Nasti, "*Caritas* and Ecclesiology in Dante's Heaven of the Sun", in *Dante's Commedia: Theology as Poetry*.

mutual illumination, enhance our appreciation of the mystery of the Incarnation as seen from the perspective of *Paradiso*. The Word as human the person Jesus, while the rose is Mary, in whose womb Jesus was conceived and generated. The Word as divine, truth itself, while the rose is the Church, in whose life the Word is made flesh insofar as it is, in charity, embodied in the words and deeds of individual persons.

It is in and through Christ, as the love incarnated in the Church that, according to Dante, human beings can achieve the perfection of their created *esse*. Indeed, it is in and through Christ that all that is was brought into being by the Love uniting Father and Son:[36]

> Guardando nel suo Figlio con l'Amore
> che l'uno e l'altro etternalmente spira,
> lo pirmo e ineffabile Valore
> quanto per mente e per loco si gira
> con tant' ordine fé, ch'esser non puote
> sanza gustar di lui chi ciò rimira. (*Par.* 10.1–6)

[Looking within his Son through that same Love/that Each breathes out eternally with Each,/the first and three-fold Worth, beyond all words,/formed all that spins through intellect or space/in such clear order it can never be,/that we, in wonder, fail to taste Him there.]

And, it is no coincidence that we should find the same term—"spira"—referring to the creation, out of nothing, of every individual human soul:

> Ma come d'animal divenga fante,
> non vedi tu ancor [. . .]
>   Apri a la verità che viene il petto;
> e sappi che, sì tosto come al feto
> l'articular del cerebro è perfetto,
>   lo motor pirmo a lui si volge lieto
> sovra tant' arte di natura, e spira
> spirito novo, di vertù repleto,
>   che ciò che trova attivo quivi, tira
> in sua sustanzia, e fassi un'alma sola,
> che vive e sente e sé in sé rigira. (*Purg.* 25.61–75)

[This creature will become a speaking child./Yet *how*, you don't yet see. [. . .] Open your heart. Receive the coming truth./Know this: when once

---

[36] For creation in the cantos of the Heaven of the Sun see Ronald Herzman, "From Francis to Solomon: Eschatology in the Sun" and Giuseppe Mazzotta, "The Heaven of the Sun: Dante Between Aquinas and Bonaventure", in *Dante for the New Millennium*.

the foetal brain is brought/to full articulation in the womb,/the Primal Cause of Motion turns in joy/to see so much of Nature's art, and breathes/new breath of spirit filled with power within,/which draws all active elements it finds/into its being and thus forms one soul/which lives and feels and turns as conscious self.]

To be human is to be an embodied, self-conscious being whose creation reflects the creative self-giving—"spira"—of the persons of the Trinity. Moreover, to be human is to be a being capable of speech ("fante"):[37] it is to enter the world in and through language, which means in and through community and human interaction.[38] It is in and through community and human interaction that we become the beings that we are, the possibility of such becoming thus being the most intimate marker of the mystery of our createdness, of our relationship with God.[39] In the light of this, we can appreciate further the theological significance of Dante's choice to craft theology as a narrative poem telling the story of a journey of transformation in and through human encounter.

V

We find, in the image of the rose developed in the *Paradiso*, full theological articulation of the idea expressed by Piccarda in *Paradiso* 3, that in God the blessed are made one while maintaining individual differences and characteristics. In turn, Piccarda's words, Dante's encounter with the contemplatives, and the image of the rose all prepare for Dante's own vision of and union with God at the end of the poem.

> Ne la profonda e chiara sussistenza
> de l'alto lume parvermi tre giri
> di tre colori e d'una contenenza;
>   e l'un da l'altro come iri da iri
> parea reflesso, e 'l terzo parea foco
> che quinci e quindi igualmente si spiri.
>   Oh quanto è corto il dire e come fioco
> al mio concetto! e questo, a quel ch'i' vidi,
> è tanto, che non basta a dicer 'poco'.
>   O luce etterna che sola in te sidi,
> sola t'intendi, e da te intelletta

---

[37] For Dante's theology of language and its poetic implications, see Vittorio Montemaggi, "In Unknowability as Love: The Theology of Dante's *Commedia*", in *Dante's Commedia: Theology as Poetry*.

[38] On language and love, see Elena Lombardi, *The Syntax of Desire: Language and Love in Augustine, the Modistae, Dante* (Toronto, Buffalo and London: University of Toronto Press, 2007).

[39] Janet Martin Soskice, "Monica's Tears: Augustine on Words and Speech", *New Blackfriars*, Vol. 83 (2002), pp. 248–258.

e intendente te ami e arridi!
    Quella circulazion che sì concetta
pareva in te come lume reflesso,
da li occhi miei alquanto circunspetta,
    dentro da sé, del suo colore stesso,
mi parve pinta de la nostra effige:
per che 'l mio viso in lei tutto era messo.
    Qual'è 'l geomètra che tutto s'affige
per misurar lo cerchio, e non ritrova,
penasndo, quel principio ond' elli indige,
    tal'era io a quella vista nova:
veder voleva come si convenne
l'imago al cerchio e come vi s'indova;
    ma non eran da ciò le proprie penne:
se non che la mia mente fu percossa
da un fulgore in che sua voglia venne.
    A l'alta fantasia qui mancò possa;
ma già volgeva il mio disio e 'l *velle*,
sì come rota ch'igualmente è mossa,
    l'amor che move il sole e l'altre stelle. (*Par.* 33.115–145)

[Within the being—lucid, bright and deep—/of that high brilliance, there appeared to me/three circling spheres, three-coloured, one in span./And one, it seemed, was mirrored by the next/twin rainbows, arc to arc. The third seemed fire,/and breathed to first and second equally./How short mere speaking falls, how faint against/my own idea. And this idea, compared/to what I saw … well, 'little' hardly squares./Eternal light, you sojourn in yourself alone./Alone, you know yourself. Known to yourself,/you, knowing, love and smile on your own being./An inter-circulation, thus conceived,/appears in you like mirrored brilliancy./But when a while my eyes had looked this round,/deep in itself, it seemed—as painted now,/in those same hues—to show our human form./At which, my sight was set entirely there./As some geometer may fix his mind/to find a circle-area, yet lack,/in thought, the principle his thoughts require,/likewise with me at this sight seen so new./I willed myself to see what fit there was,/image to circle, and how this all in-where'd./But mine were wings that could not rise to that,/save that, with this, my mind, was stricken through/by sudden lightning bringing what it wished./All powers of high imagining here failed./But now my will and my desire were turned,/as wheels that move in equilibrium,/by love that moves the sun and other stars.]

In seeing God, Dante sees a human figure—Christ's (as the Trinitarian context demands), but also Dante's (as suggested by the rich ambiguity of line 132) and that of all individual human beings (as stated with "nostra" in line 131).[40] This—the particularity of human personhood, in which individual and community can be perfectly at one—is what Dante ultimately sees in God. Why and how this should be so lie beyond creaturely comprehension. And, in realizing *this*, Dante's vision of God is perfectly realized. Which is to say that Dante finds himself to be perfectly at one with the love which God is—the charity that Piccarda had explained is the essence of heavenly being, the Creator of all that is.

It is this perfect union of creation *ex nihilo*, contemplation and charity that the *Commedia* is ultimately about. To realize this union perfectly in and as oneself is, for Dante, the final end of human creatureliness; and to invite his readers to move towards such realization is the final end of his poem. It is such realization that the pilgrim needs to come to on his journey, and this is why he has to undertake the sort of journey outlined for him by Virgil in *Inferno* 1—a journey in which movement towards God occurs in and through encounter with the individual and communal particularity of other human beings. This, I believe, is also why the poet chooses to do theology by offering us a work which, as narrative poetry, can adequately tell the story of such a journey. Through the relationship between creation, contemplation and charity, form and content can thus be seen in the *Commedia* to be perfectly at one.[41] As, ultimately, is also the case, as we have seen, with divine being and human personhood.

Using the same term—"spira"—that he uses to refer to the inner life of the Trinity and to the creation *ex nihilo* of the individual human soul, Dante tells us in *Purgatorio* 24 that his poetry is in-spired by God (52–54). And, having just been examined on his faith by Saint Peter, he tells us in *Paradiso* 25 that the *Commedia* is a "poema sacro/al quale ha posto mano e cielo e terra" [sacred work/to which both Earth and Heaven have set their hands] (1–2). In light of the role played by creation *ex nihilo* in Dante's thought, these claims ought not ultimately to be seen as an attempt to claim for the *Commedia* the same divine authority as Scripture or, for the poet, God-like divine powers.[42] They seem, rather, to be stating that if the *Commedia* is to be regarded as a truthful text, then that truthfulness ought to be seen, ultimately, as coming not from Dante but from the divine love in which all that is has its being. Indeed,

---

[40] This fertile tension between singular and plural, "mio" and "nostro", not only recalls the Eagle of the Heaven of Jupiter and Dante's profession of belief in the Trinity, but also the similar tension found in the opening two lines of the *Commedia*. In *Inf.* 1.1–2, however, the blending of individual and community is not directly associated with the figure of Christ. This difference marks the distance travelled by Dante.

[41] For the ways in which the relationship between form and content in Dante's poetry might be seen as sacramental, and in this respect be connected to the work of Aquinas and Eckhart, see Denys Turner, "How to Do Things With Words: Poetry as Sacrament in Dante's *Commedia*", in *Dante's Commedia: Theology as Poetry.*

[42] See also Chapter 2 ("Arbitrium"), in Justin Steinberg, *Dante and the Limits of the Law* (Chicago, IL: University of Chicago Press, forthcoming).

as we have seen, the story told by the *Commedia* is that of a journey of transformation towards the recognition that to be true to ourselves is to recognize our being as constituted by nothing other than divine love. The most perfectly we are able to do this and the most perfectly we can say of our human lives what Dante says about the angels: that they are loves ("amori") in, through and as which divine love can say "I am" (*Par.* 29.13–18). We can argue about the extent to which the *Commedia* actually *is* divine love configured as human language, as Dante hoped it could be.[43] But be that as it may, it is important, in reading Dante's poem as theology, to see its composition as governed by the recognition, stemming from belief in creation *ex nihilo*, that human existence and intelligence are perfected by their being transparent to their creatureliness in being contemplatively shaped as love.

The extent to which we are indeed prepared to see the *Commedia* as divine love configured as human language will depend in significant measure on the extent to which we are prepared for a text like the *Commedia* to have a transformative effect on our own lives. This need not necessarily coincide in all respects with the specific way in which the process of divinization is conceptually and imaginatively articulated by Dante in his poem.[44] But it will, in one way or another, require the kind of recognition of the radical dependence of all that is on God articulated in the doctrine of creation *ex nihilo*. Indeed, one of the theological merits of Dante's *Commedia* is its inviting us, in its narrative form as much as in its conceptual content, to reflect on just how radical that dependence might be. The *Commedia* does not simply tell us about or argue for the importance of the doctrine of creation *ex nihilo*; it attempts to show us what it might mean to fail or succeed in configuring our lives in ways that are true to the doctrine's spiritual implications. Reading a text like Dante's *Commedia* can thus help awaken us to the unfathomable depths of our createdness.

---

[43] A question that would merit serious reflection, in this respect, is that of Dante's idea of the possibility of salvation for non-Christians, raised most prominently (and somewhat problematically) by the figure of Virgil, Dante's references to Judaism and Islam, and the cantos of the Heaven of Jupiter. In reflecting on this question one would have to take into account both the fact that other religious traditions are often presented in very negative terms in the *Commedia* and the fact that the *Commedia* seems consciously to be less negative in this respect than many other medieval texts and stereotypes. One would also have to take into account both the fact that according to Dante no one will be saved who does not believe in Christ and the fact that for Dante the possibility of salvation is not necessarily tied to explicit profession of Christian belief.

[44] See also Simone Marchesi, *Dante and Augustine: Linguistics, Poetics, Hermeneutics* (Toronto, Buffalo and London: University of Toronto Press, 2011).

Modern Theology 29:2 April 2013
ISSN 0266-7177 (Print)
ISSN 1468-0025 (Online)

LUTHER'S TOPOLOGY: *CREATIO EX NIHILO* AND THE CULTIVATION OF THE CONCEPT OF PLACE IN MARTIN LUTHER'S THEOLOGY

JON MACKENZIE

How is Martin Luther to be placed within contemporary thinking? The question is barely raised in the current intellectual climate. If any answer were to be hazarded, there can be little doubt that the future development of *Lutherstudien* would be bequeathed to the historian of the late Middle Ages or the historical theologian of the Reformation period. In many respects, the Martin Luther who comes to the fore within twenty-first-century scholarship seldom steps beyond the bounds of those reductive asides in which the collapse of late-medieval ecclesiastical authority in Europe, say, or the development of modern German language, are given a number of deferential sentences before moving on to topics of greater historical interest. That is to say, it appears that Luther has little to offer the philosopher or theologian of the twenty-first century, save for those operating from within the circumscribed context of a denominational Lutheranism.

Nonetheless, the modern-day neglect of Martin Luther as a creative source for a constructive philosophy or theology manifests a clear break with earlier periods of intellectual history within the West. For it is impossible to evaluate the development of European thought through the last four centuries without perceiving Luther's influence lingering below the surface. In many cases it is indirect: for example, Kant belonged to a Lutheran faction of Pietism and, despite being critical of his native Christianity, the vestiges of the Lutheran influence upon Kant's project have not gone

Jon Mackenzie
Faculty of Divinity, West Road, Cambridge CB3 9BS, UK
Email: jrm94@cam.ac,uk

unnoticed.[1] Soon after Luther rose to prominence, appeals to his ideas became commonplace within both philosophy and theology, appearing periodically throughout the rise and fall of German Idealism, uncovered in thinkers as disparate as Hegel, Kierkegaard and Heidegger, and coming to be formative to such twentieth-century theological *virtuosi* as Karl Barth, Wolfhart Pannenberg, Jürgen Moltmann, Eberhard Jüngel and Robert Jenson. How then is this displacement of Luther as a creative starting-point within intellectual thought to be regarded? What has altered within the academic climate to reverse the tendencies of the last four-hundred years of European intellectual history?

In answering these questions, it is beneficial to take a step back and return to a time when Luther still commanded a place within the intellectual sphere. A number of academic studies produced across the twentieth century have dissected Luther's theology, linking it to various contemporary modes of philosophical thinking. On the one hand, a number of negative volumes appeared from predominantly Catholic scholars who criticised Luther for cultivating an intrinsic subjectivism, placing him at the head of a line of thinkers who would go on to become seminal for the formation of German Idealism.[2] For instance, Jacques Maritain, in his book *Three Reformers*, charges Luther with having developed a notion of the subject which could be viewed as the source of the latent individualism perceptible in western society. He argues: "Luther's self becomes practically the centre of gravity of everything. . . . The Reformation unbridled the human self in the spiritual and religious order, as the Renaissance unbridled the human self in the order of natural and sensible activities."[3] In expanding this claim, Maritain went on to write:

> And so in Luther the swollen consciousness of the self is essentially a consciousness of will, of realization of freedom, as German philosophy said later. We should have to stress too his egocentrism, and show how the self is the centre for him . . . from the claim of the individual will, cut off from the universal body of the church, to stand solitary and naked before God and Christ in order to ensure its justification and salvation by its trust.[4]

In a later study, *The Ego in Faith*, Paul Hacker makes this link to German Idealism even more explicit, claiming that:

---

[1] For instance, Martin Heidegger explored the effects of Luther's thinking upon Kant's philosophy of religion in a colloquium which he arranged with Julius Ebbinghaus, "Über die theologischen Grundlagen von Kant, Religion innerhalb der Grenzen der bloßen Vernunft, nach aus gewählten Texten" (1923).

[2] See the section entitled *"Katholische Einwände: Luther läßt die Personalität des Menschen ontologisch außer acht"* in Wilfried Joest, *Ontologie der Person bei Luther* (Göttingen: Vandenhoech & Ruprecht, 1967), pp. 21–27.

[3] Jacques Maritain, *Three Reformers: Luther, Descartes, Rousseau* (London: Sheed & Ward, 1928), p. 14.

[4] Maritain, *Three Reformers*, p. 35.

This tendency [towards subjectivism] need only be generalized and secularized, and the result will be a transformation of anthropocentric religion into epistemological idealism or spiritual monism. The philosophers of German idealism were certainly right in acknowledging their gratitude to Martin Luther.[5]

On the other hand, a number of more positive philosophical works appeared in the latter part of the twentieth century within which Luther's thinking was incorporated into a broader genealogy of western thought.[6] By reading the Reformer through a generally Kantian hermeneutic, these scholars rendered Luther's doctrine of justification by faith as a rudimentary equivalent to Kant's own methodological transcendentalism. Rudolf Malter goes so far as to posit that:

> In his teaching of justification by faith, Luther thinks that human knowledge in its metaphysical determination is received from without and yet is received nevertheless as knowledge. The doctrine is the centre of the whole Reformation thinking—as basic and yet, at the same time, as highly complex as Descartes' conception of the Cogito or Kant's notion of the transcendental deduction.[7]

Yet in both Catholic and non-Catholic depictions there is an implicit assumption of a normative account of philosophical method operating beneath the surface of the analysis. In the first case, the Catholic critics begin *externally* with a hackneyed version of the modern self—solipsistic, self-transparent, autonomous—and read Luther *into* this form of thinking. As a result, any reference to the "human subject" or the "individual" encountered within Luther's writings is *de facto* correlated to this predetermined version of subjectivity. Alternatively, on the part of the philosophers reading Luther into the Kantian lineage, the normativity is *internal*, operating out of an assumption that a transcendental methodology is a necessary philosophical starting point. It is only insofar as Luther can be interpolated into this Kantian ancestry that he is to have any place at all within this late nineteenth-century form of modernity. By regarding Luther's doctrine of justification by faith as a basic methodological principle which grounds "human knowledge in its metaphysical determination", these scholars projected a tacit methodological framework onto Luther's thinking which he may or may not have accepted. In both cases, Luther is placed firmly within the domain of modern thought, regardless of the predominantly positive or negative approach of either inquiry.

---

[5] Paul Hacker, *The Ego in Faith: Martin Luther and the Origin of Anthropocentric Religion* (Chicago, IL: Herald, 1970), p. 96.

[6] See Joest, *Ontologie der Person*; Rudolf Malter, *Das reformatorische Denken und die Philosophie: Luthers Entwurf einer transzendental-praktischen Metaphysik* (Bonn: Bouvier, 1980) and Reiner Schürmann, *Broken Hegemonies*, trans. R. Lilly, (Bloomington, IN: Indiana University Press, 2003).

[7] Malter, *Das reformatorische Denken*, pp. 140–141.

Ulrich Asendorf offers a timely reminder to those tacitly situating Luther within the modern period when he writes, "Luther's theology always has a different form than that of the thinkers of modernity who, since Descartes, are orientated to methodology, just as much as to hermeneutics."[8] As Asendorf is careful to highlight in his book of the same title, Luther always self-defined as a *"Lectura in Biblia"*, a lecturer in the Old Testament, and so, any reading of Luther's theology as a whole must never under-emphasise its scriptural-hermeneutic foundation. On this reading, "the sweeping scope of scripture must be maintained as a priority, because Luther himself moves in different traditions and in different contexts to modernity."[9] By returning the analysis to Luther's own attempts at biblical exegesis, a more faithful rendering of Luther's theological method appears which calls into question the modernist framework into which Luther's theology is all too often compressed.

Consequently, any consideration of Martin Luther within the contemporary milieu must be attentive to the great distance which opens up between the reformer and the twenty-first century world. By adopting him as their own, the past interpreters of Luther have constructed a distorted reconstruction of his thinking which anchors him firmly within the ambit of the modernist methodological *Weltanschauung*. In the remainder of this article, I shall argue that, although he does develop a fascinating concept of the human subject within his writings, Luther *does not make this subjectivity methodologically basic*. Instead, for Luther, human subjectivity is located within a more fundamental framework of "place". However, understandably, this concept of place is developed across an academic career which spans thirty years and so it can be seen to mature from its earliest appearances, as a corollary of the *theologia crucis*, into a more expansive framework for Luther's later thinking. This cultivation of the concept of place within Luther's theology will be briefly sketched as it is traced through to its apex: the *Genesisvorlesung* delivered in the final ten years of Luther's life. Through an analysis of the concept of place within the *Genesisvorlesung*, the subsequent prominence of the doctrine of creation, particularly the language of *creatio ex nihilo*, will be examined. Thus, by means of an investigation into the function of the doctrine of *creatio ex nihilo* as it appears within the *Genesisvorlesung*, the initial moves will be made to re-place Luther more constructively within contemporary thinking.

The Simul *Space of Human Being*

The claim that Luther locates the human subject within the more basic framework of place needs to be clarified. In the introduction to his book, *Getting Back into Place*, Edward Casey remarks that, "in the past three centuries in the

[8] Ulrich Asendorf, *Lectura in Biblia Luthers Genesisvorlesung (1535–1545)* (Göttingen: Vandenhoeck & Ruprecht, 1998), p. 13.
[9] Asendorf, *Lectura in Biblia*, p. 13.

West—the period of modernity—place has come to be not only neglected but actively suppressed. Owing to the triumph of the natural and social sciences in this same period, any serious talk of place has been regarded as regressive or trivial."[10] Starting from this presupposition, the substance of much of Casey's subsequent work has been of a genealogical nature, tracing the rise and fall of place from the earliest cosmogonic narratives up until its more recent postmodern utilisations.[11]

Casey's diagnosis of the implicit disregard for place which arises within modernity emphasises the importance of the shift in the West towards a culture predominantly influenced by the natural and social sciences—something Husserl called the "natural attitude". In a critique akin to those implemented by some members of the Radical Orthodoxy group,[12] Casey observes a methodological development which occurs around the beginning of modernity in which ensues a prioritisation of the concept of "space", scientifically conceived, over the concept of place. According to Casey, this relationship came to be formulated along the same lines as the Enlightenment distinction between the "general" and the "particular". Thus, "by 'space' is meant a neutral, pre-given medium, a tabula rasa onto which the particularities of culture and history came to be transcribed, with place the perceived result."[13] As a consequence, the distinction within the modern period between localised (i.e. "placed") human experience and universal (i.e. "spaced") knowledge was carried through to the configuration of the relationship between space and place. The methodological dualism which undergirded modern epistemology could now be expounded with reference to the distinction between the universal (space) and the particular (place). In this system, human experience could only be taken seriously in so far as it could be related back to the universal domain of "space". As Casey puts it, "Generality, albeit empty, belongs to space; particularity, albeit mythic, belongs to place; and the twain meet only by appeal to a procedure of superimposition that is invoked ex post facto."[14] In effect, the place within which human experience occurred came to be seen as merely a "representation" of the more general space of neutral mathematical extension.

---

[10] Edward S. Casey, *Getting Back into Place: Toward a Renewed Understanding of the Place-Word*, (Bloomington, IN: Indiana University Press, 1993), p. xiv.

[11] This trajectory was heralded in by *Getting Back into Place*, but Casey's genealogical project was most evident within *The Fate of Place* which appeared four years later. See Edward S. Casey, *The Fate of Place: A Philosophical History* (Berkley, CA: University of California Press, 1997). See also "How to Get from Space to Place in a Fairly Short Stretch of Time: Phenomenological Prolegomena", in S. Feld and K. Basso (eds), *Sense of Place* (Santa Fe, NM: School of American Research Press, 1997), pp. 13–52.

[12] One only has to recall the opening to John Milbank's *Theology and Social Theory*: "Once, there was no 'secular'. And the secular was not latent, waiting to fill more space with the steam of the 'purely human', when the pressure of the sacred was relaxed." John Milbank, *Theology and Social Theory* (Oxford: Blackwell, 2003), p. 9.

[13] Casey, "How to Get from Space to Place", p. 14.

[14] Casey, "How to Get from Space to Place", p. 15.

As Casey goes on to argue, the point at which this modern configuration of space and place collapses is at the level of phenomenology. It is simply not the case that the human experience begins with general categories of knowledge onto which are mapped localised experiences of external "sensations". All human knowledge arises within, and remains within, place; that is to say, there is no *general* knowledge which is not, in some way, *local* knowledge. The human subject does not reside hermetically within an ephemeral field of haphazard packets of "sense data" but dwells within a world which always precedes her and within which her subjectivity arises. Thus, any human experience of the world in which we live is indubitably coloured by the place within which this experience arises.[15]

As a result of this phenomenological counter-argument, Casey is led to question, "what if things were the other way around? What if the very idea of space is posterior to that of place, perhaps even derived from it?"[16] By returning to the pre-modern concept of place, not the sub-division of the neutral infinity of mathematical extension but rather the "structure that encompasses a number of distinct but interrelated components",[17] the methodological dualism of the Enlightenment might be replaced by an account of human existence in which individual human experience and the objective space within which this experience occurs are taken equally seriously. As Jeff Malpas proposes, "the idea of place thus provides the framework within which the complex interconnections of *both* subjective and objective spatiality can be understood."[18] In this sense, a conception of subjectivity is possible which does not become methodologically basic but is located within the broader framework of place, along with a number of other equally basic concepts. The remainder of this article will argue that, to appropriate Bruno Latour's famous maxim, Luther "has never been modern" and therefore operates with a richer conception of place than the scientifically-neutered space proposed by modernity.

To claim that Luther's theology is structured around a concept of place is hardly innovative. Whilst the particular terminology used by the various philosophers of place does not arise within the prevailing readings of Luther's theology, the functional account of place they developed finds a correlate in Luther's doctrine of the *theologia crucis* which pervades Luther's theology. At the heart of the *theologia crucis* is a simple methodological attitude which locates Luther's theology firmly within the place of created existence. As he wrote in his *Lectures on Galatians* of 1535:

---

[15] See Casey, "How to Get from Space to Place", p. 14–19.

[16] Casey, "How to Get from Space to Place", p. 16.

[17] Jeff E. Malpas, *Place and Experience: a Philosophical Topology* (Cambridge: Cambridge University Press, 1999), p. 69.

[18] Malpas, *Place and Experience*, p. 70.

Begin [any theological investigation] where Christ began—in the Virgin's womb, in the manger, and at his mother's breast. For this purpose he came down, was born, lived amongst men, suffered, was crucified, and died, so that in every possible way He might present Himself to our sight. He wanted us to fix the gaze of our hearts upon Himself and thus prevent us from clambering up into heaven and speculating about the Divine Majesty.[19]

The *theologia crucis* is a reminder not to attempt to look beyond creation for the divine. It is not only futile, for the human subject cannot comprehend the "Divine Majesty",[20] but it also overlooks those countless instances of revelation within the place of human existence where God reveals himself. At its heart, then, is the cross of Christ, the place in which God reveals himself most fully to be both who he is, and who we least expect him to be. To discover who God is, according to Luther, one must be brought to this place at the feet of the crucified Christ. Luther's theology is, therefore, indubitably "placed" from a very early point within its conception.[21]

This concept of place as it arises in the theology of the early Luther is never fully explicated by him at any point. In many respects, it is on a reading of the *Genesisvorlesung* from the final years of Luther's academic career that the concept of place, indirectly inferred from the *theologia crucis*, can be seen to have reached a high point. The question becomes: what changes between the inauguration of Luther's *theologia crucis* in his early theology and the sophisticated form which appears in the *Genesisvorlesung*? The argument which will be propounded here is that Luther came to realise the correspondence between the conception of place, as it appeared within his early account of the *theologia crucis*, and the doctrine of creation, as it developed later on in his career. But that is to arrive at a conclusion before the development of place is traced through Luther's thinking.

The importance of the notion of place manifests itself across the development of Luther's theological writings. Even as early as the *Dictata Super Psalterium* of 1515, the significance of place is evidenced. Steven Ozment touches upon this "spatiality" of Luther's early theology in his exploration of Luther's anthropology, *Homo Spiritualis*. Although place is not the main topic of investigation, in the initial chapter dealing with Luther's thought, Ozment explores one of the binaries which underpins much of Luther's theology: the

---

[19] *Luther's Works* [LW], Jaroslav Pelikan and Helmut T. Lehmann (eds) (St. Louis, MO: Concordia, and Philadelphia, PA: Fortress Press, 1955–1986), 26:29; *Dr. Martin Luthers Werke* [WA] (Weimar: Böhlau, 1883–1993), 40[1]:77–78.

[20] *LW* 26:28–29; *WA* 40[1]:78.

[21] It must be noted that the *theologia crucis* operates with a late-medieval concept of the apprehension of temporal simultaneity, allowing Luther to speak of the "place of the cross" *post factum*. Benedict Anderson explores the notion of the "apprehension of time" in the late-medieval period in his book, *Imagined Communities*, revised edition, (London: Verso, 2006), pp. 22–24.

distinction between the flesh and the Spirit.[22] Ozment argues that the scholarship has tended towards one or other of a dichotomy between a "Neoplatonic" reading of the distinction, in which there is a stark dualism erected between the visible and the invisible world, and an "Existentialist" interpretation, in which the distinction between flesh and Spirit is spoken of in terms of "*Existenzmöglichkeiten*", the difference between a dispositional "living before God" or "living before the world".[23] After rebutting the Neoplatonic argument, Ozment turns his attention to the Existentialist approach which he finds the more satisfying. Crucially, however, he suggests that simply reducing the spheres of the flesh and the Spirit down to mere dispositional attitudes overlooks Luther's concern for an "objective context" within which the distinction can be situated. He writes:

> Luther's primary focus here is upon two opposed objective references, two opposed "objective contexts", two opposed "places" to which and in which the heart of man directs and locates its hope and fear, and from which it receives its joy and suffering.[24]

That is to say, the division between the flesh and the spirit which underlies Luther's theology operates around a topological distinction, between "two opposed places" in which the human person finds herself located. However, these are not to be held in an irreconcilable binary but brought together into a unity, or as Luther will term it, a *simul*. Ozment continues:

> Luther is primarily concerned not to distinguish and oppose irreconcilable entities, but to reconcile distinct and opposed entities. He seeks neither the "both-and" nor the "either-or", but the *simul*.[25]

In line with Luther's later approach to Christology, the emphasis moves away from the *distinction* between Spirit and flesh to the "comprehensive objective framework" (Ozment's phrase) within which the distinction is to be conceived.[26] Within the broader compass of created existence, the human person is either grounded in the flesh or the Spirit and it is by this distinction that the human person is defined in Luther's thinking. This distinction, however, is not between two different ontological states (although the distinction may manifest itself ontologically), but rather between two different

---

[22] Steven E. Ozment, *Homo Spiritualis: A Comparative Study of the Anthropology of Johannes Tauler, Jean Gerson and Martin Luther (1509–16)* (Leiden, E. J. Brill, 1969), ch. 8.

[23] Ozment opposes the work of A. W. Hunzinger and Gerhard Ebeling as the two paradigms of such thinking. See Ozment, *Homo Spiritualis*, pp. 87–104.

[24] Ozment, *Homo Spiritualis*, pp. 103–104.

[25] Ozment, *Homo Spiritualis*, p. 131.

[26] In the *Third Disputation against the Antinomians*, Luther himself emphasises the importance of the "comprehensive objective framework" within Christology. See *WA* 39¹:507.

loci within the same ontological state: the place of human existence. The believer and the non-believer experience the same world, but from different locations within it.

In light of his exploration of Luther's *simul*, Ozment strengthens his argument with a discussion of Luther's explication of the concept of *substantia* as it appears in the *Dictata Super Psalterium*.[27] Unsurprisingly, Luther eschews the traditional philosophical accounts of substance for a "scriptural reading" of the concept in which *substantia* is described in metaphorical terms as a "place where one can stand firm and settle down" (*substaculum seu subsidentia*).[28] That is to say, the concept of substance as Luther employs it comes to signify those things by which one subsists or sustains her life. As Ozment elucidates, *substantia* "concerns 'qualities,' not 'quiddities of things.' 'Where' one lives and 'how' one lives constitutes his 'substance' in this life."[29] Applying this account of *substantia* to the doctrine of justification by faith, the person living "according to the flesh" can be said to be standing, and therefore finding her substance in, the objective context of the law: in works, in active righteousness, solely within the remit of the "this worldly".[30] Conversely, the Christian life is grounded in *fides* and *spes*, as the human person exists within the "objective context" of the divine action for the world, an existence in the interstice between the remembered past and promised future works of God.[31] Foundational for Luther's anthropology, therefore, is a concept of *substantia* which operates out of "objective contexts", that is, which requires some notion of "being-in-a-world". However, in Ozment's words, these "objective contexts" require a more "comprehensive objective framework" which is to function as the broader domain within which the various distinctions of Luther's theology are to be located. The methodological processes evinced within the *Dictata Super Psalterium* reveal an approach in direct contrast to that proposed by the modern interpreters of Luther: rather than attempting to reduce the complexities of human existence down to a universal methodological starting point, Luther prefers to hold in tension the various complexities of human existence necessitating the invocation of the language of place.

However, despite the great advantages that Ozment's careful reading of Luther's anthropology offers in shedding light on the "objective contexts" of human existence, by expressly reducing the contexts within this "broader framework" to only the objective, Ozment risks following the modern hegemony of merely objective space without giving any regard to the place of human experience. No doubt such a move signals a wariness on Ozment's

---

[27] Ozment, *Homo Spiritualis*, pp. 105–111.
[28] Ozment offers citations from *WA* 3:419–420.
[29] Ozment, *Homo Spiritualis*, p. 105.
[30] Ozment, *Homo Spiritualis*, pp. 106–107.
[31] Ozment, *Homo Spiritualis*, pp. 107–108.

part to risk falling too easily into a simple reaffirmation of the Existentialist reading of Luther. And yet, even on the most cursory reading, Ozment's formulation of the "objective contexts" which underlie Luther's anthropology necessarily entails concepts of both objective *and* subjective space. The *substantia* of the individual is not merely described in terms of the objective space of physical extension, but requires the corollary concept of subjective space which is the particular experiential context of each human individual—something akin to the Heideggerean concept of "horizon". It does not only comprise the neutral "where" of objective space but insinuates the particularised "where" of the human individual as they find themselves located within an objective context, within a world.[32] To be situated in the objective context of the law or of the Gospel, therefore, can never simply entail the "placeless" disposition of the post-Kantian subject just as little as it can be adequately spoken of in Ozment's language of merely "objective contexts": the two are ineluctably and irreducibly interdependent; the individual finds her feet in *this* place or *that* place within the world. Thus, the radical conclusion of Luther's anthropology in the *Dictata* is that it is the places within which they find themselves that make human persons who they are.[33] In the complex interplay between the subject and her environment, the subject is formed by her objective contexts just as much as those contexts are "appropriated" by the subject. To promote either the space of the subject or the objective world in which she is found into a position of methodological priority, is to miss the *simul* at the heart of Luther's anthropology; it is to squeeze Luther into the framework of a modernist methodological normativity.

At the root of Luther's anthropology, then, there lies the *simul*—a refusal to construct a distinction between the Spirit and the flesh along the lines of a "substance dualism". Both the saved person and the sinful person dwell within the place of human existence: where they differ is in finding their feet in different *loci*. As a result of this *simul*, there arises the necessary development of a concept of place with the capacity to hold together the disparate facets of human existence in such a way that one is not emphasised to the detriment of the other. Accordingly, there *is* an account of subjectivity in Luther's theology, albeit one defined very differently to that of modernity:[34] the subject can never be amputated from the objective world in which she is

---

[32] As indicated in the "Where are you?" of God to Adam in the Garden of Eden.

[33] Luther's comments on Jacob's wrestling with God in the place called Peniel is a good example of this interrelation between the subject and their environment. Importantly, Luther highlights the placed character of Jacob's struggle in the naming of the place in which it occurs. See *LW* 6:144; *WA* 44:108.

[34] In this sense, for Luther, the subject and object adopt a meaning far closer to their Latin etymologies of *subiect* (lit. "thrown under") and *obiect* (lit. "thrown against"). See Martin Heidegger, "Phenomenology and Theology" in Martin Heidegger, *Pathmarks*, edited by William McNeill (Cambridge: Cambridge University Press, 2009), pp. 57–58.

found—the one is impossible without the other. The subjectivity evident within the lines of the *Small Catechism* is not the individualistic subjectivity of post-Enlightenment philosophy but arises out of the interaction between the subject and the world in which she finds herself: "I believe that God has created me along with all creatures; that He has given me my body and soul, eyes, ears, and all my limbs, my reason, and all my senses, and still preserves them".[35] Consequently, the *simul* of Luther's anthropology demands the irreducible co-existence of objective and subjective space *within the broader framework of the place of human existence*. Throughout the development of Luther's theology, this place which offers a comprehensive framework for Luther's anthropology is increasingly presented as "being-in-a-world"; not the characterless world of infinite extension promoted by modern thinkers, but the world created to be the stage upon which the drama between Creator and creature could be played.

The Place of Creation as the Place of Justification

As a result of the concept of place underlying his anthropology, the concept of place becomes operative beneath the surface of Luther's corresponding discussion of the doctrine of justification by faith. Given that the human subject is defined by the places in which she finds herself, the problem of soteriology in Luther's writing becomes one of re-location: how does the sinful person *change place* from her grounding in the context of the law to that of the Spirit? Or, to render it in the language used above: how does the human person "find her feet" in the *fides* and *spes* of righteousness rather than in life "according to the flesh"? Such a claim necessitates a re-evaluation of the standard readings of Luther's doctrine of justification far surpassing the limits of this article.[36] What is important to note here is that the account of the human subject drawn up by Luther within his early theology extends beyond the bounds of soteriology; whilst this "placed" anthropology impinges upon the doctrine of justification, it is not reducible to it. The concept of subjectivity precedes the doctrine of justification by faith *by virtue of its location within the broader context of place*.

Theologically speaking, this invokes the awareness that underlying Luther's soteriological schema is a doctrine of creation which must, in some way, orientate his language of salvation.[37] The particularities of Luther's account of the *theologia crucis* entail a doctrine of creation in which God

---

[35] *Shorter Catechism*, II, 6.

[36] The work of Piotr Malysz is innovative in this regard when he writes, "The impact of the light of grace is not only epistemological; it also has far-reaching ontological consequences. By living in an identity-bestowing relationship with God, the believer exists as properly placed." Piotr J. Malysz, "Luther and Dionysius: Beyond Mere Negations", *Modern Theology*, Vol. 24 no. 4 (October 2008), p. 687.

[37] David Löfgren, *Der Theologie der Schöpfung bei Luther* (Göttingen; Vandenhoeck & Ruprecht, 1960), p. 22.

creates the world, maintains the world, and comes into the world in order to interact with individuals—individuals who become aware of themselves and aware of him *in place*.[38] To return to the language of the *Small Catechism*, the language of human subjectivity is placed within a broader confession of the creation of the world by the God who seeks to interact with his creation: "I believe that God has created me along with all creatures".[39] It is because human experience was created as "placed" that the concept of revelation— expounded through the doctrine of the Word of God—becomes so funda- mental to Luther's theology.[40] In his Romans commentary, for example, Luther describes the human faculties as created *"pro perceptione verbi auditi"*— "for the perception of the Word".[41] For Luther, therefore, subjectivity and objectivity are natural corollaries of a Creator God who wants to be in rela- tionship with the Other. Or, to put it more forcefully, you cannot have the subjective without the objective, nor the objective without the subjective; they are held together in a mutual dependence circumscribed by the doctrine of creation.[42] Subjectivity is not limited to the realm of soteriology, as many of Luther's critics seem to suppose, but flows out of a more basic account of God's relating to the Other before the fall.[43]

Through time, it appears that Luther recognises the significance of this doctrine of creation operating beneath the surface of his doctrine of justifica- tion by faith and can be seen to be situating any language about justification within the more comprehensive framework of the doctrine of creation. In view of this genetic reading of Luther's theology, it is unsurprising that many of the modern interpretations of Luther's notion of subjectivity have gleaned their accounts of justification by faith from Luther's earlier writings, particu- larly the *Dictata Super Psalterium* (1513–1515), the *Lectures on Romans* (1515– 1516), the *Freedom of the Christian* (1520) and *De Servo Arbitrio* (1525). Although not entirely absent from these early works, the situation of justifi- cation within the place offered by creation becomes increasingly perceptible

---

[38] Heiko Oberman points to the importance of the Franciscan paradigm (which came to Luther through his exposure to the *Via Antiqua*) for this movement towards the interactive God of the late medieval period. See Heiko H. Oberman, "Luther and the Via Moderna: The Philo- sophical Backdrop of the Reformation Breakthrough", *Journal of Ecclesiatical History*, Vol. 54 no. 4 (2003), p. 649.

[39] *Shorter Catechism*, II, 6.

[40] See Ingolf U. Dalferth, "Luther on the Experience of Faith", *The Heythrop Journal*, Vol. 20 no. 1 (1980), pp. 50–56.

[41] *LW* 25:418; *WA* 56:426.

[42] This interdependence of subjectivity and objectivity within creation is at the heart of Barth's famous assertion that "Creation is the external—and only the external—basis of the covenant." See Karl Barth, *Church Dogmatics* (Edinburgh: T & T Clark, 1958), III/1, p. 97.

[43] Oswald Bayer's resolution of this issue stresses the expansive scope of the language of "justification", impinging as it does into the realm of the doctrine of creation. In this sense, creation is, in itself, a form of justification. See Oswald Bayer, "The Doctrine of Justification and Ontology", trans. Christine Helmer, *Neue Zeitschrift für Systematische Theologie*, Vol. 43 no. 1 (2001), pp. 44–53.

as Luther's theology develops, a phenomenon which Rowan Williams labels his "conversion to the world".[44] For example, in the *Disputation on Justification* of 1536, the doctrine of justification is contextualised so as to remind the audience that it is to be related not only abstractly to the human person but to include the full orb of God's salvific dealings with the creation.

> 29. For Justification is healing for sin, which slays the whole world eternally and brings it to destruction with its infinite evils.

> 30. For this reason that divine work of justification is too great to allow any reckoning or consideration of our activity or work to hold here.[45]

Implicit within the wording of thesis 30 is the supposition that human subjectivity, here spoken of in Luther's preferred language of "activity" or "works", should not assume a basic priority in the discussion concerning the doctrine of justification *precisely because* justification operates within the ambit of "the whole world eternally".

This "emplacement" of the doctrine of justification in the *Disputation on Justification* is mirrored in the introduction to Luther's second attempt at lecturing through the book of Galatians. Within the overview of the argument of the book, Luther offers the following explication of the Law/Gospel distinction:

> We set forth two worlds, as it were, one of them heavenly and the other earthly. Into these we place these two kinds of righteousness, which are distinct and separate from each other.[46]

Again, the doctrine of justification in the second *Lectures on Galatians* is situated within a comprehensive worldly context, albeit one divided into earthly and heavenly "objective contexts". Accordingly, Luther goes on to imply that the two forms of righteousness, although "distinct and separate from each other", are *simultaneously* functional within the broader level of created existence. This is accentuated in the final paragraph of the introduction to the argument of the book of Galatians where Luther avers:

> When I have this righteousness within me, I descend from heaven like the rain that makes the earth fertile. That is, I come forth into another kingdom, and I perform good works whenever the opportunity arises. . . . In short, whoever knows for sure that Christ is his righteousness not

---

[44] Rowan Williams, *The Wound of Knowledge* (London: Darton, Longman and Todd, 2003), p. 155.
[45] *LW* 34:156; *WA* 39¹:86.
[46] *LW* 26:8; *WA* 40¹:46.

only cheerfully and gladly works in his calling but also submits himself for the sake of love . . . in this present life.[47]

Once again, Luther affirms that the doctrine of justification by faith is not something which takes place *outside* created existence but occurs within the conditions of time and space as the human individual "finds her feet" not merely within the realm of the earthly, but in the more substantial sphere of *fides* and *spes* in God's work in Christ, and his future promises. In this sense, the human person's *substantia* is defined not by the flesh but in the Spirit, an activity which locates that person even more firmly within the created world. It is the human person who lives in faith, denying that the world is "all that is the case", who can then truly live within the world.[48] The justification of the human person takes place within the "comprehensive framework" of the created world, a world within which objective space and subjective space interrelate so that human subjects become aware of themselves, aware of the world in which they dwell, and aware of the God who created it.

The apex of this so-called "conversion to the world" is to be found in Luther's final major theological project, the *Großen Genesisvorlesung*, composed as lectures between 1535 and 1545, the year before Luther himself would die. Within the text, the doctrine of justification by faith is illustrated through the exegesis of the passage in Genesis 12 concerning Abram's call out of Ur. Here Luther emphasises the "emplaced" character of salvation as Abram is not called to live monastically outside of the world but is rather called to inhabit the world more radically than before. Luther writes of Abram and Sarai:

> Thus they live in the world at all times. They do indeed concern themselves with the affairs of the home and of the state, govern the commonwealths and rear families, till fields, carry on commerce or manual occupations. . . . They make use of the world as an inn from which they must emigrate in a short time, and they do not attach their hearts to the affairs of this life. They tend to worldly matters with their left hand, while they raise their right hand upwards to the eternal homeland.[49]

Here the *simul* nature of human existence is maintained with the double imagery of left hand and right hand; the standpoints of flesh and Spirit are maintained within the broader context of the particular world which Abram

---

[47] LW 26:11–12; WA 40¹:51.

[48] As Ingolf Dalferth puts it: "Ordinary experience thus acquires a new significance without being stripped of its original content; rather it is preserved as an element of a more comprehensive pattern which improves our understanding of it by providing a context and perspective which brings out its real significance more adequately." Dalferth, "Luther on the Experience of Faith", p. 52.

[49] LW 2:253; WA 42:441–442.

and Sarai inhabit. Rather than offering a theoretical account located simply in an abstract space, Luther offers the concrete example from the text of scripture itself, from within the subjectively-located experience of Abram and Sarai. In this manner, Luther does not attempt to offer a conjectural model of God's justification of the human person but instead recounts the narrative of God's salvific action as it occurred *within the place of creation.*

The *Großen Genesisvorlesung* unites the parallel conceptions of space which have been observed operating under the surface of Luther's anthropology: on one side, the "rootedness" of all human activity within the space of subjective experience; on the other, the necessary reliance of this subjective experience upon the broader objective space of the world out of which it arises in the first place. Exegesis of the text of Genesis affords Luther the opportunity to attend to both concerns, as the biblical narrative offers Luther a concrete place within which to speak of the human subject in the world.[50] Read this way, the Genesis text presents a microcosmic depiction of the broader account of God's action within the world. The "rootedness" of this description of the Creator's relation to his creation within the text of Genesis prevents the theologian from detaching the human subject from its context, thereby precluding an abstract account of subjectivity situated outside the "space and time" of God's creative action. In this fashion, Luther gives weight both to creation, as the establishment of the place within which God will interact with humanity, as well as to scripture, as the biblical narrative offers a temporal rendering of this place of divine activity.[51] The *Genesisvorlesung* therefore offers the pinnacle of Luther's theological endeavour: a theological work which accomplishes the ultimate interplay between biblical exegesis and theological loci, postulating the inextricability of the hermeneutic character of created reality.[52] For Luther, theology is always hermeneutical, an interpretation of God's dealings in the world by individuals from within the world.[53] The human person engages with the divine in the domain of the creative action of God, within the world which God created, and she perceives this relation from within that same place.[54]

---

[50] "Into this garden, which the Lord Himself had planted with such special care, He placed man. All this, I say, is historical." *LW* 1:89; *WA* 42:68. "Moreover, just as Moses above makes various differences between the brutes and man, who shares with the brutes their origin from the ground, so in this passage he sets man apart by the particular place and abode which the Lord planted for man and, as it were, constructed with greater sumptuousness and with more careful application than all the rest of the earth." *LW* 1:90–91; *WA* 42:69.

[51] The close correspondence between the place of creation and the place of scripture in the *Genesisvorlesung* must not be overlooked. Throughout its pages, Luther chooses to use the Latin noun "*locus*" to speak both of the physical place in the narrative (e.g., "Jacob went down into that *place* . . .") as well as the textual reference in scripture (e.g., "As it says in this *place* . . .").

[52] See Asendorf, *Lectura in Biblia*, p. 11.

[53] *LW* 1:68; *WA* 42:51.

[54] Löfgren, *Die Theologie der Schöpfung*, p. 31.

This subjective space of human existence is reflected in the text of the *Genesisvorlesung* as the biblical narrative recounts the dealings of God with various individual characters in the place offered by creation. Throughout Genesis, God encounters human persons—making them aware of themselves as subjects within the world created by him, and bringing them into relationship with himself. It is at this point, therefore, that the function of *theologia crucis* can be seen to retain its place within Luther's theology. The theologian cannot simply speculate beyond the creative event towards a general paradigm by which to encompass the salvific activity of God because God does not interact with his creation generally, but rather particularly, within the bounds of the place created for this relationship. This final methodological move by Luther, utilising the book of Genesis as the text for his theological dialogue, allows him to balance the dual concepts of objective and subjective space without allowing either one or the other to assume a position of priority. The broader framework of place allows Luther to speak of the giving of the human individual the space to experience being in a world where genuine, unique encounters can occur: encounters with the world, with others within the world, and with the divine. Thus, the movement towards place, begun in the early *theologia crucis*, has reached its endpoint in the *Genesisvorlesung*. What has changed, however, is not Luther's original theological methodology—this remains the same as it ever was—but his realisation of the crucial function of the doctrine of creation out of which the concept of place must necessarily operate.

A Place Arising Ex Nihilo

Read from the perspective of the "place-character" of the remainder of the work, the doctrine of creation encountered within *Genesisvorlesung* reads less like a cosmogonic description of the emergence of bare materiality than a careful rendering of the institution of the place within which divine and human interaction will occur. Accordingly, Luther passes hurriedly over the opening verses of the book of Genesis in which the "crude and formless masses of the crude heaven and earth" were brought into being, preferring to concern himself with the "ordering" and "shaping" of these masses to generate the place of human existence.[55] Across the remainder of the opening chapters of the book of Genesis, Luther emphasizes this "place-character" of creation, maintaining that:

> [Holy Scripture] plainly teaches that God created all these things in order to prepare a house and an inn, as it were, for the future man, and that He governs and preserves these creatures by the power of His Word, by which He also created them. Finally, then, after everything that belongs

---

[55] *LW* 1:6–7; *WA* 42:6.

to the essence of a house is ready, man is brought, as it were, into his possession that we may learn that the divine providence for us is greater than all our own anxiety and care.[56]

In the *Genesisvorlesung*, therefore, the doctrine of creation is not simply an attempt to answer the problematic of the primordial Whence of materiality—it is not ontological in the connoted sense of contemporary scientific thought—but rather concerns itself with the richer ontological sense of the framework *within which* human existence is rooted. It is not just the quiddity of human existence which is considered in Luther's doctrine of creation, but also the structural underpinnings by which this material is organised and through which human existence can be seen to function.[57] The world is created to be the place within which the divine comes into relationship with human subjects and so the doctrine of creation necessarily informs any concomitant descriptions of human subjectivity. As a consequence, the doctrine of creation in the *Genesisvorlesung* directly impinges upon the subjectivity of the *Genesisvorlesung*.

At the heart of the doctrine of creation encountered in the *Genesisvorlesung* is the problem of "differentiation", something denoted by Robert Sokolowski's expression "the Christian distinction between God and the world, the denial that God in his divinity is part of or dependent on the world".[58] By relocating theological discussion within the broader domain of the place of divine-human encounter, Luther's approach in the *Genesisvorlesung* accentuates the radical tension inherent in such close coincidence of Creator and creature. The question becomes: How does one prevent the ontological distinction between Creator and creature spanning too great a distance or being brought so close as to eradicate the distance altogether? To counteract this predicament, Luther makes the standard theological move: he introduces the important doctrine of *creatio ex nihilo* as a methodological tool whereby the Creator-creature distinction can be maintained correctly. However, as a result of his decision to situate theology within this framework, Luther's account of *creatio ex nihilo* takes on a different nuance than do many of the standard treatments. Just as the doctrine applies to the broad framework of created existence, it also corresponds to both the objective and subjective facets encompassed by the place offered in creation. In the remainder of this section, this dual function of the *creatio ex nihilo* formula within the text of the *Genesisvorlesung* will be more closely examined.

---

[56] *LW* 1:47; *WA* 42:35.

[57] The distinction here is something like the Heideggerean distinction between ontic/ontological, although, of course, Heidegger would claim that any reference to the doctrine of creation by the philosopher would not be ontological at all.

[58] Robert Sokolowski, *God of Faith and Reason* (Washington, DC: Catholic University of America Press, 1995), p. 37.

That Luther should utilise the doctrine of *creatio ex nihilo* in these lectures is hardly remarkable. Nevertheless, on a close reading of the *Genesisvorlesung* it becomes apparent that, rather than restricting the *creatio* formula to the chapters of Genesis dealing with creation proper, Luther applies it throughout the lecture series, using it as a theological device to speak of all divine action within the world. In this way, when Luther speaks of the inexplicable conception of Isaac by the aged Abraham and Sarah; or the depreciation in Joseph's social status from father's favourite to slave in Egypt, and his subsequent restoration; or Abraham's being considered righteous in Genesis 15; in all of these situations, Luther employs the language of *creatio ex nihilo*, seeing these divine actions within the world as instances of creation out of nothing.[59] So far-reaching is the semantic of *creatio ex nihilo* that Johannes Schwanke, in his book-length treatment of the employment of the *creatio ex nihilo* formula in Luther's Genesis commentary, declares that "the formula is, therefore, not a peripheral concept concerning divine action, but rather the basic matrix of his dealings with humanity and the world."[60] In this sense, the doctrine of *creatio ex nihilo* offers a hermeneutic by which the dealings of God within creation might be interpreted. Within the pages of the *Genesisvorlesung*, there is no aspect of God's dealing with creation which takes place outside of the event of *creatio ex nihilo*. As Luther later writes in the *Genesisvorlesung*, "it is a perpetual and unparalleled rule of the works of God to make all things out of nothing."[61]

Given that the *Genesisvorlesung* functions as an elucidation of a scriptural text, Luther nowhere explicitly lays out a precise formulation of this utilisation of the doctrine of *ex nihilo*. As Ulrich Asendorf has emphasised,[62] the *Genesisvorlesung* exhibits a reciprocal interplay between textual exegesis and theological ideas, both elements directed toward the other. The best expression of the formula is therefore to be found interspersed throughout Luther's interpretation of the text of Genesis. The most extensive citation articulating the function of the concept of *creatio ex nihilo* is found in Luther's interpretation of the narrative of Joseph.[63] Luther writes:

> For we believe in that God who is the almighty Creator, who produces all things from nothing, the best things from those that are evil, and salvation from what is despaired of and lost. In Rom. 4:17 this is attributed to him when it is stated that he "calls into existence the things that do not exist." And 2 Cor. 4:6 speaks of God who ordered light to shine out of darkness—not a spark from a coal but light out of darkness, like life from

---

[59] Johannes Schwanke, *Creatio Ex Nihilo: Luthers Lehre von der Schöpfung aus dem Nichts in der Grossen Genesisvorlesung (1535–1545)* (Berlin: W. de Gruyter, 2004), p. 4.

[60] Schwanke, *Creatio Ex Nihilo*, p. 5.

[61] LW 7:210; WA 44:455.

[62] Ulrich Asendorf, *Lectura in Biblia*, p. 11.

[63] Schwanke explores this section of the *Genesisvorlesung* as the "Grundtext für die Bedeutung der Formel 'creatio ex nihilo' in der Großen Genesisvorlesung". See Schwanke, *Creatio ex nihilo*, pp. 65–72.

death, righteousness from sin, the kingdom of heaven and the liberty of the children of God from enslavement to the devil and hell.[64]

It is obvious just how wide-ranging a function the doctrine assumes, even on the basis of this text. Initially, there is the basic ontological function which the doctrine performs, in which the creation is brought into being by the Creator out of nothing (*producens ex nihilo omnia*) and held in its existence by him. In this manner, Luther is able to articulate the absolute dependency of the creature upon the divine, thus offering a basic configuration of the Creator-creature distinction. God is the one who creates *ex nihilo*, the creature is the one who is created *ex nihilo*. Any reversal of this ontological relationship will result in the inversion of the distinction, positing the creature over the divine, and ultimately collapsing the ontological difference between creation and its Creator. Thus, the ontological aspect of the *creatio ex nihilo* formula represents the institution of the place within which the human subject will be situated. It is created out of nothing by God, is maintained through time by him, and is therefore completely dependent on him.

This complete receptivity of the creaturely forms the mainstay for the doctrine itself, and gives rise to the subjective aspect of the formula; since God creates *ex nihilo*, there is no way that the creature can "look behind" the place of God's creative action to determine the causality which motivates it. David Löfgren writes, "between God as 'agent' and the creation as 'effect' there always stands a 'nothing' which excludes every relation of causality in the standard sense."[65] Or to put it differently, the human subject is reminded that all human awareness is *necessarily* limited to the place of creation and to those phenomena experienced within its sphere. Luther adopts the *ex nihilo* formula as a hermeneutic in the *Genesisvorlesung* precisely in order to protect the Creator-creature distinction from becoming inverted. By reminding the human subject of her rootedness within the place of human existence, Luther cautions the reader of Genesis against limiting God to the strictures of created place. The *creatio ex nihilo* formula calls attention to the difference between the Creator and his creation, precluding the divine from being "subjected" to the logic of causality which the human subject generally attributes to worldly phenomena.

In this way, the notion of the human subject as it arises within Luther's theology is circumscribed by a dual receptivity: in the first place, classically, the creation of the world out of nothing entails the complete dependence of the created upon the divine for its existence and perdurance. That there is objective space at all is the result of the gift of God in creating *ex nihilo*. Secondly, however, the location of the subject within the place offered by creation occasions the articulation of the subjective space within which the

---

[64] *LW* 8:38; *WA* 44:175.
[65] Löfgren, *Die Theologie der Schöpfung*, pp. 23–24.

subject experiences the world. Again, this subjective space is circumscribed by a form of receptivity, not of bare existence, which is included within the objective range of the *creatio ex nihilo* formula, but rather a receptivity of experience, as all encounters of the objective world come to them from beyond the subject, including their interactions with the divine. However, this receptivity of subjective experience is bounded by the *ex nihilo* character of human existence whereby the human subject is reminded of the situation of human subjectivity within the place of created existence. The subjective aspect of the *creatio ex nihilo* formula reminds the reader of the limits of human subjectivity, preventing any transgression beyond the domain of the divine creative event, making the objective and subjective aspects of the doctrine of *creatio ex nihilo* opposite sides of the same coin. Read this way, the task of the theologian becomes the exegesis of the human experience of place so as to disclose the presence of the divine as it emerges within the phenomena of the every-day world.[66]

This account of subjectivity, circumscribed as it is by the account of *creatio ex nihilo*, clearly differentiates Luther's theology from the versions of subjectivity ascribed to the thinkers of the late-modern period. To speak of the human subject as it occurs within Luther's writings is to speak of a subject who emerges as a subject at the moment of her creation *ex nihilo*: as she is "subjected" (*lit.* "thrown under") within the place within which all human experience occurs. Whilst there is a self-reflexive element to this subject, this is not basic to the subject: the subject both *has* a world (reflexivity) and is *part* of a world (non-reflexivity). By inhabiting particular places within the world, the human subject is enabled to undergo experiences which make her who she is, experiences which will lead to complex ideas of self-understanding and self-awareness. However, this subjectivity is always bounded by the *ex nihilo* character of created existence, reminding the subject of the receptivity of her being and experience through the creative power of the Word.[67] In this sense, the human subject developed by Luther is "empty", not containing within itself the conditions for the possibility of its own existence or, as the Christian tradition has put it, the human subject looking within herself will always be drawn outside herself.[68] Through a careful analysis of the subjectivity emerging within the pages of Luther's theological writings, the conjecture with which the article began resurfaces: Luther has never been modern.

---

[66] Nothing has been said so far regarding the importance of the doctrine of the Eucharist for the concept of place in Luther's thinking. In many respects, it could be argued that the debates surrounding the presence of Christ in the place of the world are the efficient cause of Luther's later realisation of the importance of the concept of place in his thinking. The most significant work in this regard is the *Confession of Christ's Supper*, in which the famous "three modes of presence" are discussed. Given that this was written in 1528, seven years before the *Genesisvorlesung* was delivered, the natural development of this concept seems likely.

[67] LW 6:344; WA 44:257.

[68] Eberhard Jüngel, *The Freedom of a Christian: Luther's Significance for Contemporary Theology* (Minneapolis, MN: Augsburg Fortress, 1988), p. 63.

The doctrine of *creatio ex nihilo* comes to occupy an important and unique position in the *Genesisvorlesung*. However, despite any originality in its usage, the *ex nihilo* formula merely offers a more thorough underpinning to the methodology propounded by the earlier *theologia crucis*: the human subject is to remain rooted within the place of the world created for divine–human encounter. Across the span of a thirty-year career as a *Lectura in Biblia*, Martin Luther came to realise just how fundamental the doctrine of *creatio ex nihilo* was for his theological topology. For Luther, without the careful circumscription of *creatio ex nihilo*, there would be no place for the human subjects to experience the world and no place for the Creator to come into relationship with his creation.

Final Thoughts

How is Martin Luther to be re-placed within contemporary thinking? Three *loci* present themselves as pertinent in this regard. Firstly, Luther's topology lends itself to interesting comparisons in contemporary philosophies of place. This correspondence need not be limited simply to Edward Casey and Jeff Malpas, but may open interesting vistas upon the thinking of such disparate philosophers as Heidegger, Bachelard, Lefebvre, Deleuze and Guattari, amongst others. Secondly, our tentative treatment of Luther's account of subjectivity needs expanding, as the interplay between the human subject and her creation *ex nihilo* is brought to light. The human subject in Luther, circumscribed by the *nihil* of creation, takes on a different manifestation from the self-subsistent subject of modernity (if such a manifestation ever existed). This "empty" subject finds interesting resonances with a number of contemporary accounts of human subjectivity. The provocative work of Slavoj Žižek (via Lacan) heralds a growing faction of scholars who talk of subjectivity in terms of "nothingness", with Badiou, Agamben, and Vattimo being the main protagonists. Furthermore, the work of Merleau-Ponty, with its invocation of *écart*, or "rupture", allows an incursion into the ambit of phenomenological accounts of pre-reflexive human subjectivity which may prove fruitful. This Merleau-Pontyian detour generates the third *loci*: the field of phenomenology proper. Very little work has been done on the relationship between Luther's *theologia crucis*, "calling a thing what it actually is", and the sphere of phenomenology, "a return to the things themselves" (Husserl). In this regard, the work of Eilert Herms offers the best example, but a more thorough treatment of Luther's theology might advance the foundations for an interesting account of theological phenomenology. Each of these *loci* would open avenues to Christian theology which could prove mutually beneficial to the theologian and the philosopher. And so, in due course, Martin Luther may be returned to his place within contemporary thinking.

Modern Theology 29:2 April 2013
ISSN 0266-7177 (Print)
ISSN 1468-0025 (Online)

THE WONDER OF IMMANENCE: MERLEAU-PONTY AND THE PROBLEM OF CREATION

ANDREAS NORDLANDER

La position de Dieu ne contribue en rien à l'élucidation de notre vie. Nous avons l'expérience non pas d'un vrai éternel et d'une participation à l'Un, mais . . . d'une participation au monde.

Maurice Merleau-Ponty[1]

If there is no God, then nature is not a creation. . . . If God were dead, so would nature be.

Erazim Kohák[2]

Most of us keenly feel the attractions of immanence: we tend to think that if a philosophy leads us away from concrete life here and now it ought to be rejected; we place great value on embodiment and the sensuous; we suspect that emphasizing a deeper meaning might lead us to forget the quite ordinary meaning and comfort of the everyday, of "the wife, the heart, the bed, the table, the saddle, the fire-side, the country," as Herman Melville has it.[3]

Theologians are certainly not insensitive to the attractions of immanence. Indeed, because they have so often been accused of depreciating the

---

Andreas Nordlander
Centre for Theology and Religious Studies, Lund University, CTR, Allhelgona Kyrkogata 8
SE-22362 Lund SWEDEN
Email: andreas.nordlander@teol.lu.se

[1] "The positing of God contributes nothing to the elucidation of our lives. We experience, not a genuine eternity and a participation in the One . . . we experience a participation in the world" (emphasis omitted). Maurice Merleau-Ponty, *Phénoménlogie de la perception* (Paris: Éditions Gallimard, 2005), p. 455; *Phenomenology of Perception*, Colin Smith (trans.), (London: Routledge Classics, 2002), p. 459. [Hereafter *PhP*. Where appropriate, references to Merleau-Ponty's work will be given by the page number of the original before that of the translation.]

[2] Erazim Kohák, *The Embers and the Stars: A Philosophical Inquiry into the Moral Sense of Nature* (Chicago, IL and London: The University of Chicago Press, 1984), p. 5.

[3] As quoted in Hubert Dreyfus and Sean Dorrance Kelly, *All Things Shining: Reading the Western Classics to Find Meaning in a Secular Age* (New York, NY: Free Press, 2011), p. 168.

immanent sphere in their desire for a transcendent deity—a predominately modern critique brilliantly chronicled in Charles Taylor's *A Secular Age*—they have all the more begun to stress the wonder and value of immanence. It is true, as Taylor argues, that this "immanent frame" in which we live *can be* "spun" both in the direction of openness to a transcendent referent and in the direction of closure; nonetheless, a closed immanence seems to be something of a default position not least in the academy.[4] In this context of sensitivity to the wonder and value of immanence not a few theologians have felt it necessary to reject the transcendence of God altogether, at least in the radical form that follows from the doctrine of creation *ex nihilo*. However, both the secular critique and the immanentist theology (for lack of a better expression) accommodating this critique by rejecting creation *ex nihilo* seem to share one crucial assumption—this assumption is that immanence and transcendence should be understood according to a contrastive logic. They have assumed, in other words, that the created world is the Creator's "other" according to a straightforward dialectic, such that more God equals less world, and vice versa. On such a construal, affirming the immanent must of course imply negating the transcendent.

At this point the defender of creation *ex nihilo* may retort saying that this is a complete misunderstanding of the subtle logic of the doctrine, and in a sense this is certainly true. However, there are reasons not to dismiss the critique too quickly. For one thing, Gnostic escapism *is* Christianity's constant companion and the critique of transcendence forces theology to remember this in articulating its vision for creation—a vision that arguably *does* embrace the wonder and value of the immanent sphere as God's good creation. But it is also useful for theology to be pressed to say something, not only about its affirmation of immanence in general, but about how this is worked out concretely. My point is that it is not enough for theology to invoke a formula; rather, there is a sense in which each generation needs to rediscover the doctrine of creation and to articulate its implications in dialogue with concerns that are alive within that particular context. These implications, I believe, have often been poorly communicated.

Kathryn Tanner makes a similar point when she argues for the importance of rhetoric in the articulation of Christian theology: it is simply not enough for theological discourse to keep to the formal "rules" of what makes such

---

[4] Charles Taylor, *A Secular Age* (Cambridge, MA and London: The Belknap Press of Harvard University Press, 2007), pp. 539–593. In describing the cultural framework of emerging modernity as an "immanent frame," Taylor means to suggest the ubiquity of this framework as a context for believers and unbelievers alike. However, in contrast to mainstream secularization theory he claims that this immanent frame does not necessarily imply a rejection of transcendence; it may lead to such a rejection, but it may also retain a notion of transcendence. The modern predicament is thus *not* that we are barred from transcendence, but that we must choose to affirm or reject it—this is not any more a given. In this sense, immanence is lived as either "open" or "closed," and it becomes interesting to explore what motivates people to opt for one or the other of these positions.

discourse hang together in a coherent way. For even if it is coherent from a theological point of view, it may be misapprehended due to the pre-understanding of the particular cultural context in which it is received. What is needed, therefore, is a sort of rhetorical sensitivity that not only keeps to the rules of coherent Christian talk, but that also understands the way in which such talk will be heard in the given situation.[5] In the present context, wanting to affirm the wonder and value of immanence while denying that this requires closure, how should one therefore proceed to articulate the doctrine of creation *ex nihilo* and its consequences?

An important first step is arguably to enter into conversation with thinkers who have a keen appreciation for the wonder of immanence, to learn from what they are saying, with the purpose of connecting this to the theology of creation. With this in mind I suggest existential phenomenology, and especially that of the French philosopher Maurice Merleau-Ponty (1908–1961), as an important dialogue partner for theology. Merleau-Ponty's philosophy is a sustained effort to elucidate the creative power inherent in the world, all the way from simple life forms to the complexities of human thought, and always defending the integrity of the immanent sphere against reductions of various sorts. For this reason his philosophy has recently been taken up by a number of thinkers in diverse fields who share a desire to develop holistic and more ecologically sensitive alternatives to materialistic reductionism and classical dualism alike.[6]

To illustrate the resonance between Merleau-Pontian phenomenology and the theology of creation, I want to focus especially on two themes that are very much at the heart of Merleau-Ponty's philosophical vision. These are themes that also resonate strongly with our contemporary attraction to imma-nence: on the one hand, the desire to belong within nature—to be natural—and to feel oneself, as it were, at home in the world, and, on the other, the desire to partake in the unfolding sense of the world and in the course of its history as free agents of change, at work to bring out meaning. We might think of these as the desire to be *at home in the world*, as well as to be *at work in the world* (where "work" is used in the widest possible sense).

Merleau-Ponty, however, clearly thought that we can only truly be at home and at work in the world if divine transcendence is rejected—in this sense he inhabits a closed immanence. On the other hand, his critique of the regnant

---

    [5] Kathryn Tanner, *God and Creation in Christian Theology: Tyranny or Empowerment?* (Oxford: Blackwell, 1988), pp. 120–123.
    [6] See in particular, David Abram, *The Spell of the Sensuous: Perception and Language in a More-Than-Human World* (New York, NY: Vintage Books, 1996); Ted Toadvine, *Merleau-Ponty's Philosophy of Nature* (Evanston, IL: Northwestern University Press, 2009); Suzanne Cataldi and William Hamrick, (eds.), *Merleau-Ponty and Environmental Philosophy: Dwelling on the Landscapes of Thought* (Albany, NY: State University of New York Press, 2007); Evan Thompson, *Mind in Life: Biology, Phenomenology and the Sciences of Mind* (Cambridge, MA: The Belknap Press of Harvard University Press, 2007); and Alva Noë, *Out of Our Heads: Why You Are Not Your Brain, and Other Lessons from the Biology of Consciousness* (New York, NY: Hill and Wang, 2009).

paradigms finally led him to articulate something of an enchanted naturalism in his "ontology of flesh". In contrast to Merleau-Ponty himself, I believe that this enchanted naturalism is deeply congruent with the Christian under-standing of creation—if by naturalism we mean a philosophy that sees human beings as integral parts of the natural world, and not its antithesis. To begin to see this, the logic of creation *ex nihilo* needs initially to be clarified.

The Logic of the Doctrine of Creation

While the historical emergence of the doctrine of creation *ex nihilo* is complex, its main lines of argument can be briefly stated. On the one hand, early Christian theologians argued for the absolute sovereignty and freedom of God against the Platonic idea of a plurality of original principles existing in parallel with God and constraining his activity, as well as against the Neo-platonic idea that God created out of an inner necessity rather than out of freedom. On the other hand, theologians defended the inherent goodness of the created world against various forms of Gnostic escapism and disdain of the material world. Hence, Christian theologians came to agree on a doctrine according to which God created the world constrained neither by recalcitrant matter, nor by any other necessities or hindrances, and that the world was therefore entirely good in virtue of having been so created.[7] This context is important if we are rightly to evaluate the contemporary relevance of the doctrine, as we shall see.

From these basic statements of the Christian doctrine of creation, however, a number of more subtle consequences necessarily follow. First, creation *ex nihilo* teaches us that God is not a being among other beings, one more item in the universe, albeit the biggest and the best. Rather, God is to be distin-guished from the universe of beings as their creator. But this also means that this distinction is one of a kind—*sui generis*—and that it must therefore work in a very unusual way. Ordinary distinctions, of which philosophers are so fond, work by means of contrasts within a common context: we look for the *differentia specifica* within a common *genus*. The distinction between God and the world, however, cannot operate like this, since God is not one more item within the common context of the universe or the natural whole, which is the normal context for human reflection. Rather, God is the creator of the whole *ex nihilo* and would be just as much God even in the absence of the world created. This is one aspect of saying that there is no necessity bridging God and world, since God did not have to create; rather, creation is seen as an utterly gratuitous gift contingent upon nothing but the gracious will of God.

---

[7] For more on the historical context of the emergence of the doctrine, see Gerhard May, *Creatio ex Nihilo: The Doctrine of "Creation out of Nothing" in Early Christian Thought* (Edinburgh: T&T Clark, 1994); and Janet M. Soskice, "Creatio ex Nihilo: its Jewish and Christian Founda-tions", in David Burrell, Carlo Cogliato, Janet M. Soskice and William R. Stoeger, (eds.), *Creation and the God of Abraham* (Cambridge: Cambridge University Press, 2010).

In contemporary philosophical theology no one has done more than Robert Sokolowski to elaborate on the peculiarity of this distinction, which he calls "the Christian Distinction".[8] Sokolowski shows that the Christian distinction ushered in an understanding of both God and the world hitherto unknown to classical thought: God as absolutely transcendent in relation to the world, and the world as radically contingent upon God's creative act alone. This has far-reaching consequences for how we understand the notion of creation in the first place, and the relation holding between the Creator and creation. Of particular importance is the recognition that "no distinction made within the horizon of the world is like this, and therefore the act of creation cannot be understood in terms of any action or any relationship that exists in the world."[9] That is to say, whenever we think of God acting in the world in the same manner and on the same level as any other cause—when we think, for instance, that among the forces of the world there are gravitation, strong and weak nuclear force, electromagnetism . . . and God—we are making a *theological* mistake.

With this insight we are already at a second important consequence flowing from the doctrine of creation *ex nihilo* via the Christian distinction—what I, inspired by the work of Kathryn Tanner, shall call the principle of non-contrastive transcendence.[10] If God is not another item in the universe, but is as radically transcendent as the Christian distinction suggests, it follows that God cannot be related to the things of this world as they are related to each other; God cannot be contrasted with the world or with anything in the world in the way that things in the world in various ways stand in contrastive relations to each other. For God is not just another competing part of nature, but the one without which these competing parts would not be in the first place. The influence of God upon created things should therefore not be construed like that of the influence of created things upon each other, which arguably always contains an element of violence.[11] Earlier theologians spoke in this context about God sustaining creatures not from without but from within. Thus, for instance, Augustine says that "it is one thing to establish and administer creation from the *inmost and supreme pivot of all causes* . . . it is another matter to apply activity from outside."[12] And Aquinas continues: "in all things God himself is properly the cause of

---

[8] See Robert Sokolowski, *The God of Faith and Reason: Foundations of Christian Theology* (Washington, DC: The Catholic University of America Press, 1995). See also David Burrell, "The Christian Distinction Celebrated and Expanded", in his *Faith and Freedom: An Interfaith Perspective* (Oxford: Blackwell, 2004).

[9] Sokolowski, *God of Faith and Reason*, p. 33.

[10] See Tanner, *God and Creation*, pp. 42–48.

[11] This is an observation already made by Thomas Aquinas. See *The Summa Thelogica of St. Thomas Aquinas*, The Fathers of the English Dominican Province (trans.), (Notre Dame, IN: Christian Classics, 1948), Ia, q. 103, art. 1.

[12] Augustine, *De Trinitate*, Edmund Hill, O.P. (trans.), (New York, NY: New City Press, 1991), III.2.16 (my emphasis).

universal being *which is innermost in all things . . .* in all things God works *intimately.*"[13] In our terms, the transcendence of God must not be contrasted with the immanence of creation, as if divine transcendence were somehow antithetical to immanence; rather, it is because God is not just generically "other" but transcendent in this peculiar way that God can establish the immanent sphere with its proper integrity. It is with this understanding of the logic of the doctrine of creation that I now turn to Merleau-Ponty's attempts to elucidate and defend the integrity and wonder of immanence.

At Home and at Work in the World

"True philosophy," says Merleau-Ponty in *The Phenomenology of Perception*, "consists in relearning to look at the world."[14] Phenomenology, as a philosophical method, is a perpetual apprenticeship to learn a particular kind of vision; "it is as painstaking as the works of Balzac, Proust, Valéry or Cezanne—by reason of the same kind of attentiveness and wonder, the same demand for awareness, the same will *to seize the meaning of the world* [*saisir le sens du monde*] or of history as that meaning comes into being."[15] In other words, phenomenology is concerned with understanding how the world comes to be meaningful or structured in particular ways. This concern for meaning—and indeed, for the ontology such meaning presupposes—is arguably at the heart of Merleau-Ponty's philosophical program, being replayed in different keys throughout his several works.

Following certain suggestions in Edmund Husserl's phenomenology, Merleau-Ponty pioneers a philosophical approach to the body, seeing it as the primary locus of human meaning-making. But if that is so, he argues, meaning can no longer be seen as residing in a subjective order entirely other to material nature, such as in a transcendental ego; the body is after all one material body among others in a shared world. On the other hand, this body is not merely an inanimate object, but an experiencing body, a "lived body" [*corps vécu*].[16] Investigating this lived body, Merleau-Ponty

---

[13] Aquinas, *Summa Theologica* Ia, q. 105, art. 5 (my emphases).

[14] *PhP.*, p. 21/xiii.

[15] *PhP.*, p. 22/xxiv (my emphasis).

[16] The expression "lived body" harkens back to Husserl's distinction between *Körper* and *Leib*, where the former signifies the objective body, as observed from a third-person perspective, and the latter signifies the body as experienced and experiencing, that is, from a first-person perspective. For Husserl realized that there is something it is like to be a body (or to have a body), ways in which our embodiment has an irreducible subjective dimension, and he also realized that by virtue of the bodies we have, the world is disclosed to us in particular ways. Most importantly, Husserl realized the role of bodily movement in the constitution of the world. See e.g. Edmund Husserl, *Ideas Pertaining to a Pure Phenomenology and to a Phenomenological Philosophy. Second Book: Studies in the Phenomenology of Constitution*, Richard Rojcewicz and André Schuwer (trans.), (Dordrecht: Kluwer Academic Publishers, 1989), §§ 18, pp. 35–42. For a lucid discussion of this theme in Husserl, see Dan Zahavi, *Husserl's Phenomenology* (Stanford, CA: Stanford University Press, 2003), pp. 98–109.

believes he has discovered "a third genus of being" [*un troisième genre d'être*], making it possible to overcome traditional dualistic stalemates.[17] The lived body, then, designates a material body which as such is clearly a part of nature, but precisely in its function as agent in the world—as intentionality, as subjectivity.

The crucial characteristic of the lived body is that it is *meaningfully* related to its surroundings in a pre-objective or pre-cognitive way, through practical projects. It is not the case that the body without the higher cognitive functions of the mind is devoid of the sort of intentionality that results in a meaningful relation with the world. Rather, the body has its own ways of disclosing the world through its "motor intentionality" [*intentionnalité motrice*],[18] or what can generally be called its sensorimotor capacities. In the same way that *Dasein*, for Heidegger, is primordially involved in the world so as to make it meaningful without the assistance of thematic thought or cognitive representation, the lived body, for Merleau-Ponty, is meaningfully related to the world through the body's own intentionality long before and also always behind reflective thought.[19]

This leads to a re-articulation of transcendental philosophy from the point of view of embodiment. Merleau-Ponty is clearly a transcendental philosopher within the historical trajectory going from Kant and the Romantics through Husserl and phenomenology, which means that he is interested in the way in which pregiven subjective structures inform experience and shape the way that the world is given.[20] Yet with the discovery of the corporeal subject he breaks with this tradition in two important respects: first, by showing that the constituting structures are not primarily in the mind, as categories or concepts, but in the body as an acquired schema for sensorimotor interaction; and, second, by consequently insisting that constitution must be reciprocal *between* the subject and the world rather than unidirectional *from* some otherworldly subject. Significantly, the lived body is always in the world, as part of the world, and this means that a sharp distinction between the subjective and the objective orders cannot be clearly drawn.

This brief sketch of one of Merleau-Ponty's most important basic insights—that of the lived body and its relation to the perceived world—already allows us to see how his philosophy connects with the twin desires of immanence articulated above: being at home in the world, and being at work in the world. For it is precisely because the subject is a material subject that a

---

[17] *PhP.*, p. 407/408.

[18] *PhP.*, p. 141/127.

[19] On the relation between Heidegger's and Merleau-Ponty's projects, see Alphonse de Waelhens introduction, "A Philosophy of the Ambiguous", in Maurice Merleau-Ponty, *The Structure of Behaviour*, Alden L. Fisher (trans.), (Pittsburgh, PA: Duquesne University Press, 1963).

[20] For an elucidating discussion of the continuities and ruptures between the transcendental tradition and Merleau-Ponty's project, see Martin Dillon, "Apriority in Kant and Merleau-Ponty", *Kant-Studien: Philosophische Zeitschrift der Kant-Gesellschaft*, Vol. 78 (1987), pp. 403–423.

meaning can emerge in its interaction with the material surroundings, according to an enactive logic transpiring on an embodied level. But this requires the motor intentionality of the lived body, which in turn requires a history of intimate coupling between body and world. Meaning, in short, emerges because the subject belongs to the world and is at work in the world to bring forth its latent meaning.

In fact, the first thing that strikes the reader of Merleau-Ponty's descriptions of the phenomena of perceptual meaning is the way he stresses the very intimate relation between the lived body and the world: "Our own body is in the world as the heart is in the organism: it keeps the visible spectacle constantly alive, it breathes life into it and sustains it inwardly, and with it forms a system."[21] David Abram draws attention to the "dynamic blend of receptivity and creativity" implied in these descriptions.[22] For Merleau-Ponty it is never the case that perceptual meaning is passively received by the subject, nor that it is only the result of active creation—rather, it is a *dialogue* in which the subject and the world both participate.[23] Abram suggests that the concept of *participation*, as it was developed by the early French anthropologist Lucien Lévy-Bruhl, captures the relation Merleau-Ponty describes: "By asserting that perception, phenomenologically considered, is inherently participatory, we mean that perception always involves, at its most intimate level, the experience of an active interplay, or coupling, between the perceiving body and that which it perceives."[24]

Against this background we can understand the import of the above epigraph: to "participate in the world," for Merleau-Ponty, means both to be an integral part of the world—at home—*and* to actively partake in the unfolding sense of the world—at work. Initially this takes place at the level of sensorimotor activity, but as we shall now see this is only the beginning: out of the body's primordial sense-making arises the entire spectrum of human meaning.

The Contingent Unfolding of Meaning

The development of meaning from its beginnings in perceptual dialogue to the rich world of cultural meaning coincides with the development of the subject from a "pre-personal" corporeal subject to the speaking, thinking,

---

[21] *PhP.*, p. 245/235. Merleau-Ponty never tires of inventing metaphors for the intimate relation between the lived body and the world perceived. In the *Phenomenology* it is described, for instance, as the relation between the sleeper and his slumber [*du dormeur et de son sommeil*] (p. 256/245); as sacramental communion [*une communion*] (pp. 257/246, 258/248); as communication [*communication*] (pp. 302/296, 373/370), symbiosis [*symbiose*] (pp. 373/370), and coition [*accouplement*] (p. 376/373); and as primordial contract [*contrat primordial*] (p. 261/251).

[22] Abram, *Spell of the Sensuous*, p. 50.

[23] *PhP.*, pp. 375–376/372–373.

[24] Abram, *Spell of the Sensuous*, p. 57. See also Lucien Lévy-Bruhl's classic *How Natives Think* (Princeton, NJ: Princeton University Press, 1985), chap. 2 in particular.

self-reflective cogito. Says Merleau-Ponty: "The 'mental' or cultural life borrows its structures from natural life and . . . the thinking subject must have its basis in the subject incarnate."[25] I have no space here to discuss the intricacies and potential problems of Merleau-Ponty's treatment of this development, so I shall only indicate the basic structure of his approach.

Merleau-Ponty follows a logic that he borrows from Husserl and his notions of *Fundierung* (or *Stiftung*) and sedimentation.[26] *Fundierung* names a kind of circular or reciprocal relation that can play itself out on many levels.[27] In general, it designates a whole meaning-structure in which present meaning builds on previously acquired meanings, which in turn builds on an originally instituted meaning-formation (*Urstiftung*).[28] Such a structure is characterized by a kind of teleology towards increasing complexity, as more complicated structures grow from the originally instituted meaning—as in geometry, to take Husserl's example, where incredibly complex structures nonetheless build upon a relatively small set of founding insights. This struc-ture is also characterized, however, by the return of founded terms upon founding terms so as to imbue them with an altered signification. *Fundierung* therefore names not just a linear edifice, but instead a kind of circularity of influence.[29] In another context, Merleau-Ponty describes it as follows: "Husserl has used the fine word *Stiftung*—foundation or establishment—to designate first of all the unlimited fecundity of each present."[30] The important upshot of this is that the already sedimented repository of meaning is at any given moment pregnant with endless possibilities of new formations of meaning, even as they are never guaranteed or simply caused by the past. They need to be taken up and actualized.

It is important to underline that on Merleau-Ponty's construal there is no necessity in the development of meaning-structures. If each present holds

---

[25] *PhP.*, p. 235/225.

[26] Cf. Maurice Merleau-Ponty, *Signes* (Paris: Gallimard, 1960), pp. 172–177; *Signs*, Richard C. McClearly (trans.), (Evanston, IL: Northwestern University Press, 1964), pp. 217–223; *PhP.*, pp. 226–231/216–221, 448–455/451–459.

[27] Husserl puts the logic of *Fundierung* to fruitful use not least in his later work on the constitutive role of tradition, as for instance in his "Origin of Geometry," where he undertakes an "inquiry back into the most original sense in which geometry once arose, was present as the tradition of millennia, is still present for us, and is still being worked on in a lively forward development." Edmund Husserl, "The Origin of Geometry", in *The Crisis of the European Sciences and Transcendental Philosophy: An Introduction to Phenomenological Philosophy* (Evanston, IL: Northwestern University Press, 1970), p. 354.

[28] See e.g. "Origin", pp. 362–363. There is a peculiar sort of foundationalism in the logic of *Fundierung*, but as Merleau-Ponty uses it this is not an epistemological foundationalism, which would require what Merleau-Ponty denies—a secured access to the foundation. In contrast to Husserl, Merleau-Ponty is more interested in the layered structure of *meaning* than in epistemol-ogy as such.

[29] It is to indicate this circular non-identical repetition within the relation that I here keep the German *Fundierung* as a technical term, rather than translating it as *foundation*, which has a straightforward, linear connotation.

[30] Merleau-Ponty, *Signs*, p. 73/59.

"unlimited fecundity," this means that its potentiality can be taken up, expressed and developed in many different ways. We have a cultural repository of meaning but it contains numerous possibilities of creative appropriation. The sense of the world is therefore neither given once and for all—objectively there just waiting to be mirrored in human thought—nor is it merely a subjective projection upon an in itself meaningless substratum. Meaning—perceptual, linguistic, ideal—emerges as subjectivity actively engages with a world always already "pregnant with meaning" [*prégnante d'un sens*].[31] We live the sense of the world as though "perched on a pyramid of past life"[32] and what will be is contingent on the creative participation of free agents. Our work matters—"our world . . . is an unfinished task."[33] It is this rich notion of human creative participation that I wish to indicate when speaking about being at work in the world. It must be noted, however, that if such creative participation is to be possible the world must contain a measure of contingency. This is because contingency is a condition of freedom, and freedom is the necessary condition of being genuine participants in the game, rather than pawns moved about by external forces. As Merleau-Ponty understands it, this rules out not only reductive materialism as well as dualistic idealism, but also the idea of divine creation.

Theology Against Contingent Meaning-Making

According to Merleau-Ponty, then, we are at home in the world, entirely rooted in the sensuous domain. We are also at work in the world so as to unfold its sense, first through very basic sensorimotor activities and then in the sublimated forms of language, culture, politics and science, all of which remain rooted in the primary carnal dimension of human existence.[34] Finally, this unfolding of meaning is a contingent affair, leaving room for human participation. We are now in possession of the elements we need in order to understand Merleau-Ponty's critique of Christian doctrine, especially of the idea that God transcends the world by virtue of having created it *ex nihilo*.

If one follows Merleau-Ponty's explicit interaction with Christian thought it appears that it is fundamentally governed by an insistence on closed immanence, which is itself motivated by the perception of a *contrastive understanding* of the relation between transcendence and immanence as it is

---

[31] Cf. *PhP.*, pp. 45/25, 340/356, 492/498; and Maurice Merleau-Ponty, *The Primacy of Perception and Other Essays on Phenomenological Psychology, the Philosophy of Art, History and Politics*, James M. Edie (trans.), (Evanston, IL: Northwestern University Press, 1964), p. 12.

[32] *PhP.*, p. 453/457, quoting Proust.

[33] Merleau-Ponty, *Primacy*, p. 6, quoting Malebranche.

[34] Says Taylor Carman: "Merleau-Ponty's philosophical purpose is thus basically the same in his phenomenology of perception and in his reflections on language, art, and history, namely, to show that all forms of meaning are rooted in the bodily intelligibility of perception." *Merleau-Ponty* (London: Routledge, 2008), p. 23.

worked out in Christian experience and theology. Starting from these premises, Merleau-Ponty's critique takes different forms depending on whether his focus is on philosophical method, praxis and politics, or ontology. Having no space here to follow these themes through Merleau-Ponty's writings, I shall illustrate his basic assumptions by looking at one central text from his middle period, and then return to the thematic in relation to his late ontology.[35]

In 1953 Merleau-Ponty delivered the inaugural lecture as the youngest ever to hold the chair of philosophy at the Collège de France, entitled "In Praise of Philosophy" [*Éloge de la philosophie*]. Towards the end of the lecture Merleau-Ponty engages in a polemic with Henri de Lubac and Jacques Maritain. The principal problem for Merleau-Ponty concerns the nature of philosophy as antithetical to the absolute in any and every form, which is to say that philosophy, as a paradigmatic example of human meaning-making, is premised on contingency. He accuses de Lubac and Maritain of assuming that any philosophy that does not seek and affirm the absolute must end up in the utterly dissolute, as if there could be no philosophy that refused the absolute but nonetheless witnessed to the birth and development of human meaning. On a theological construal, Merleau-Ponty thinks meaning is absolute because it reposes in the mind of God; the transcendent realm entirely governs the immanent world. It is in this sense that "promethean humanism's" absolute denial of the world's meaning, locating it instead in the mind of man, is merely the inversion of "explanatory theology," reproducing its absolutist and objectivist logic in a different key.[36] Genuine philosophy, on the other hand, admits that there is meaning in the world, but also that this meaning is never absolutely given, is not preordained, secured or static.

> The [true] philosopher does not say that a final overcoming of human contradiction is possible and that the completed human awaits us in the future: like everyone else, he does not know anything about that. He says—and that is a very different thing—that the world begins, that we cannot judge its future from what has been its past, that the idea of a destiny in things is not an idea but a vertigo, that our relations with nature are not fixed once and for all, that *no one can know what freedom may do*.[37]

---

[35] For a more extensive treatment, see my *Figuring Flesh in Creation: Merleau-Ponty in Conversation with Philosophical Theology*, Doctoral Dissertation at Lund University, 2011.

[36] Cf. Maurice Merleau-Ponty, *Éloge de la philosophie et autres essais* (Paris: Gallimard, 1953), pp. 50–51 [all translations mine].

[37] "Le philosophe ne dit pas qu'un dépassement final des contradictions humaines soit possible et que l'homme totale nous attende dans l'avenir: comme tout le monde, il n'en sait rien. Il dit,—et c'est tout autre chose,—que le monde commence, que nous n'avons pas à juger de son avenir par ce qu'a été son passé, que l'idée d'un destin dans les choses n'est pas une idée, mais un vertige, que nos rapports avec la nature ne sont pas fixés une fois pour toutes, que *personne ne peut savoir que la liberté peut faire.*" *Ibid.*, p. 52 (my emphasis).

Can theology accept and wonder at such a fragile and contingent formation of meaning emerging out of immanence? Merleau-Ponty believes that it cannot, at least not as understood by de Lubac and Maritain. "For theology observes the contingency of human being only to derive from it a necessary Being, that is, to get rid of it; it uses philosophical wonder only to motivate an affirmation that terminates it."[38] What Merleau-Ponty seems to be saying is that only a thinking that affirms the contingency, not only of humankind, of meaning and the progression of history, but of being itself can remain in the philosophical attitude. De Lubac, in his 1944 book *Drame de l'humanité athée*, had claimed that the ultimate metaphysical question of why there is something rather than nothing is indeed the problem that "has let God be born in human consciousness."[39] And in the face of its explicit intentions, de Lubac accuses modern atheism of being *insufficiently* sensitive to the problem of contingency—indeed, of eliminating it. Merleau-Ponty retorts that he is not the one eliminating contingency, but rather that he radicalizes it. The philosopher "makes it [the problem of contingency] radical, he raises it above 'solutions' that choke it."[40] In other words, the philosopher recognizes contingency as a fundamental and principal enigma, for which no solution could or should be sought.[41] Merleau-Ponty here bases his rejection of the "solution" of divine creation on an understanding of the nature of philosophy: without contingency there is no wonder, and without wonder no genuine philosophy. But deeper assumptions are clearly at work under the surface of this exchange, assumptions about the relation between creation, contingency and human meaning-making.

To make sense of this it may be useful to draw a distinction between *absolute* and *relative* contingency—the former referring to the very existence of the world, of human being and of the possibility of meaning; the latter signifying the fact that the forward development of meaning is not determined and fixed, that there is room for creative participation in its unfolding. In his discussions of the nature of philosophy and the wonder it requires, Merleau-Ponty seems mostly to be concerned with relative contingency, as in the quote above: "no one can know what freedom may do." Again, nature is not to be understood as a deterministic stretch of cause and effect—"our relations with nature are not fixed once and for all"—whether couched in theological or naturalistic vocabulary, but as an open structure in which human beings participate.

---

[38] "Car la théologie ne constate pas la contingence de l'être humain que pour la dériver d'un être nécessaire, c'est-à-dire pour s'en défaire, elle n'use de l'étonnement philosophique que pour motiver une affirmation qui le termine." *Ibid.*, p. 53.

[39] Quoted by Merleau-Ponty in *ibid.*, p. 53.

[40] *Ibid.*, p. 53.

[41] Cf. with what Merleau-Ponty in another context says about religion: "As a questioning, it is justified on the condition that it remains answerless." *Signs*, p. 257/203.

However, what seems to be at stake in de Lubac's charge and Merleau-Ponty's riposte is the different (though of course related) question of absolute contingency, what Merleau-Ponty in another place calls "ontological contingency" [*contingence ontologique*]; that is, the very question of why the world *is* in the first place.[42] The confusion of this exchange of ideas, it seems to me, is caused in no small part by the fact that Merleau-Ponty is less than clear about what absolute contingency has to do with the relative contingency that meaning-making requires. Why does Merleau-Ponty need to affirm the brute facticity of the world, human existence and meaning so strongly? The answer turns out to be intimately bound to theology. Simply put, Merleau-Ponty believes that an affirmation of divine creation as a response to the enigma of ontological contingency implies a denial of intra-mundane relative contingency; he believes, that is, that a transcendent Creator implies a fully determined creation and therefore the loss of the human phenomenon, its freedom, and its creative meaning-making. He indicates as much when he says, in his response to de Lubac, that "it is the same thing to establish [*constater*] [the contingent unfolding of sense] against every naturalistic explanation as it is to liberate [it] from every sovereign necessity [i.e. God]."[43]

At this point we return to the Christian distinction—which, we may note, was the cultural background against which the question of absolute contingency was first pondered—and to the principle of non-contrastive transcendence. For it is evident that Merleau-Ponty's concern presupposes a contrastive logic of transcendence, one that does not follow from the Christian distinction between God and creation. Here it plays itself out principally in the realm of causality, as Merleau-Ponty understands the presumed divine "cause" of the world to be much like any other cause in the world, only of course more powerful. Moreover, the divine cause and ordinary causes are assumed to work at the same level, such that they are in competition. On such a setup, naturally, God wins and the creature loses. But, as suggested above, this is not how Christian theologians have normally understood the logic of creation. In this matter Karl Barth's discussion of the divine accompanying of the creature—the divine *concursus*—and especially his discussion of the theological legitimacy of using the philosophical concept of "cause," is very helpful.[44] Barth argues that Catholic and Protestant theologians rightly appropriated the philosophical notion of causality to speak both of God as creator and sustainer of the world [*causa prima*] *and* of creatures as causes in their own right [*causae secundae*], such that God can be spoken of as the cause of all causes [*causa causarum*]. However, he adds that while earlier theologians were indeed formally correct in this linguistic usage, they did not sufficiently guard against its attendant dangers, and Barth goes on to argue

---

[42] *PhP.*, pp. 459/462–463.
[43] Merleau-Ponty, *Éloge*, p. 54.
[44] Karl Barth, *Church Dogmatics* III.3 (London: T&T Clark, 2009), pp. 94–107.

that several qualifications must be constantly kept in mind if the notion of cause is not to lead theology astray. Many of these fall back on the same non-contrastive logic spelled out above. For instance, (1) *causa* must not be understood, under the influence of modern natural science, to operate in a mechanistic way; (2) the meaning of *causa* must not be understood to be univocal when applied to God and to human beings; (3) the qualitative distinction between the Creator and creation means that their causal agencies must not be thought to be operative on the same level.

What Merleau-Ponty criticizes is a Christian theology oblivious of these points, and which therefore ends up with a necessitarian and mechanistic conception of the world. Ironically, this brings him rather close to the concerns of the traditional Christian theology discussed by Barth: both want to affirm the genuine efficacy of the causal matrix of the world and of human beings in particular. As Barth puts it, "God rules in and over a world of freedom."[45] But why is it that Merleau-Ponty and Barth come to such different conclusions about the consequences following from affirming a divine creation of the world, given that they share a commitment to the wonder and value of immanence?

To clarify this, let us return to that "wonder in the face of the world" without which Merleau-Ponty believes there would be no philosophy. Perhaps we could say that there are two fundamental reasons for philosophical wonder and questioning: that there is a world *and* that it is such as it is for us—*that* it is and *how* it is. If, for the sake of argument (and only for the sake of argument), we concede to Merleau-Ponty that divine creation puts a stop to the first kind of wonder, we would still have the possibility of the second kind of wonder—which is in fact the one that most occupies him (phenomenology as learning to see the unfolding sense of the world). Unless, of course, a necessary connection is perceived between the first kind of wonder and the second, if that is, it is assumed that eliminating the first kind of wonder automatically eliminates the second. But why would it do that? This inference only works if it is assumed that divine creation implies a world stripped of its own integrity, reduced to a passive effect of the divine creative intention. This is, of course, Merleau-Ponty's assumption—for which, I might add, he does not argue. When in his debate with de Lubac he says that theology "uses philosophical wonder only to motivate an affirmation that terminates it," we ought therefore to understand him as saying that theology, by affirming a divine creation of the world, immediately terminates the first kind of wonder and then also the second, through the ontological connection holding between them. At one fell swoop theology manages to get rid of absolute and relative contingency together, and with them all reasons for wonder and philosophy, as well as all possibility of human participation in

---

[45] *Ibid.*, p. 93.

the unfolding sense of the world. In short, the *how* of the world follows necessarily from the *that* of the world—we are left with a mechanism, not an organism.

However, the emphasis on divine freedom in the doctrine of creation would seem to deny the possibility of knowing anything about the way in which the created world operates simply from the fact that it is created. Again, there simply is no necessary connection between a world contingent upon divine creation *ex nihilo* and the contingencies or necessities holding within that world as a result. While God could have created a mechanistic world, it cannot be excluded that God could also have created a world with a significant amount of contingency and in particular with creatures endowed with the power of a qualified self-determinacy—indeed, with creatures who participate in the unfolding sense of the world so created. And when we look at how theologians such as Augustine or Aquinas conceived of the matter, it is unsurprising that creatures are conceived of as existing in such a framework and as having such powers. It is true, of course, that the co-creative role of human subjectivity does not become a central focus of philosophy until modernity. Nonetheless, long before modernity theologians understood that creation *ex nihilo* implies the inherent goodness and integrity of creation, and that this extends to the proper action of creatures. Aquinas, for instance, insists that divine creation is what establishes the efficacy of the creature, such that "the dignity of causality is imparted even to creatures."[46] By this way of reasoning, it seems to me, traditional theologians opened up a fertile area of reflection, one which they nonetheless did not explore very much, and which therefore remains for us to investigate in greater depth and with the conceptual tools at our disposal. Merleau-Ponty's contribution to that set of tools cannot be adequately evaluated until his later ontology is taken into account.

Towards a New Philosophy of Nature and Meaning

Towards the mid-1950s Merleau-Ponty begins to develop a new philosophy of nature and the so called "ontology of flesh." These developments can be seen as an attempt to fully and consistently articulate the ontology that was only partially and inconsistently revealed in the earlier works. He writes that this projected new work, or the first volume of it, "takes up again, deepens and rectifies my first two books," and that it is "entirely carried out within the perspective of ontology."[47]

---

[46] Aquinas, *Summa Theologica* 1a, q. 22, art. 3. An insightful modern discussion of this theme is found in Barth, *Church Dogmatics* III.3, pp. 90–94.

[47] Maurice Merleau-Ponty, *Le visible et l'invisible: suivi de notes de travail*, Claude Leforte (ed.), (Paris: Gallimard, 1979), p. 220; *The Visible and the Invisible, Followed by Working Notes*, Alphonso Lingis (trans.), (Evanston, IL: Northwestern University Press, 1968), p. 168.

Whereas the *Phenomenology* retained certain vestiges of dualism, Merleau-Ponty believes he has now pressed on to a deeper understanding of the unity of being—in which human being is included. The earlier work had suggested that the *sine qua non* of meaning is a relation of some kind, a correlation or dialogue between the corporeal subject and world. The very possibility of this relation, however, is what is at stake in the later ontology, its ontological roots: how can the world and the subject be *for each other*? Merleau-Ponty's answer, *in nuce*, is that the intentional relation is possible because subject and object are rooted in a differentiation within the same being, which he calls *flesh* [*chair*]. This answer is crystallized in the expression: *J'en suis*—I belong to it. This expression and its variations return often in Merleau-Ponty's last and unfinished work, *The Visible and the Invisible*, and it signifies Merleau-Ponty's fundamental insight, the original and peculiar unity of being, to which subjectivity and objectivity alike belong "as the two halves of an orange."[48] What we see in the later philosophy, then, is a deepening of the theme of belonging, of truly being at home in the world.

This, in turn, has implications for the question of meaning. Merleau-Ponty begins to de-emphasize somewhat the necessary role of human subjectivity in the emergence of meaningful structures. The origin of meaning is now to be sought in nature, or being itself, characterized after the model of the body as a unity-in-difference, a unity described as being always already in rupture [*écart*], but also always chiasmically intertwined [*entrelacé*]—a single thread of being intricately woven like a spider's web, a single fabric infinitely folded back over itself.[49] Rather than meaning arising as the relation of two orders, then, Merleau-Ponty suggests that being (which is here equivalent with nature) is self-expressive in ascending orders, and that humankind is a particularly rich expression of being, through which being comes to self-reflection. This means that the transcendental function, if that is still an appropriate expression, has descended from consciousness, through the body, all the way into being itself—being as expressive of meaning, as auto-affective of its own proto-intelligible structures. So much is this so that a humanist like Jean-Paul Sartre can complain that "at times, it would seem that being invents man in order to make itself manifest through him."[50] But Merleau-Ponty never denies the importance of human being for the emergence of meaning in the world; he is trying to think the radical continuity of nature and human consciousness in such a way as to fully acknowledge the crucial transcendental function of human consciousness without making it—*per impossibile*—the primordial

---

[48] *Ibid.*, p. 174/133.

[49] These terms, which take on a technical as well as metaphorical significance, are elaborated in the highly intricate and dense fourth chapter of *The Visible and the Invisible*, entitled "The Intertwining—The Chiasm" [*L'entrelacs—le chiasme*].

[50] Jean-Paul Sartre, "Merleau-Ponty Vivant", in *The Debate Between Sartre and Merleau-Ponty*, John Stewart (ed.), (Evanston, IL: Northwestern University Press, 1998), p. 616.

origin of meaning as such. "What lives in Nature is not mind or spirit, but rather the beginning of meaning in the process of ordering itself, but which has not fully emerged. . . . The subject has to intervene in order to bring meaning out fully."[51]

Merleau-Ponty understands the flesh, then, as a structured lattice that admits of contingency and human participation. On the other hand, it is still not clear how this would tie into the question of divine creation. At first sight, it may seem that the new understanding is only an opening towards theology if the flesh is itself taken to be divine, according to something like a pantheistic logic, but there is very little, if any, support for this reading in Merleau-Ponty's texts. In fact, in the later writings Merleau-Ponty's understanding of the incompatibility of nature's integrity and divine creation is given an even more explicitly ontological foundation. This is perhaps most clearly seen in his lecture series on *Nature* at the Collège de France in the years 1956–1960. Contrasting it with the concept of nature he wants to defend, Merleau-Ponty once more suggests that the Judeo-Christian tradition has led to the modern conception of nature or the world as a lifeless product, lacking creativity of its own—*naturata* rather than *naturans*. All that could have been interior to nature (its inherent potentialities) takes refuge in God, and nature becomes thoroughly subjected to linear causality, that is, it becomes regulated by law—a gigantic object fully constituted by God.[52] The world thus becomes intrinsically meaningless; meaning is to be sought elsewhere: "Nature loses its interior; it is the exterior realization of a rationality that is in God."[53] Granted, these are Merleau-Ponty's descriptions of the Cartesian understanding of nature. It seems clear, however, that he believes such a conception of nature to be an outworking of the assumptions of Christian theology, and equally clear that he describes the essence of the position to which he intends to oppose his own understanding. Criticizing modern conceptions of nature, he says that

the very concept of Nature, such as it is often allowed by scientists, belongs to a conception that is entirely theological in its infrastructure. . . . The world is positive, full. At bottom, this conception is a theological affirmation, the affirmation of a view of totality capable of subtending all evolution of the world.[54]

---

[51] Maurice Merleau-Ponty, *La nature: notes, cours de Collège de France* (Paris: Éditions du Seuill, 1995), p. 68; *Nature: Course Notes from the Collège de France*, Robert Vallier (trans.), (Evanston, IL: Northwestern University Press, 2003), p. 43 (my emphasis).

[52] *Ibid.*, p. 26/9.

[53] *Ibid.*, pp. 27–28/10.

[54] "Le concept même de Nature, tel qu'il est souvent admis par les savants, appartient à une conception entièrement théologique dans son infrastructure. . . . Le monde est positif, plein. Au fond, cette conception est une affirmation théologique, c'est l'affirmation d'une vue de la totalité capable de sous-tendre toute l'évolution de monde." *Ibid.*, pp. 123–124/88–89.

Thus "Judeo-Christian ontology" and modern scientific ontology, according to Merleau-Ponty, share the common assumption that the world, or nature, is devoid of potentiality. There can therefore be no progression or unfolding with which subjectivity could freely assist, insofar as subjectivity is seen as that which realizes some of the manifold potentialities inherent in the world.[55]

In relation to the earlier works, the later philosophy of Merleau-Ponty adds a dimension to the problem of divine creation: not only does it eliminate philosophical wonder and the possibility of human participation in the unfolding sense of the world, it is now seen to lead to a mistaken ontology, to a view of nature leaving no room for an "autoproduction of meaning," out of which human being emerges to continue the unfolding of sense in freedom and creativity.[56]

From the perspective of the desire to be at home and at work in the world, Merleau-Ponty's later development is suggestive. Especially his reformulation of the transcendental tradition of philosophy in terms that are—frankly—much more naturalistic. The strength of the transcendental tradition in philosophy was always that it was able to think the human contribution to the meaningful structures of the world—it allowed human beings to be at work in the world, ultimately giving birth to an activist philosophy. However, it was at the same time always tainted by a dualistic presumption in that the transcendental subject had to be seen as other to the natural world—human subjectivity could never truly belong within the world, never be at home.[57] When Merleau-Ponty first begins to investigate embodied subjectivity, and then the ontology of flesh, he indicates a way out of this "correlationist circle" of modern philosophy and proposes instead that the natural world is an auto-productive source of meaningful structures, creative in its own right.[58] Human beings arise out of this world and belong to it; indeed, they are a particularly rich structure, through which being comes to self-reflection, turning back upon itself to realize ever more of its inherent possibilities: consciousness, language, culture. On this understanding, then, human beings are not re-placed, but are rather firmly *placed* within the world with an important task. Merleau-Ponty's later philosophy, I contend, succeeds better than most other articulations of modern thought in preserving the wonder of immanence.

With regard to the later critique of theology, the response is a variation on the earlier theme: Merleau-Ponty, operating on the assumption of contrastive

---

[55] There can still be a sort of progression, but if so this progression must follow from antecedent conditions by causal necessity, or at least as specified by law.

[56] *Ibid.*, p. 19/3.

[57] Cf. Kohák, *Embers and the Stars*, pp. 3–5.

[58] The expression "correlationist circle", as well as a useful analysis of the transcendental tradition from that point of view, is found in Quentin Meillassoux, *After Finitude: An Essay on the Necessity of Contingency* (London: Continuum, 2008), pp. 5–9.

transcendence, takes the presumed productive power of God and the productive power of nature to operate on the same level and to be antithetical: if
God is a productive power, nature cannot be. However, from the vantage
point of the Christian distinction we see that it is one thing for God to be the
absolute productive power of the world *ex nihilo*, and quite another for the
world to be given its own productive powers. It is one thing for God to
establish a causal matrix within which human beings can exist, and quite
another for human beings to be causes in their own right, co-workers, as it
were, with the divine in bringing out the various layers of meaning inherent
in creation.

In conversation with Merleau-Pontian phenomenology, as well as with
contemporary voices sharing the same concerns about the theology of creation, this must be repeated: creation *ex nihilo* does not imply a mechanistic
conception of the world. In fact, from the logic of creation sketched above it
follows that theology must expect the exact opposite of a mechanistic world,
which is to say a living world with contingency, freedom, intentionality and
a rich potential for development.[59] Such a world, it seems to me, is what
Merleau-Ponty's description of flesh is after, which actualises a more constructive question: how should theology respond to a view of the world
such as that finally proposed by Merleau-Ponty? I suggest that reading the
flesh in light of creation *ex nihilo* is a useful theological exercise. Appropriating the language of the ontology of flesh would allow the theologian to
hold together *coming to be* and *becoming*, where the former refers to the
gratuitous divine gift of existence, and the latter to the open structures of this
creation, in and by which subjectivity has a significant role to play in the
bringing forth of its latent meaning.[60] This is interesting, because with regard
to human participation in the unfolding sense of the world of which we are
an integral part, contemporary theology stands in need of development. This
is not to say that the topic has been absent from contemporary debates, or
that it is absent from pre-critical theological traditions, as is sometimes
assumed when the history of Western philosophy is periodized with Kant as
the great watershed. Nonetheless, much needs to be done to flesh out how
such participation actually takes place on a number of interrelated creational
levels, as well as in relation to the divine.[61] This article has suggested that

---

[59] From this perspective, a statement such as the following is almost incomprehensible: "An
utterly programmed world would have to be created *ex nihilo*; a world created *ex nihilo* should
have been utterly programmed if the programmer knew what he was doing." John Caputo, *The
Weakness of God: A Theology of the Event* (Bloomington and Indianapolis: Indiana University Press,
2006), p. 76. Not only is this a *non sequitur*, but it is also not true to the historical understanding
of the doctrine, against which this statement is meant to polemicize.

[60] On the distinction between coming to be and becoming, see William Desmond, *God and the
Between* (Oxford: Blackwell Publishing, 2008), pp. 248–249.

[61] One recent attempt at this is found in Alexander Broadie, "Scotistic Metaphysics and
Creation *ex Nihilo*", in Burrell et al. (eds.), *Creation and the God of Abraham*, pp. 53–64. However,
Broadie argues for a reconciliation of the doctrine of creation *ex nihilo* with the philosophies of

Merleau-Ponty is a key philosophical resource in this endeavour, especially in a cultural context deeply drawn to the value and wonder of immanence. The auto-productive power inherent in nature, and the participation of human subjectivity, on any number of levels, in the unfolding sense of the world in no way implies a rejection of creation *ex nihilo* and the concomitant notion of divine transcendence. On the contrary, it can be argued that these wonders of immanence are not only vaguely compatible with the doctrine of creation, but even implied in its non-contrastive logic: A world so created must have its own integrity established by the one who sustains it at the very fount of its existence.

Hume and Kant, and thus with the modernist notion that the human *mind* is what is creative. The upshot is an idealist proposal that essentially leaves us with three distinct entities: God, mind and world. Needless to say, I believe the Merleau-Pontian approach sketched above not only better captures what actually goes on in constitution (meaning-making), but also that it is a more adequate response to the wonder of immanence and the desire to belong within it rather than to stand above it.

Modern Theology 29:2 April 2013
ISSN 0266-7177 (Print)
ISSN 1468-0025 (Online)

CREATIO EX NIHILO AND THE DIVINE IDEAS IN AQUINAS: HOW FAIR IS BULGAKOV'S CRITIQUE?

JOHN HUGHES

What is the place of the divine ideas in the doctrine of creation *ex nihilo*? Are they a Platonic hangover that properly belongs in a Demiurgic model of creation such as the *Timaeus* and contaminates creation *ex nihilo* with a vestige of pantheistic necessary emanation? Or is it rather that, properly understood and reconceived in the light of the revealed truth of creation *ex nihilio*, the divine ideas actually guard *against* the notion of necessity in creation (as Aquinas claims), and also prevent this doctrine from falling into extreme voluntarism? The latter position has been suggested by a number of writers (e.g. Roger Arnaldez) but requires further explanation.[1] It is commonly claimed that the doctrine of creation *ex nihilo* was developed out of the revealed experience of divine sovereignty and freedom—there is nothing over and against God restricting his creative intention. Creation, according to Jews, Christians, and Muslims, should be understood as a *free* intentional act, rather than according to a scheme of necessary emanation. Yet this leaves the question of how this divine freedom should best be imagined. Or to put it another way, if creation *ex nihilo* means that creation proceeds solely *ex Deo*, then is this from the "nothingness" of arbitrary divine choice, or rather does it proceed somehow from the plenitude of form which is the divine wisdom and essence (yet without necessity)? If Arnaldez thinks that the divine ideas prevent Christian understandings of creation *ex nihilo* from descending into voluntarism, others have taken the opposite view: that it is the notion of divine ideas

John Hughes
Jesus College, Cambridge CB5 8BL, UK
Email: j.hughes@jesus.cam.ac.uk

[1] Roger Arnaldez, "*Intellectualism et voluntarisme dans la pensée Musulmane*" in 1274, *année charnière: mutations et continuités* (Paris: Editions du centre nationale de la recherche scientifique, 1977), p. 125: "*La première conséquence de ce volontarisme, c'est la negation des Idées exemplaires en Dieu; . . . De la négation des Idées résulte la négation des natures et des lois naturelles.*"

as an infinite timeless warehouse of essences from which God "chooses" a world to create which leads to voluntarism. According to this view, the divine ideas are a Platonic world of ideal essences which detracts from the "existentialist" priority of the actual, which, it is claimed, is the great achievement of Aquinas and his Aristotelian revolution.[2] While I shall be mainly following Arnaldez in arguing that the divine ideas help to understand creation *ex nihilo* as neither necessary nor purely voluntarist in an arbitrary sense, we shall see that there are certain conceptions of the divine ideas that can suggest a priority of the possible and thus open the door to voluntarism.

Bulgakov's Reading of Aquinas on Creation

In this article I hope to explore these debates through the particular lens of Sergei Bulgakov's critique of Aquinas on creation *ex nihilo*. Bulgakov's own sophiological method is particularly concerned with this question of the relation between divine and creaturely being. In *The Bride of the Lamb*, written by 1939 as the third of his trilogy on Divine-Humanity, but only published posthumously in 1945, Bulgakov begins with a survey of classical, patristic, and medieval views on creation before offering his own "Sophianic" account. Christian views of creation need, he says, to avoid two alternative positions: "pantheistic or atheistic monism on the one hand and the dualistic conception of creation on the other."[3] Because the world is created *ex nihilo* "the world exists only in God and by God".[4] Sophia, or wisdom, thus names, for Bulgakov, both the existence of the world in God, the divine ideas or prototypes of all creatures eternally pre-existing in the mind of God (the "divine Sophia"), and the existence of God in the world, the potential divine life and form in all creatures ("creaturely Sophia"). According to Bulgakov's account of the history of "sophiology", the Christian tradition has not clearly formulated this question, but has remained under the unhelpful influence of pagan sophiologies which do not fully grasp the Trinitarian logic of creation.

---

[2] This seems to be the fear for Gilby (see Thomas Aquinas, *Summa Theologiae*, vol. 8, [London: Eyre and Spottiswoode, 1967], pp. xxv, 149) and also for David Burrell (*Freedom and Creation in Three Traditions* [Notre Dame, IN: University of Notre Dame Press, 1993], p. 63). R. J. Henle speaks of the "awkwardness" of the Divine Ideas in Aquinas's thought, *Saint Thomas and Platonism* (The Hague: Martinus Nijhoff, 1956), p. 360, while W. Norris Clarke, describes them as an aspect of Neo-Platonism which "stubbornly resists coherent assimilation" in Christian thought (*The Creative Retrieval of St Thomas Aquinas* [New York, NY: Fordham University Press, 2009], p. 88). These authors see the ideas as contrary to the Christian valuing of creation, history, and incarnation, and claim that Aquinas only incorporated this alien element into his metaphysics of act out of deference to St Augustine. Bergson, who, via Gilson, may be behind much of this tradition, spoke of "la maladie des archetypes" (cited in Vivian Boland, *Ideas in God according to Saint Thomas Aquinas: Sources and Synthesis* [Leiden: E. J. Brill, 1996], p. 327).

[3] Sergius Bulgakov, *The Bride of the Lamb* (trans.) Boris Jakim, (Edinburgh: T & T Clark, 2002), p. 3 (hereafter "BL"). For an introduction to Bulgakov's sophiology, see Bulgakov, *Sophia: The Wisdom of God* (Hudson, NY: Lindisfarne Press, 1993).

[4] BL, p. 7.

What is Bulgakov's specific critique of Aquinas's account of creation? He begins with the familiar charge of twentieth-century Orthodox theologians (and some Protestants) against Western scholastic theology, that it is contaminated by the excessive influence of Aristotle: "As his point of departure Thomas Aquinas takes not the Christian dogma of the personal, trihypostatic God, but Aristotle's impersonal divinity".[5] As evidence of this Bulgakov points to Aquinas's understanding of God as prime mover (*primus motor*) and efficient cause (*causa efficiens*) and particularly to Aquinas's position on the eternity of the world. Although Aquinas rejects this Aristotelian doctrine, he does so, according to Bulgakov, for purely *fideistic* reasons, admitting its theoretical possibility. For Bulgakov this is "a compromise between Moses and Aristotle, a compromise that is unconvincing for Aquinas himself as a theologian and philosopher, and that exposes in this question his hidden or unconquered Aristotelianism."[6] The relationship between God and the world in Aquinas is understood according to these Aristotelian categories of motion and causation, according to Bulgakov, and is therefore defined "statically, so to speak, not dynamically".[7] Although Bulgakov admits that a more Trinitarian account of creation *ex nihilo* exists in Aquinas he argues that this account is mixed with Aristotelian metaphysics in a way that does "not form an organic unity".[8] The influence of Aristotle is particularly evident for Bulgakov in Aquinas's account of the relationship between God's knowledge and will in creation, which brings us to the tension between necessity and freedom. "Aquinas uses both *intellectus* and *voluntas* without any reference to the personal God", claims Bulgakov.[9] For Aquinas, the knowledge of God is the cause of things (*scientia Dei est causa rerum*) *and* the will of God is the cause of things (*voluntas Dei est causa rerum*).[10] Although it is necessary that God knows things other than himself and God's knowledge is eternal, yet creation is not.[11] Aquinas therefore distinguishes two modes of God's knowledge: knowledge of that which will exist at any time ever (the knowledge of vision, *scientia visionis*) and knowledge of that which is possible but will never be (the knowledge of simple understanding, *scientia simplicis intelligentiae*). "This is a highly obscure and arbitrary distinction", says Bulgakov, "which admits in God an abstract, unreal thinking of bare possibilities, contrary to the fact that God's thoughts are also his deeds. This is pure anthropomorphism."[12] While Bulgakov recognises that the notion of will is an advance upon the Aristotelian view of God as impersonal thought thinking itself, he

---

[5] BL, p. 19.
[6] BL, pp. 20–21.
[7] BL, p. 21.
[8] BL, p. 22.
[9] BL, p. 22.
[10] Thomas Aquinas, *Summa Theologiae* (hereafter ST), 1a, qq. 14 and 19.
[11] ST 1a, q. 14, aa. 5 and 8.
[12] BL, p. 22.

claims that Aquinas's position, that "God's knowledge necessarily causes the existence of things while his will freely causes this existence", is inconsistent, an abstract account of the faculties of will and mind in God.[13]

Bulgakov sees the same problems even more acutely manifest in Aquinas's treatment of the divine ideas, where he says Platonism is "brought into the very heart of Christian philosophy".[14] "The doctrine of ideas is", he says, "*not* brought into a connection with the doctrine of the Holy Trinity, does not belong to the Trinitarian doctrine, but refers, so to speak, to the pre-trinitarian or extra-trinitarian (more Aristotelian than Christian) doctrine of God as mind, *noesis.*"[15] For Aquinas, forms or ideas of things exist in the mind of God. God does not simply create by chance, or will alone, but according to his intellect, intentionally, like an artisan, so these divine ideas are the exemplary causes in the mind of God of all things. God knows other things through his own essence, which is the likeness of all things. Although the divine mind is absolutely simple and without composition, nevertheless the divine ideas are plural for Aquinas, following Augustine, because they are the various ways in which diverse creatures participate in the divine nature.[16] But here again the same tension arises for Bulgakov as before, in that Aquinas distinguishes the ideas according to those which are realised and are therefore exemplars, by which God creates in the manner of an artisan, and those which are mere possibilities (*rationes*) never to be realised and therefore known speculatively (*per modum sepeculationis*)[17] "What a strange, contradictory, and unreal notion of abstract 'speculation' in God", exclaims Bulgakov.[18] Bulgakov sees in Aquinas's account of creation a conflict between a "doctrine of the Divine Sophia and the creaturely Sophia in their identity and difference" and residual Platonism and Aristotelianism. He is particularly concerned by the inclusion of "thoughts of God that never become a reality", in opposition to Aquinas's own position that the divine knowledge is the cause of things (*scientia rerum est causa rerum*).[19] Bulgakov sees this as connected to another significant problem with Aquinas's doctrine of creation, that the world is not understood as "unique in its design and perfect" but "as imperfect, only one of many possible types of worlds".[20] This is opposed to healthy cosmology, anthropology, and Christology for Bulgakov, and "introduces an element of irrational accident and arbitrariness in the relation of the Creator to creation."[21] We are left with "a quantitative noncorrespondence of ideas and

---

[13] BL, p. 23.
[14] BL, p. 24.
[15] BL, p. 24.
[16] ST, 1a, q. 15.
[17] ST, 1a, q. 15, a. 3.
[18] BL, p. 25.
[19] BL, pp. 25–26.
[20] BL, p. 26.
[21] BL, p. 26.

things. . . . The domain of ideas is larger than the domain of things; divine Sophia does not coincide with creaturely Sophia."[22] But if the divine ideas were originally introduced as the exemplary prototypes of things, what would be the point of unrealised ones?, asks Bulgakov.

From all this we can sum up Bulgakov's critique of Aquinas on creation and the divine ideas, which, it is worth noting, is not directed against Aquinas alone, but is part of a larger account of the "unfinished" nature of sophiology in patristic as well as scholastic thought, in the East as well as the West. For Bulgakov, Aquinas's account of creation and the divine ideas is insufficiently Trinitarian and too much influenced by Platonic and Aristotelian philosophy. As a result it works with an overly anthropomorphic account of the faculties of divine intellect and will in creation, with intellect being identified with necessity, and will with arbitrariness. This distinction "brings into divinity the element of accident and arbitrariness", pure occasionalism.[23] The divine ideas likewise are pictured as the speculative surplus of possible worlds in the divine essence from which God arbitrarily selects some to be exemplars for the creation of this world, which as such is neither unique nor perfect. The ideas on this account are not understood "sophiologically", but merely extrinsically, instrumentally, in their relation both to God and the world. They are left "ontologically suspended in the air; . . . situated somewhere between God and the world."[24] But is this a fair reading of Aquinas?

Aquinas on Creation and the Divine Ideas

The claim that Aquinas's thought is too pagan and philosophical and insufficiently Christian is of course not a new one. First made by some of his more conservative contemporaries, anxious about his use of the "dangerously secular" new Aristotelianism, these charges have been repeated by many since, especially amongst Protestants and Catholics of a more Augustinian temperament. In the mid-twentieth century, when Bulgakov was writing, this view reached something of a crescendo, perhaps in reaction to the textbook approach to Aquinas taken by the Leonine Neo-Thomists and anti-modernists who used him as the basis for an independent "natural theology" and rationalist apologetics. This criticism of Aquinas often focused on the structure of the *Summa* and the placing of the discussion *de Deo uno*, built upon the supposedly universal purely rational foundations of the *quinqae viae*, before coming to the revealed doctrine of God as Trinity only in question 27. It is frequently claimed that this move unwittingly establishes a Deist account of God at the foundation of Aquinas's thought. Not only Barth, Moltmann, Pannenberg, and Gunton, amongst Protestants, and Lossky

---

[22] BL, p. 26.
[23] BL, p. 31.
[24] BL, p. 33.

amongst the Orthodox, take this view, but perhaps more surprisingly Rahner and von Balthasar express similar misgivings.[25] Another critique of Aquinas's indebtedness to Aristotle, which may also have influenced Bulgakov, is made from a rather different philosophical position by Heidegger, who famously attacked the account of God as *causa sui*.[26] But if these readings of Aquinas have been widespread, they have not been universal. Indeed, the defence of Aquinas has been vigorously made by many Thomists, particularly in the French tradition of Maritain, Gilson, and Chenu, which has often laid more stress on Aquinas as theologian rather than simply a philosopher. As various authors have pointed out more recently, the structure of the *Summa* need not be construed as giving priority to natural theology before revelation; rather the initial account of the Divine Unity can be understood instead in terms of the unfolding of salvation history and Israel's confession of faith in one God which preceded the revelation of God's triune nature.[27] While the five ways certainly all have classical precursors, they are set by Aquinas firmly in the context of the revelation of the divine name "I AM THAT I AM" to Moses and the Scriptural claim that "the invisible things of him from the creation of the world are clearly seen" (Romans 1:20), indicating that there is no bracketing of revelation here, but rather Aquinas's thought is inseparable from revelation from the beginning. More importantly for the questions raised by Bulgakov, it is not clear that the adoption of non-Scriptural categories from pagan antiquity such as "motion" and "causation" necessarily involves the wholesale importation of their original metaphysical contexts. Indeed it seems ironic that Bulgakov should object to such adoption of non-Christian language when he himself faced similar accusations from other Orthodox theologians in relation to his use of German idealism in his sophiology. It is equally plausible to maintain that Aquinas freely moulds and develops Platonic and Aristotelian categories to do new and different tasks within his own Christian metaphysics. In particular it seems unfair of Bulgakov to accuse Aquinas of a purely impersonal and mechanical account of creation, when Aquinas goes to such considerable lengths to distinguish free, intentional creation from necessary emanation. Aquinas insists that God acts by will not by natural necessity (*Deum agere per voluntatem, non per necessitatem naturae*[28]), and puts as much stress on the more personal and intentional

---

[25] See Fergus Kerr, *After Aquinas: Versions of Thomism* (Oxford: Blackwell, 2002), pp. 181–183.

[26] Kerr, pp. 85–88.

[27] Kerr, pp. 183–184, Josef Pieper, *Guide to Thomas Aquinas* (trans.) Richard and Clara Winston, (New York, NY: Pantheon Books, 1962), p. 93, and A. N. Williams, "Mystical Theology Redux: The Pattern of Aquinas's *Summa Theologiae*" in *Modern Theology*, Vol. 13 no. 1 (January 1997), pp. 53–74. Cf. also Robert Jenson, cited in Kerr, p. 205: The five ways "occur within a specifically biblical apprehension already in place" because "the entire body of Thomas Aquinas's *Summa Theologiae*, encompassing alike the propositions supposed to be available by nature to all humans and those attributed to historically specific revelation alone, is shaped by a narrative of creational-incarnational procession from and return to God".

[28] ST, 1a, q. 19, a. 4, rep.

modes of causation (exemplary and final) as upon what we might think of as more naturalistic modes such as efficient causation and motion (indeed some see an ascent within the ordering of the five ways from lower models of creation towards higher more personal ones).[29] Likewise the charge that Aquinas reduces God to the first in a series, on the same ontological plane as his creation, seems to ignore the point noted by so many commentators, that Aquinas goes to great lengths precisely to stress the absolute uniqueness and therefore relative incomprehensibility of creation, the distinction between God who has being and all other things which receive their being from him, and the at most analogical rather than univocal nature of the five ways. For example, Aquinas stresses that although our spatio-temporal minds cannot help but picture it in these terms, creation cannot actually be a change or motion for there is nothing that precedes it to be acted upon ("creation is not a change", *creatio non est mutatio*[30]). It is hard not to suspect therefore that Bulgakov's allergy to images of causation and motion for creation says more about his own (post-Kantian) position, and perhaps the distortions of Aquinas presented by textbook apologetics, than about Aquinas himself. As Fergus Kerr puts it: "Thomas's God is not the perfect being of Greek metaphysics, the supreme entity at the top of a hierarchy of atomistically conceived substances. . . . Whatever else is to be said, Thomas is plainly out to save God from being turned into one more entity."[31]

If it is unfair to accuse Aquinas of a purely philosophical, Aristotelian, mechanistic, and impersonal account of creation, is he nevertheless guilty of being insufficiently Trinitarian? Would Bulgakov's critique be more plausible if we restricted the claim to saying that Aquinas's account of creation is generically monotheistic and not truly Trinitarian and Christian? In particular is it more dominated by the anthropomorphic faculties of divine intellect and will rather than shaped by the Trinitarian life? While this might seem an initially plausible accusation, it does not obviously stand up so well to closer inspection. For in fact the treatment of divine knowledge and will (qq. 14, 15, and 19), although it precedes the articles on the Trinity, is very obviously neither Aristotelian (Aristotle's deity does not have any will to speak of), nor anthropomorphic in some univocal way. Rather these questions are already oriented towards the discussion of the Trinity, in that divine intellection and will are, following St Augustine, identified with the internal processions of the Son and the Spirit respectively.[32] When Aquinas says that God's intellect and will are the cause of things he is making precisely the Trinitarian claim that the Father creates through the Son and the Spirit:

---

[29] See Robert Slesinski's interesting unpublished essay "Bulgakov's Sophiological Conception of Creation", which helps to explain Bulgakov's hostility to the "mechanistic" language of motion and causation.

[30] ST, 1a, q. 45, a. 2, ad 2.

[31] Kerr, pp. 200, 204.

[32] ST, 1a, q. 27, aa. 1–5, q. 45, a. 7.

Deus est causa rerum per suum intellectum et voluntatem, sicut artifex rerum artificiatarum. Artifex autem per verbum in intellectu conceptum et per amorem suae voluntatis ad aliquid relatum operatur. Unde et Deus Pater operatus est creaturam per suum Verbum, quod est Filius, et per suum Amorem, qui est Spiritus Sanctus.[33]

Bizarrely Bulgakov quotes these very articles before concluding "the creator of the world is, strictly speaking, the impersonal Aristotelian divinity".[34] The implication seems to be that Bulgakov believes the Trinitarian processions are being subordinated to an abstract prior account of divine will and intellect, whereas it is surely more plausible that the opposite is the case, that intellect and will are being understood in a Trinitarian fashion. Creation, according to Aquinas, is absolutely rooted in the Trinitarian inner life of God: "The comings forth of the divine Persons are causes of creation", *processiones divinarum Personarum sunt causa creationis.*[35]

Yet, if Aquinas's account of creation can be said to be not only personal but also Trinitarian, nevertheless Bulgakov's charge that intellect is identified with (eternal) necessity in God's own life and will with (external) freedom in creation is harder to dismiss and potentially troubling. Will in God is not understood quite as anthropomorphically as Bulgakov suggests, as pure arbitrariness. God's will is free in the sense of not being determined by any external cause (*nullo modo voluntas Dei causam habet*[36]) and in being intellectual and intentional rather than a matter of natural necessity, like the appetite of a plant or animal (*Deum agere per voluntatem, non per necessitatem naturae*[37]). But this does not mean that it is therefore empty and contentless, like many more modern notions of the will. For God's will is not, according to Aquinas, a "seeking what is not possessed" but a "delighting in what is".[38] As will is, for Aquinas, a tending towards a good, so God's will is the possession of his own goodness, which is his nature (*objectum divinae voluntatis est bonitas sua, quae est essentia; unde cum voluntas Dei sit eius essentia*[39]). Aquinas can compare God's will to the sun (following Dionysius[40]) and even speak of it as having a certain necessity in itself, in common with the divine knowledge: *sicut*

---

[33] ST, 1a, q. 45, a. 6, rep.: "God is the cause of things through his mind and will, like an artist of works of art. An Artist works through an idea conceived in his mind and through love in his will bent on something. In like manner God the Father wrought the creature through his Word, the Son, and through his Love, the Holy Ghost."

[34] BL, p. 27.

[35] ST, 1a, q. 45, a. 6, ad 1.

[36] ST, 1a, q. 19, a. 5, rep.: "God's willing is not in any way caused".

[37] ST, 1a, q. 19, a. 4, rep.: "he works through will, and not . . . through necessity of his nature".

[38] ST, 1a, q. 19, a. 1, ad 2.

[39] ST, 1a, q. 19, a. 1, ad 3.: "The objective of God's will, however, is his own goodness, and this is his nature".

[40] ST, 1a, q. 19, a. 4, ad 1.

divinum esse in se est necessarium, ita et divinum velle et divinum scire.[41] But then he goes on to make significant qualifications to this claim: God's being, unlike that of creation, is "not of a determinate kind, but contains in itself the whole perfection of being" (*esse divinum non sit determinatum, sed contineat in se totam perfectionem essendi*[42]), so it seems as if whether any *particular* idea is realised or not in reality is determined by God's will, which is not necessary (*quia forma ut est in intellectu tamen non determinatur ad hoc quod sit vel non sit in effectu, nisi per voluntatem*[43]). Thus, according to Aquinas, God wills his own goodness absolutely necessarily, just as our will is necessarily ordered towards our own happiness (*bonitatem suam Deus ex necessitate vult, sicut et voluntas nostra ex necessitate vult beatitudinem*[44]), but everything other than himself that he wills through his happiness he does not will absolutely. This is because God could will his happiness though different means, just as, Aquinas says, we could choose to take a journey by horse or on foot. Although God wills creation for his goodness, he does not need creation and it adds nothing to his perfection so he does not will it *absolutely* necessarily (*alia a se eum velle non sit necessarium absolute*[45]). Creation does however have a *hypothetical* necessity, because what God wills he wills from eternity and cannot be unwilled (*quod velit, non potest non velle, quia non potest voluntas eius mutari*[46]). We might think that Bulgakov would be sympathetic with the subtle argument that Aquinas is developing here: that creation adds nothing to God, is not needed by him, and is therefore personal and free, against all pantheistic schemes of necessary emanation (the Latin Averroeists are presumably the immediate concern). Yet, despite all the careful qualifications, and the repeated insistences that will and intellect are ultimately one in God, there is undoubtedly an alignment here of intellect with internal necessity and will with external freedom and contingency, which remains troubling. This means that creation is at times conceived surprisingly anthropomorphically, not simply as free, but as an act of free *choice, liberum arbitrium.*[47]

Where does this leave the divine ideas? They seem to be in danger of being conceived anthropomorphically as an infinite set of possible worlds known by God, not really identical with the goodness of his nature, from which he arbitrarily chooses one to create. This is, as we saw earlier, the heart of Bulgakov's criticism of Aquinas's account of creation *ex nihilo*: "The domain

---

[41] ST, 1a, q. 19, a. 3, ad 6.: "As the divine existing is essentially necessary so also is the divine knowing and the divine willing".

[42] ST, 1a, q. 19, a. 4, rep.

[43] ST, 1a, q. 19, a. 4, ad 4.: "Whether an idea conceived in the mind is or is not realised in fact depends on the will".

[44] ST, 1a, q. 19, a. 3, rep.

[45] ST, 1a, q. 19, a. 3, rep.: "there is no absolute need for him to will [things other than himself]".

[46] ST, 1a, q. 19, a. 3, rep.: "on the supposition that he does will a thing it cannot be unwilled, since his will is immutable".

[47] ST, 1a, q. 19, a. 10.

of ideas is larger than the domain of things; divine Sophia does not coincide with creaturely Sophia."[48] The evidence for this claim can be seen in questions 14 and 15 of the *prima pars*, but their interpretation is not straightforward.[49] Aquinas follows Augustine and others in saying that "God's knowledge is the cause of things", for "God's knowledge stands to all created things as the artist's to his products" (*scientia Dei est causa rerum. Sic enim scientia Dei se habet ad omnes res creates, sicut scientia artificis se habet ad artificiata*[50]). Then, perhaps fearing that this could imply that creation follows necessarily from God's necessary knowledge, he adds that "an intelligible form does not indicate a principle of activity merely as it is in the knower, unless it is accompanied by an inclination towards producing an effect; this is supplied by the will". Therefore God's knowledge is the cause of things "when it is conjoined with his will" (*secundum quod habet voluntatem conjunctam*) and this is termed "knowledge of approbation", *scientia approbationis*.[51] This invocation of will is surely correct, yet need not in itself imply a choosing between things, unless the relationship between intellect, will and goodness is conceived extrinsically. Such a notion does however appear in the following article where Aquinas asks if God has knowledge of non-existent things. This question leads him to distinguish between God's knowledge of things that are or ever have been or will be existent and his knowledge of those things that will never exist, following on St Paul's expression in the letter to the Romans: "Who calls the things that are not, as the things that are" (Romans 4:17). Those things which will exist at any time are known by God's knowledge of vision, *scientia visionis*, while those things which never are, except potentially in the mind of God, are known by his knowledge of simple understanding, *scientia simplicis intelligentiae*.[52] Of these things that only ever exist potentially, God has a purely speculative knowledge as he does of his own nature; while all things that actually exist are known by God through practical as well as speculative knowledge.[53] This is the crucial distinction and the will is brought in to justify the difference between the two: "it is not necessary that all that God knows should exist at some time, past, present or future, but only such things as he wills to exist or

---

[48] BL, p. 26.

[49] See also *De Veritate* 1:3; *Scriptum in IV Libros Sententiarum*, 1, 36, 2, 1; *De Spiritualibus Creaturis* 10, ad 8; *Lectura super Ioannem*, 2:77. The best overviews of this are Vivian Boland, *Ideas in God according to Saint Thomas Aquinas: Sources and Synthesis* (Leiden: E. J. Brill, 1996); John F. Wippel, *Thomas Aquinas on the Divine Ideas* (Wetteren: Universa, 1993), and Gregory T. Doolan, *Aquinas on the Divine Ideas as Exemplar Causes* (Washington, DC: The Catholic University of America Press, 2008). See also: Étienne Gilson, *The Philosophy of St Thomas Aquinas* (trans.) E. Bullough, (Cambridge: Heffer and Sons, 1924), pp. 111 ff.; Rudi te Velde, *Participation and Substantiality in Thomas Aquinas* (Leiden: E. J. Brill, 1995), pp. 102–116.

[50] ST, 1a, q. 14, a. 8, rep.

[51] ST, 1a, q. 14, a. 8, rep.

[52] ST, 1a, q. 14, a. 9, rep.

[53] ST, 1a, q. 14, a. 16.

permits to exist".[54] When Aquinas comes to say more of the divine ideas, he preserves this same distinction. Ideas are forms existing apart from the things themselves and can serve two purposes: "either to be the exemplar or pattern of the things whose form it is said to be", corresponding to practical knowledge, or "the principle of knowing that thing", corresponding to speculative knowledge.[55] It seems as if there are two sorts of divine ideas: those that are realised and those that are not. The ideas used by practical knowledge are exemplars, while the ideas that are never realised and known only speculatively are purely principles, *rationes*.[56] Such an account does indeed seem to have the elements of anthropomorphism and arbitrariness of which Bulgakov accuses it. For *why* does God choose to realise these ideas and not others, to make this world and not different ones? This does appear to represent an opening for both later voluntarism and possibilism. And is not a wedge driven here between the necessary intellect and the arbitrary will in God, which by extension means also between the Son and the Spirit? But this is only because freedom and necessity are being understood all too humanly. Bulgakov's alternative account is surely more convincing here when he says that in God "all is equally necessary and equally free" and that "against the idea of different and manifold *possibilities* in God, actualised and unactualised, we must oppose the idea of the *uniqueness* of the ways of God, a uniqueness that excludes all other unactualised possibilities".[57] In fairness we should note that there are moments when Aquinas seems to lean more in this direction. He does, for example, insist that "God's knowledge has the same extension as his causality" (*intantum se extendit scientia Dei inquantum se extendit eius causalitas*[58]), and his entire account of the divine ideas emphasises their intentional dynamic creative exemplarity, after Dionysius's *paradeigmata*, as against purely cognitive views of the ideas.[59] Similarly, Aquinas often speaks of the divine ideas more in terms of a single perfect plan, identical with God's own wisdom or essence, and not simply an unconnected collection of thoughts: *Idea in Deo nihil aliud est quam eius essentia*.[60] Likewise, as more recent anti-Platonist commentators are keen to point out, Aquinas frequently insists that the ideas are not a separate realm of forms existing "between God and the world", nor even really distinct relations in God, but only the diverse ways that God knows his own nature as imitable by creatures, and that therefore the ideas are extended, beyond the Neo-Platonists

---

[54] ST, 1a, q. 14, a. 9, ad 3.

[55] ST, 1a, q. 15, a. 1, rep.

[56] ST, 1a, q. 15, a. 3, rep.

[57] BL, p. 31.

[58] ST, 1a, q. 14, a. 11, rep.

[59] Wippel, pp. 37–38. See also Boland, ch. 3, where he stresses how Dionysius fuses the Platonist tradition of the ideas with more explicitly Biblical, intentional notions such as "predestinations".

[60] ST, 1a, q. 15, a. 1, ad 3.: "an Idea in God is simply the divine essence".

and Avicenna, to individuals and matter.[61] In this respect, David Burrell is surely correct when he wishes that Aquinas had taken the analogy of the artisan to its radical conclusion and rejected the residual Aristotelian priority of speculative over practical reason. For an artist does not "choose" from a set of options whether to create this work of art or that one, "like a jury in an architectural contest", as Burrell puts it.[62] Rather those other possibilities which were never realised have at most a shadowy, virtual existence, merely "penumbral" to this practical knowledge which creates.[63] It is not that the ideas are the problem which must be abandoned, but rather that they must be understood in this more integral, intentional, practical way, or, as Bulgakov puts it, in a more Trinitarian and Sophiological way. And at times this is exactly what Aquinas seems to say, restricting the divine ideas in their truest sense to those which are exemplars, and describing the *rationes* of those things which never exists as merely virtual.[64] All these elements of Aquinas's account of the divine ideas certainly seem to reduce their instrumental and accidental character, of which Bulgakov is so afraid, but they do not altogether do away with the problems we have noted.

These problems, concerning the existence of a surplus of unrealised divine ideas, from which God arbitrarily chooses some to actualise, do in the end seem to leave a certain ambivalence towards the very goodness of creation, despite all Aquinas's supposed affirmation of the world. As Bulgakov claimed, the world is not understood as "unique in its design and perfect" but "as imperfect, only one of many possible types of worlds".[65] This can be seen in Aquinas's discussion of divine power. Here, having repeated that "God can do what he does not do" (*Deus potest facere quod non facit*[66]) and "can make things differently from how he has made them" (*Deus potest alia facere quam quae facit*[67]), he makes the strange and speculative claim "God can make a better thing than anything he has made" (*qualibet re a se facta potest Deus facere aliam meliorem*).[68] Aquinas goes on to qualify this: God could not improve *this* universe without upsetting its harmony, but he could "make other things, or add them to those he has made, and there would be another

---

[61] ST, 1a, q. 15, a. 2, rep.; cf. Henle, p. 361.

[62] Burrell, p. 111.

[63] Burrell, p. 110.

[64] Wippel notes how Aquinas's position on this seems to shift slightly from the commentary on the Sentences, where he is unclear as to whether purely possible things have ideas of their own, through the *De Veritate*, where they are known actually as *rationes* by *scientia simplicis intelligentiae*, but only virtually as exemplars, to the *Summa Theologiae*, where they are not known as exemplars at all, but only as *rationes* (pp.36–37, 46–48). See also Doolan, pp.22–3 and *passim* on this gradual restriction of the term exemplar, under the influence of Dionysius, to things which are actually made.

[65] BL, p. 26.

[66] ST, 1a, q. 25, a. 5, sed contra.

[67] ST, 1a, q. 25, a. 5, rep.

[68] ST, 1a, q. 25, a. 6, rep.

and better universe" (*et esset aliud universum melius*).[69] The reasoning behind this position is, exactly as Bulgakov claimed, because the divine Sophia does not coincide with the creaturely Sophia: God's power is limited by his wisdom (*divina sapientia totum posse potentiae comprehendit*[70]), but this is not exhausted by the current course of events. Therefore "divine wisdom is not limited to one fixed system in such a manner that no other course of things could flow from it".[71] If, as Aquinas says, it is the divine will which chooses which aspects of divine wisdom are to be realised, then this will seems only accidentally or instrumentally related to divine wisdom, not intrinsically.

It is worth returning to the role that the divine ideas are meant to perform in Aquinas's account of creation *ex nihilo*. According to the *De Veritate*, the divine ideas are essential to a correct view of creation.[72] For the ideas simultaneously rule out the view that everything is simply a matter of chance, as Aquinas claims the Epicureans believed, *and* the view that everything is simply determined by natural necessity, as he believed Empedocles and others to have thought. Plato is thus praised by Aquinas for avoiding these two options, while he also accepts Aristotle's criticisms of an independent realm of substantial forms by embracing the Augustinian position that the ideas exist in the mind of God. But Aquinas is even more explicit about the connection of the divine ideas with a Trinitarian view of creation: he cites Augustine's claim "whoever denies the existence of the ideas is an infidel because he denies the existence of the Son" (*qui negat ideas esse, infidelis est, quia negat filium esse*[73]) and also insists that a knowledge of the Trinity is needed in order to have a right view of the creation of all things.[74] Because we know that God made everything by his Word and his Love we avoid thinking of creation as necessary (*excluditur error ponentium Deum produxisse res ex necessitate naturae*) and that he made creatures from his own goodness, not because of any need or compulsion (*neque propter aliam causam extrinsecam, sed propter amorem suae bonitatis*).[75] For Aquinas, the divine ideas are clearly not some hangover from Platonic demiurgic or emanationist schemes of creation, but rather, understood according to the logic of the Trinity, are crucial to understanding creation as truly free and personal rather than proceeding from natural necessity, but also as in accordance with the intrinsic order of divine goodness and wisdom rather than simply formless, random,

---

[69] ST, 1a, q. 25, a. 6, ad 3.

[70] ST, 1a, q. 25, a. 5, rep.: "divine wisdom covers the whole range of power".

[71] ST, 1a, q. 25, a. 5, rep.

[72] *De Veritate*, q.3, a. 1

[73] *De Veritate*, q. 3, a. 1.

[74] In the light of this claim by Aquinas, it is difficult to agree with those whose anti-Platonism makes them determined to see the divine ideas as unimportant and out of place in Aquinas's thinking, or with those who see his account of creation as deistic and non-Trinitarian.

[75] ST, 1a, q. 32, a. 1, ad 3: we avoid the error of those who held that God's nature compelled him to create things' [he created] "not because he needed them nor because of any reason outside himself, but from love of his own goodness".

and arbitrary. And yet it seems that in one particular respect, as we have seen, there is an instability in this account which can introduce an element of arbitrary will into the picture.

In conclusion, I have argued that some of Bulgakov's criticisms of Aquinas on creation reflect the widespread prejudices of his time against Leonine Thomism and do not stand up to closer attention. It is not the case that Aquinas's account of creation is impersonal, mechanistic, or non-Trinitarian. Bulgakov's sophiological concerns do however draw attention to the way that the divine ideas were crucial in Christian understandings of creation *ex nihilo*. It seems that the image of the artisan and the divine ideas, understood according to a Trinitarian logic, enabled Christian theologians to articulate creation *ex nihilo* in terms that avoided both necessary emanation and arbitrary choice. God creates not without any reason or order, according to the arbitrariness of pure will, nor according to some external plan constraining his freedom, but according to the divine ideas which are his own self-knowledge, his intellection of himself and the ways in which creatures can participate in his being. He creates not simply by thinking these thoughts, in some passive or speculative necessary manner, but simultaneously by actively willing them as goods, or as participations in his own goodness. This creation by the ideas, in and through God's thought and will, enabling creatures to share in his own truth and goodness, is a form of practical reason, comparable to the way an artist brings his ideas to fruition. But the inevitable limitations of this analogy when applied to the unique case of the act of creation by the entirely simple, perfect, and eternal One leave a number of potential dangers of anthropomorphism. Principal amongst these is how we should understand the uniqueness of this creation in relation to divine knowledge and will. Is it really appropriate to imagine a surplus of unrealised divine ideas from which God chooses, apparently without reason, to make this particular creation? Here Aquinas's mode of expression, perhaps intended to avoid the necessitarianism of the Averroeists, may well have unwittingly opened a door to later more extreme forms of voluntarism and possibilism, against which he is normally presented as an heroic champion of the priority of actual existence.[76]

---

[76] These tensions can be seen in the debate generated by James Ross's article "Aquinas's Exemplarism; Aquinas's Voluntarism" in *American Catholic Philosophical Quarterly*, Vol. LXIV no. 2 (1990), pp. 171–198, followed by the replies of Armand Maurer, Lawrence Dewan, and Ross in *American Catholic Philosophical Quarterly*, Vol. LXV no. 2 (1991), pp. 213–243. Ross argues that Aquinas's Aristotelian metaphysics meant that he effectively rejected any residual "photo-exemplarism" despite paying lip-service to Augustine's account of the divine ideas. This determination to resist any account of possibilism, of really distinct ideas of things before they exist (like a "row of tin soldiers"), which Ross shares with Maurer and the Gilson tradition, leads him to assert a voluntaristic view of creation which they generally do not share. Dewan on the other hand seeks to defend the surface meaning of Aquinas's position on the divine ideas (particularly their inclusion, even if only virtually, of things which will never actually exist, especially in the *De Veritate*), although at times this leads him in the direction of the sort of possibilism about which Ross and in a different way Bulgakov are not unreasonably concerned.

Modern Theology 29:2 April 2013
ISSN 0266-7177 (Print)
ISSN 1468-0025 (Online)

CREATION *EX NIHILO* AS MIXED METAPHOR

KATHRYN TANNER

This article makes the following three programmatic points.[1] First, an under-standing of divine transcendence, prominent in Christian theology's apo-phatic strain, developed in tandem, both historically and logically, with ideas about creation that eventuated in a creation *ex nihilo* viewpoint. Such an account of divine transcendence, second, fosters an account of creation (and a general understanding of the God/world relationship) that typically mixes both natural and personalistic images and categories. The loss of such an account of transcendence since the early modern period, I suggest thirdly and in conclusion, is therefore responsible in great part for the dualistic, mutually exclusive alternation between a deistic, interventionist God and pan(en)theism so common in modern Christian thought.

Divine Transcendence

Divine transcendence is not a doctrinal affirmation in any ordinary sense but a grammatical remark about theological language: it signals a general lin-guistic disturbance, the failure of all predicative attribution, in language about God. Following one common way of making this point, one could say that God is not a kind of thing: God is beyond every genus. For that reason, talk about God systematically violates the usual canons of sense making.

At the most basic level, God's transcendence means that God is not one instance among others of a general sort of thing, distinguished from (and

---

Kathryn Tanner
Yale Divinity School, Yale University, 409 Prospect Street, New Haven, CT 06511, USA
Email: kathryn.tanner@yale.edu
    [1] For a more thorough, technical explication of my first point, along with some of the methodological background in support of the second, see Kathryn Tanner, *God and Creation in Christian Theology* (Oxford: Basil Blackwell, 1989) chapters one and two.

ranked hierarchically with respect to) those others by the supreme degree to which it exhibits the designated quality. In other words, divinity is not a class term; and therefore things within the world cannot be differentiated and ordered by the degree to which they exhibit such a (non-)predicate.

Affirmations about God, as a result, do not imply corresponding denials. Talk about God violates the Spinozistic dictum, maintained in ordinary language about things, that all determination is negation; and vice versa. In other words, language about God contravenes the way in ordinary speech that the affirmation of certain qualities implies the denial of others, and the denial of certain properties implies the affirmation of others. For example, when one denies that God is a body it does not follow that God is spiritual (or whatever is ordinarily incompatible with materiality). And the reverse holds as well: when one affirms that God is immaterial one is not denying that God has bodily existence. Similarly, when one denies that God can be rendered by images, one is not implying that God is an abstractly definable concept; and the reverse. In sum, God transcends the application of all ordinarily contrastive terms.

Since God is in this way incapable of absorption into a general category, God has a non-predicative identity. God is identified, in other words, by this very failure to mean. God becomes the paradigmatic inassimilable Other, the (paradoxically non-predicatively grounded) paradigm for all that remains indigestible to sense-making practices that insist on the exhaustive, homogenizing subsumption of particulars under general concepts. God becomes the model for resistance to the Same, which all those who resist the status quo might follow, I believe, in a solidarity that involves none of the usual group identifications by way of mutually exclusive categories.

What it means to say that God is transcendent cannot, as a result, be captured semantically in the particular statements that affirm it—such statements as, "God is beyond identity and difference." Such statements do not, in other words, effectively convey a meaning for the term "transcendence." That "meaning" is instead merely displayed or shown in the non-semantic surplus of theological language itself, in the failure to mean that haunts all theological claims, in the unclosable gap between the recognition *that* theological claims signify and the inability to specify *what* it is, conceptually, that they convey.

This account of transcendence has the following implications for theological method. The first is that no set of concepts or images is proper to theology. A theology that abides by these apophatic commitments makes do with whatever categories are at hand, twisting and violating them according to its own fundamentally non-semantic purposes. Theological discourse is therefore always a hybrid discourse, in two senses. First, theology is always haunted by the resonances of the categories and images proper to other fields of discourse, resonances that it draws upon and disturbs in the process of its own discursive self-constitution. It always contains what it is working discursively to set itself against; borrowed language always carries the undertones appropriate to that language's more usual field of application, no matter how perverse its new theological employment. Theological discourse is therefore never simply itself—never simply religious in sharp distinction from the secular, or Christian in simple opposition to what is pagan or Jewish. It arises as an internal modification of that over against which it comes to define itself. Second, this sort of theology makes do with almost anything to hand, in an apparently indiscriminately profligate raiding of multiple fields of discourse. It borrows from all sides to produce a seemingly anarchic bricolage, fundamentally "disciplined" by only a thoroughgoing refusal of sense, by the systematic repudiation of all ordinary canons of sense making.

Theology of this apophatic sort does not, moreover, respect the proper boundaries of the particular concepts or images it deploys. This is an important subsidiary form of linguistic disturbance beyond the basic forms mentioned earlier: basic canons of sense-making are violated, but so too are particular linguistic habits about what follows from what, habits based on established boundaries of the meanings of particular terms. This sort of semantic violation—of particular categories and images—means, first of all, that mutually-exclusive categories (for example, categories of both intentional agency and natural causation) can be used to the same end. The divisions among those disciplines or fields of discourse in which these categories or images have their proper employ (for example, ethics and natural science, respectively) are consequently blurred. Secondly, the "same" categories, conversely, are susceptible to widely disparate uses. Links of presupposition and implications among statements that follow a category's ordinary sense are often disrupted in different ways, by different theologians or by the same theologian, depending on the purpose to be served. Moreover, any new links of presupposition and implication formed by such theological disruption are highly fragile and far more susceptible to breakage than is the case, for example, with the more firmly established habits of everyday speech that theologians are often re-working. This fragility holds for discursive links in the broad sense of both language and action. For example, while creation *ex nihilo* may be linked to what Catherine Keller calls *tehomophobia*, fear of the deep with all its gendered resonances, as a kind of practical orientation toward the world, it need not. There are no necessary—and in that sense proper—consequences of theological claims. Theological claims can easily be made to do an uncommonly wide variety of things.

Divine Transcendence and Creation Ex Nihilo

This sort of account of divine transcendence arises in tandem with an account of creation *ex nihilo* by way of an internal modification of a widely-held Greco-Roman problematic or dilemma surrounding the question of how a God different from the world can be intimately involved with it (or, perhaps better stated, directly responsible for it and for the qualities it displays). The dilemma is this: God is either like some of the things one finds in the world and then there is no problem saying that God is intimately involved with the world. God is intimately involved with just those things that are most like it. Or, God is radically different from the world—not like anything in it—but then God cannot have anything very directly to do with it.

The principle behind the dilemma would seem to be "like is involved with like." Supporting such a principle is the commonsensical idea that, were unlike things to be intimately involved with one another, their natures would be compromised. Some things, one could say, are essentially defined by not being like other things and were these different kinds of things to be too intimately associated with one another they would corrupt one another's natures. The boundaries that essentially define a kind of thing have to be guarded against those things that it is defined as not being.

Christians would resist either pole of the dilemma (and therefore the principle upon which it rests) to the extent they want to hold that nothing in the world is like God (a version of monotheism), and yet affirm that God is intimately involved with the world as its creator and redeemer. Certain distinctively Christian preoccupations with Jesus would, moreover, make such resistance imperative. There is a growing desire, in at least some Christian quarters in the first few centuries CE, to affirm a peculiarly heightened intimacy between God and Jesus which nevertheless does not compromise the difference between God and humanity: God in the highest (and not merely some lesser, mediating deity) is to be identified with Jesus, who is a human being like any other in respect of his humanity (and therefore not some superman, some quasi-divine human, mediating between divinity and ordinary humans).

A way out of the dilemma is found when accounts of both God's transcendence and God's involvement in the world as creator are radicalized. The result is a consistently apophatic view of divine transcendence and a doctrine of creation *ex nihilo*.

This Christian position is produced as an internal modification of the Greco-Roman problematic, and therefore that problematic has to be explored with some thoroughness. Consider the first horn of the dilemma, where God is like the world and directly involved in it. One finds a supposition of that sort in popular Greco-Roman polytheism. Greek and Roman gods and goddesses are very much like human beings, the chief differences being their immortality and superhuman powers. Humans can indeed become gods after death: emperors are deified; heroes are too. The flip side of this similarity to humans is that gods are quite integral to the normal run of human events. The gods are the source of those things that regularly and normally occur in human life. They have very particular domains corresponding to their characters. For instance, the belligerent Ares is the God of war. As a whole they represent all the things that commonly befall a person and that he or she must take into account and adjust to if things are to go well, and all those things that one can go against only at one's peril.

In the rational theologies that follow Greco-Roman criticism of this popular polytheism—for example, the rational theologies of Plato and his followers, Stoicism, Aristotle and his followers—one finds a similar dynamic in more sophisticated form. Divinity is generally still a class name, a sortal term, specifying those principles within the world responsible for order, pattern, and regularity. The characteristics of divinity, how divinity is defined, follow from those functions: what is divine is eternal, stable, unchanging, simple, and rational. Any number of things can therefore be called divine: (a) The cosmos as a whole can be called divine insofar as it is thought to be eternal and harmonized by proportion among its parts. (b) Heavenly bodies can be called divine in that they are thought to be eternal (because immaterial) and in that they move in regular circular motions. (c) Principles of mathematics—number, geometrical figures, proportions—can be considered divine in that they seem to be ordering principles par excellence, to be eternal truths and to capture a kind of ideal perfection never instantiated in fact. (d) Forms or ideas in a Platonic or Aristotelian sense of that can also be called divine insofar as they provide intelligibility, enable one to generalize about the nature of things, and appear to have a stability, permanence and ideal quality not found in the multiple, changing and impermanent things to which they give shape. (e) Finally, soul can be considered divine as a self-propelling source of motion that is assumed to be regular in accord with intelligible ideas. All these instances of divinity can be ranked by degrees; some are more divine than others. Soul, for example, usually has a lower rank than forms or ideas since as a principle of movement it is part of the world of time and change and may work only in tandem with, and therefore is inextricably bound up with, changeable, impermanent material bodies.

If divinity is one principle among others that are necessary to explain the way the world is, then there is obviously no problem in saying that divinity is intimately involved with the workings of the world. Divinity is simply one of the world's essential factors or components. Divinity is primarily responsible for a particular aspect of the world as we know it: its ordered, regular aspects, just those aspects of the world that are most like divinity.

But often no sharp distinction is drawn between non-divine and divine aspects of the world in order to make the integration of diverse principles within the world seem plausible. In Stoicism for instance, the divine world soul is itself material along with the world it pervades and arranges—soul is just a more ethereal or fiery form of matter. That similarity of nature seems to be why the two—soul and body—can be so well integrated. In Plato, too, material things, despite their impermanence and mutability, can share or participate in the eternal forms. The form of Life can therefore have something directly to do with living things because changing and impermanent embodied things can be like the form Life; they can share in its qualities.

The second horn of the dilemma is found where more dualistic accounts of divinity are offered in Greco-Roman thought, accounts in which divinity is opposed to everything in the world. Consider Plato's distinction between a world of being and becoming, between an intelligible world and a material world. According to this more dualistic way of characterizing divinity, divinity does not seem to be a principle in the world but a principle quite distinct from *any* in it. The intelligible world is simply opposed to the world of time, change and motion, as a whole; the whole world—with all its components—is simply not divine. This more dualistic account of divinity comes out in Plato's more dualistic treatment of the forms in portions of the *Parmenides*, according to which things of this world do not participate in the divine forms but are merely pale imitations of them. As pale imitations of the forms, things of this world have a kind of internal sense but no intelligibility or order that is in any active way bestowed upon them by the forms. A more radically transcendent and less this-worldly notion of divinity is also suggested by Plato's account of the idea of the Good in the *Republic*, an idea that seems beyond all the forms as some sort of ineffable principle or source of their unity.

Aristotle's unmoved mover can also be interpreted as a similar propulsion of divinity outside the world of change and impermanence, although Aristotle unlike Plato would reject any claim of transcendent forms and therefore reject *that* Platonic way of making the point about divinity in opposition to the world of becoming. The unmoved mover of Aristotle seems to be setting the whole eternal cycle of motion in the heavens into motion from beyond it. The unmoved mover does not seem to be a principle in the world but outside it in some sort of sovereign indifference to the whole of what is going on there.

Some of these examples—Plato's dualistic rendering of the forms, Aristotle's unmoved mover—already suggest how the more transcendent God becomes in these Hellenistic world-pictures, the less God seems to have much to do very directly with the world as we know it. But that sort of implication is especially evident in many of the religious cosmologies of a mixed Platonic, Aristotelian and Stoic character in the second and third centuries CE—for example, in Middle Platonism. Here a high God, a supremely transcendent God, is set into the mix of fundamental principles or components of the cosmos (matter, forms, or ideas, active intelligence, and soul) as they figure in Plato's myth of world construction in the *Timaeus*. The new supreme, transcendent divine principle typically combines Aristotle's unmoved mover thinking itself with Plato's discussion of the idea of the Good in the *Republic* and some metaphysical suggestions about a supreme principle of unity in Plato's *Parmenides*. (Plato himself does not make the latter connection in the *Timaeus*, though there is some mysterious reference to the father of all as an additional principle to the ones I mentioned.) This high God or first God or supremely transcendent God seems to set off a multiplication of divine principles that are all more or less designed to explain the same thing: order and rationality in the cosmos. Divine principles are multiplied to produce a kind of buffer zone between the first God and the material world that is rationally ordered. For example, in the Middle Platonist, Albinus, there is a prime intelligence (thought thinking itself, the source of thought) then a secondary intelligence (an actualized intellect, perhaps thought thinking the forms), a potential intellect (thought capable of thinking and perhaps brought to think by an already actualized intellect), then a world soul (a living thing possessed of intellect), and then lesser divine souls or intellects with more restricted spheres of operation. The high God, consequently, is not directly concerned with ordering the world of time and change; instead these intermediary divine principles are. These lesser deities are less divine, more like what is not divine—matter—and therefore the more appropriate ordering principles for it. They can order matter in a way that will allow it to be what it is: something characterized by impermanence and change. The first God is only responsible for ordering the intellect of the second divine principle most like itself. So not only is the supreme God responsible for only what is like itself—rationality, order, pattern, proportion—but the first God is not even directly responsible for those things (at least insofar as they make up ingredient features of the world as we know it).

The transcendence of God is imaged here as distance; transcendence is understood spatially, as a distance or spatial interval occupied by intermediary divinities. And one finds much the same thing in a more straight forwardly Aristotelian cosmology that talks about the first God as simply the unmoved mover. There is the same spatialized understanding of transcendence as distance and the same multiplication of divinities to explain order in the world. The unmoved mover directly influences only what is most like itself—the single, eternal circular motions of the heavenly bodies—and it is these heavenly bodies that are themselves responsible, in turn, for the multiple and linear movements of generation and becoming on earth (for example, the growth of plants).

One also of course finds much the same thing in Gnosticism. Because they often denigrate the material world more than simple Platonists or Aristotelians would, Gnostics tend to multiply divine principles almost ad infinitum to produce a buffer zone between the high God and this world (while also including a moment of disruption and disorder within the descending scale of divine beings). Only at the end of this scale of divine beings is there a divinity dumb and disordered enough to produce the deformed and disintegrated components of the world as we know it: matter, active world-forming souls, and sparks of divinity.

Yet it is the very emanationist principles found in Gnosticism, and maintained more consistently in Neo-Platonism (that is, without a Gnostic moment of disruption and disorder and a personalistically conceived demiurge), that suggest a way beyond the dilemma. In the emanationist scheme the typical Hellenistic characterization of the first God begins to enable God's involvement in the world to be deepened in both scope and manner. There are no longer a number of independent cosmological principles (as there are in Plato or Albinus or Aristotle) but all the factors that go into the world as we know it are the ultimate productions of the first God. The first God is therefore ultimately responsible for matter as well as form or ideas; matter is also ultimately traceable back to the first God through a number of intermediary deities. And divinity is involved in the world not just as an ordering principle but as a productive principle: everything comes out of or emanates from the first God. Although clearer in a Neo-Platonist such as Plotinus, one finds the same thing in Gnosticism, despite the break in emanations with the deformed products of the last divinity (out of which the world is constructed by art): everything in the world in some way unfolds out of the divine realm. In sum, we find here a wider scope for the indirect involvement of the first God—including matter—and a deeper manner of involvement, a productive involvement.

The Neo-Platonism of Plotinus begins to reveal what it is about the characterization of the first God that suggests this widening of scope and deeper involvement. First of all, Plotinus suggests that there is something about the way the first God is characterized that breaks the like-is-involved-with-like principle. Plotinus foregrounds the very common Hellenistic idea that the first God is formless or beyond form—neither a this nor a that, not any particular kind of thing. The same thing is indicated by saying that the first God is beyond being—meaning by that that God is beyond *finite* being which is itself only by being a definite something, a particular sort of thing in contrast to other sorts of things. If the forms of things—intelligible ideas—come from the first God (these are usually in Hellenistic cosmologies the primary and immediate product of the first God), then, Plotinus points out, like is not coming from like but forms are grounded in what they are not—the formless—and the principle "like from like" does not hold. More importantly, Plotinus suggests that it is just *because* the first God is not a kind of thing that it can be responsible for more than what it is like. "The cause . . . of all existing things cannot be any one of these things."[2] Because God is not any particular kind of thing, God is able to produce any sort of thing and therefore all of them. What Plotinus seems to be suggesting here is that what limits the scope of God's involvement to a particular kind of thing—intelligibles, forms—is the characterization of God as a particular kind of thing. Talking about God as beyond kinds removes the limitation. One must avoid characterizing God in terms of one side of a contrast that applies to things in the world, because doing so makes it hard to see how God can be responsible for the contrast *as a whole*, how God can produce both sorts of thing that constitute the contrast.

---

[2] Plotinus, *The Enneads* 6.9, section 6, translated by Joseph Katz, in *The Philosophy of Plotinus* (New York, NY: Appleton-Century-Crofts, Inc., 1950), pp. 149–150.

Plotinus also suggests that something about the usual characterization of the first principle conflicts with the idea that transcendence means distance. Distance in space, separation, is not what the difference between the first God and everything else implies. The first principle is not, in other words, located at a distance from everything else in space as the spatial models of cosmic principles so common in Greco-Roman thought suggest. Even though Plotinus uses a spatial model, one should not take the model literally. Why not? Because God is different from everything else by containing no difference. That sort of characterization of the first principle—that it contains no multiplicity—is quite common in Hellenistic philosophy. Given such a characterization, Plotinus argues, the One—the first principle—cannot be absent from or far from anything, since the first principle contains no difference in itself with which to be separate from it. The One has to be perfectly present everywhere—to every sort of the thing—because it is just that one which excludes difference and exteriority. "As the One does not contain difference, it is always present (to everything)."[3]

In sum, the more transcendent God is, the more intimately involved God is with everything. The two go together. And the dilemma is thereby resolved.

Plotinus, however, fails to follow through on this insight consistently. First of all, he commonly falls back on the idea that like is directly involved only with like. The first principle produces directly only what is most like itself—Nous—the intelligible, the eternal, what is as unified as anything can be short of the One. The direct operation of the One still seems restricted by kind. Secondly, talk of the unity of the One, rather than suggesting what is beyond all contrasts between kinds, seems to involve a simple contrast with what is multiple. The One is not also beyond the contrast between the one and the multiple, but becomes a kind of thing among others, that kind of thing that is one rather than internally divided. This means that beings that include difference and multiplicity are not really present to the One as the beings they are—multiple and internally differentiated beings. To be one with the One, present to it, one must leave multiplicity and difference behind. One must become like the One to be present to it, one with it. "We are present to the One insofar as we contain no difference."[4] "The One is not absent from anything though in another sense it is absent from all things. It is present only to those who are able to receive it ... by virtue of their similarity to it" (and that means by virtue of their leaving difference and multiplicity behind).[5]

With Irenaeus, we see something like what I have suggested could be gotten out of Plotinus, the sense, that is, that Hellenistic ideas about God's

---

[3] *Enneads*, 6.9, section 8, trans. Katz, p. 152.
[4] *Ibid*.
[5] *Enneads* 6.9, section 4, trans. Katz, p. 145.

radical transcendence suggest something that most Hellenistic philosophers do not realize: God is intimately involved with everything. Particularly in Book Two of his *Against Heresies*, Irenaeus takes Gnostic ideas about divinity as a pleroma—a fullness without limit, the all, what contains everything without itself being contained (very common Hellenistic ideas about God)—and argues that they do not suggest what the Gnostics assert: that the first God has nothing very directly to do with this world, that the first God is far off at a distance and that we must escape this world, leave it in spirit and in flesh, in order to return to that first principle. The argument here is rather simple. If God is this unlimited fullness then nothing really exists outside its direct field of influence and concern, as the Gnostics assume. When the Gnostics say that the material world is produced by and under the control of a defective principle—the demiurge—who exists and exerts his influence outside the fullness of God, then they put a limit around God, they suggest that God is contained by something else, and therefore they imply that God is not really God. If God is what the Gnostics say God is—fullness without limit—then God's presence and influence are unrestricted in their range; there is nothing that exists apart from God and nothing that is not subject to God's direct influence. God is the measureless context and source for everything; everything is in God's territory, as Irenaeus puts it.

The conclusions of this argument are also used by Irenaeus to dispute the idea of divinity as a generic category and to affirm monotheism in that sense. If God is not at a distance form the world, then there is no need for, no place for, intervening divine principles to relate God to the world outside God. There is instead only one God, and all the intermediary deities that Gnostics talk about are really only names for what exists altogether and at once in that one God. Irenaeus is really replaying here the same sort of argument he used to dispute a limited scope for the first God's influence. If there are many deities at a remove from the first God and those deities appear sequentially, temporally, out of the first God by a process of emanation, then the first God again appears to be a limited being, something contained, a being circumscribed in time and place. These various deities must therefore exist in the first God—the only God there is, is that one God—and because they are in God they are all equally God and bear no relations of before and after with respect to one another.

Again, the solution to the dilemma is to show that what makes God different from what is not God is exactly what insures that God is directly and intimately related to everything. And in order to show that, one must develop in very particular ways both the claim about God's transcendence and the claim about God's involvement in the world. First, God's transcendence has to be talked about in such a way that the difference between God and the world is not like any of the differences among things within the world. And that basically means that the difference between God and the world is not to be discussed as a simple difference between kinds, the sort of difference that distinguishes sorts of beings within the world. God is neither like the world nor simply unlike it. God is beyond the difference between like and unlike, beyond simple identifications or simple contrasts. That is just what makes God different from anything else.

Second, God's involvement in the world—particularly as a productive principle—should have an unlimited scope and be utterly direct in manner. That, I take it, is the point of creation *ex nihilo*. To say that God creates by working on anything (for example, uncreated prime matter) or with (or through) anything (for example, with the help of, or by means of, other creative principles) would be to restrict the scope of God's creative activity and/or to make that activity less than immediate in its relations with at least some features of the world. Saying either one would also run counter to the radicalized account of divine transcendence, by suggesting that God is a sort of being alongside others. To claim that the world is created out of God—the other alternative to a creation *ex nihilo* position—would also run counter to this radicalized account of divine transcendence if the claim were taken to mean the quasi-divinity of the world, the world's difference from God in degree of divinity. Emanationist imagery, as I will show in a moment, is often retained in creation *ex nihilo* accounts (for obvious reasons given its importance to the move beyond what I have been calling the Greco-Roman problematic), but with significant warping.

The practical resonances of these radicalized claims about God's transcendence and creative agency need have very little to do, therefore, with support for a principle of coercive domination or for dualistic hierarchies among creatures. When seen as a modification of the Greco-Roman problematic, radicalized transcendence seems designed to prevent the divinizing of any this-worldly status quo, while relativizing the significance of differences among creatures: none of those differences makes any difference with reference to intimacy to God. (I leave out of account here the difference between good and evil, which is often a serious complicating feature of these sorts of accounts.) In contrast to views typical of the first horn of the Greco-Roman problematic, the given order and reason of things in this world (both natural and socio-political) are not likened to the divine and due respect as such. Nor are qualities associated with rationality and order privileged over against the messy realities of embodied existence.

Creation *ex nihilo* means that there is nothing outside the direct reach of God's beneficent working as creator, nothing that in its obstructing power might mean the world is fated to remain only as good as it now appears or has been up until now (as in the first horn of the Greco-Roman problematic), nothing that must simply be escaped or left behind in the search for the greater good (as in the second horn of that dilemma). One need not (as in the first horn of the dilemma) simply resign or accommodate oneself to how the world works on the supposition that this is the best that the divine cosmic principles can do given the other recalcitrant cosmological materials with which they must work. Nor (as in the second horn) does a pessimism about the messy material features of this world prompt one to pin one's hopes on extrication from those features, on refusal of them, purification from them. Instead, one can entertain extravagant hopes for a genuinely novel future good for the world as a whole, pinning one's hopes on the unconstrained productive powers of a God who gives rise to the whole world without being it rather than on the unrealistically optimistic belief that the world is really (at least potentially) much better than it has so far appeared to be.[6]

Mixed Metaphors

Creation *ex nihilo* constitutes itself as the rejection of both creation from or through something, and creation out of God. But since this relation with what it rejects is constitutive of creation *ex nihilo*, neither rejection is total. Typically, creation *ex nihilo* positions include the imagery and concepts of both these rejected viewpoints—on the one hand, personalistic images and concepts appropriate for artifactual production, and the naturalistic images and concepts associated with emanation, on the other—while violating their proper bounds. It is the mixing of the two sets of images and concepts to discuss the very same divine productive process that, one might say, distinguishes the creation *ex nihilo* position.

Usually, one or the other set of images and concepts takes primacy. For example, in the medieval period Thomas Aquinas makes the idea of God's intentional agency in creating the world primary: God conceives the world to be created, intellectually, and brings it about through an act of free will. Bonaventure is influenced more by the Dionysian emanationist language of self-diffusion: God radiates out into the world like light or flows out into the world like water from its source. Similarly, in the modern period Friedrich Schleiermacher is more inclined to talk of the natural necessity of God's operations and Karl Barth to talk of God's loving freedom in personalistic terms. These divergent emphases approximate one another, however—by way of the mixing of the two sets of images and concepts, and through the severity of the modifications made to even the preferred imagery.

Aquinas, for example, resists making emanationist categories his primary ones for a number of reasons. First, natural production (which is the model for creation out of God) suggests that what is produced is of the same kind as its producer. For instance, the effects of heat are hot; offspring are the same kind of animals as their mothers; and so on. The radical account of transcendence forbids divinity to be in this way a kind shared with the world. Second, natural causes are restricted in their effects; they tend to produce only a single sort of effect or instance. Fire only heats; mares give birth only to other horses.

---

[6] Tertullian's "Against Hermogenes" can be read to be making these practical points.

Used to talk about God's creation of the world, such language would therefore restrict the scope of what God is responsible for as creator. Aquinas associates this restriction of effects with the necessary character of natural causes' productivity: they must be productive to the extent their natural capacities are actualized; they therefore do not act by free choice. Acting on intention, on the other hand, makes possible (in principle) an infinitely extensible diversity of productions. For example, a free agent can choose to make a house, or go to the store or write a book, etc. Third, natural causes already include in themselves, in a higher form, what they give rise to. When applied to God and the world, this might slight the value and dignity of created things outside God; the world, it seems, would be better off remaining as it exists within God (where it exists *as* God).

Aquinas favors personalistic imagery, then, by default, by a kind of process of elimination, but also because he thinks such imagery helps show the all-inclusive scope of God's activity as creator—and (as I now suggest) the transcendence of God. Language of intentionality—language of knowing, believing, thinking, willing, intending—has a peculiar grammatical structure: verbs of intention have clauses for their grammatical objects ("I think *that* such and such"). The terms in those clauses therefore have what is called in modern logical parlance referential opacity, that is, the terms only refer to their objects under a particular description of them; and therefore the truth of a statement concerning intentions does not necessarily carry over when terms with a different meaning but the same reference are substituted in the object clause. (For example, if it is true that I think Barack Obama is handsome that does not imply that it is true that I think the current President of the United States is handsome, because I may not know who the current president is.) Referential opacity means that what characterizes the willing, thinking, intending, and so on, of the subject need not also characterize the referents of the terms in the object clause. Nothing, indeed, is implied one way or another. For example, my thinking ill of others may be necessary (because I am an inveterately nasty person) without that ill will or the necessity of it implying anything about the referents of my scorn. They may not be as bad as I think they are (who knows?) and if they are, they are not necessarily so because I need to think they are. If one talks about God's creating the world using intentional language (for example, if one says God creates the world by the very process of intellection and will) then one's language about God will display the idea of God's transcendence. The world need not be like or unlike God; what is said about the character of God's knowing and willing will imply nothing either way about the character of the world.

Despite this preference for personalistic language, Aquinas modifies it so severely that emanationist language is rehabilitated. God produces the world like a human being might freely choose to build a house of which she has a mental conception. That is the preferred imagery. But in God's case there are no materials; God's creation of the world presupposes nothing prior to it, upon which God works. And there are no tools, no means. Indeed, God creates the world without any intervening process at all, that is to say, immediately. The rejection of creation on or by way of anything requires all such modifications.

The last modification of personalistic agency, in particular (that is, the denial of any intervening process), was already intimated in saying above that God creates in the very process of thinking and willing. God, unlike a human agent, does not have to take any additional action to bring about what God intends. What would be intransitive acts in human beings—acts of reasoned willing that remain in the agent—are therefore transitive acts (like my picking up a hammer to build a house frame) in God, that is, they are acts that have external effects. The closest analogues here are the favorite images of the emanationist scheme. For instance, fire and sunlight produce their effects immediately, without doing anything, without any intervening process, just by being themselves. (Images of bodily reproduction are unsuitable for this purpose.)

Aquinas also severely modifies the usual presuppositions and implications of the language of free choice, so that again emanationist language re-surfaces. God's free choice of the world involves no deliberation; God never begins to so choose after a time of not doing so; God's choice involves no successive acts; and so on. The idea that God does not have to do anything in order to create the world extends, in short, even to having to make a decision. God creates the world simply by being what God always is; God creates the world insofar as God is always already in act. Everything God needs to create the world is already prepared. God does not come to decide to create the world; if that is God's intention, then God always intends to create the world. Again, the sun illuminating the air, fire heating things up, would seem the closest analogues. Fire does not need to do anything that it is not already doing to heat up what is brought near it; it is already throwing off heat. That is all just part of what it means to be fire.

Ultimately, all that is left of the idea of free choice for Aquinas is the idea of a non-necessary logical relation between God's being and nature, on the one hand, and God's intention to create the world, on the other. From God's existence and nature one cannot infer with any logical necessity that God wills the world—this one or any one at all. The latter does not follow from the former by any necessary logical implication. Aquinas thinks that personalistic imagery is better able to display this point since natural causes (that work immediately) are necessarily productive (unless hindered or defective). Fire, for example, has no choice but to heat up the surrounding air; it would not be itself without doing so.

Theologians who favor emanationist imagery are generally more wary of untoward anthropomorphic connotations of personalistic language: "God as a fussy, arbitrary little deity who, after aeons of inertia, suddenly decided to create a world."[7] To insist on God's free choice in creating (especially while reserving language of emanation for intra-trinitarian processions) is to suggest a simple contrast with agents who do not act by free choice, in violation of a radical view of divine transcendence. Repudiating language of free choice (without absolutely refusing personalistic imagery), Schleiermacher, for example, suggests that, if anything, God should be talked about as the perfect artist "who in a state of inspired discovery thinks of nothing else, to whom nothing else offers itself, save what he (sic) actually produces."[8] "[To] suppose that God also decides and produces by choice and deliberation [is] a view which from of old every form of teaching in any degree consistent has repudiated."[9] It is better simply to say that God creates the world necessarily in the way fire and light necessarily produce their effects while denying that in the case of God necessity excludes freedom. "We must . . . think of nothing in God as necessary without at the same time positing it as free, nor as free unless at the same time necessary."[10]

Indeed, theologians such as Bonaventure who favor emanationist imagery do not just assert that in God's case necessity and freedom are not at odds; they have a way of explaining the freedom of this God's necessary creation, the freedom of God who would not be God without diffusing God's own goodness outwards to the creature. God is good and the good must diffuse itself, but this diffusion of the good is already perfectly achieved in God's own trinitarian life: perfect self-diffusion results in exact equality with the one who diffuses and this is only possible if the effects of such diffusion are themselves perfectly divine. There is no need, therefore, for God to diffuse the good in creating; the God whose trinitarian life is already constituted by self-diffusion would be perfectly fecund even if there were no world. God does not need to create as if in not doing so God would suffer a lack; God creates instead because of the superfluity, the excess, of God's already achieved goodness. The imagery is now no longer simply of water but of an overflowing spring; not simply of light but of superabundant effulgence.

Creating the world can for these reasons be thought of as an act of generosity, an unforced demonstration of regard for what is other than God. (The point of God's already achieved perfection is not therefore to stress the isolated self-sufficiency of God.) Self-communication of the good, an impersonal cosmological principle maintaining that what is good naturally brings forth the good, becomes a gracious concern for the good of others. Personalistic language returns in the language of love now applied to the primarily impersonal imagery of natural causation, fire heating and light illuminating.

---

[7] A. H. Armstrong, "Platonic *Eros* and Christian *Agape*," *Downside Review*, Vol. 79 (1961), p. 111.

[8] Friedrich Schleiermacher, *The Christian Faith*, edited by H. R. Mackintosh and J. S. Stewart (Philadelphia, PA: Fortress Press, 1976), paragraph 55, p. 225.

[9] *Ibid*.

[10] Schleiermacher, *The Christian Faith*, paragraph 54, p. 217.

This argument for God's freedom in creating is, indeed, not far from Aquinas' own support for a non-necessary relation between God's existence and nature, on the one hand, and God's willing of the world, on the other. "God wills things apart from himself (sic) in so far as they are ordered to his own goodness as their end. Now in willing an end we do not necessarily will the things that conduce to it, unless they are such that the end cannot be attained without them. . . . But we do not necessarily will things without which the end can be attained. . . . Hence, since the goodness of God is perfect, and can exist without other things inasmuch as no perfection can accrue to him from them, it follows that his willing things apart from himself is not absolutely necessary."[11] Similarly, "Everyone . . . wills his ultimate end of necessity. . . . [But God's] ultimate end is not the sharing of his goodness, but rather the divine goodness itself: it is out of love for it that God wills to share it. For God does not act because of his goodness as if desiring what he does not have, but as if wanting to share what he has, because God acts not out of desire for the end, but out of love for the end."[12] In short here, too, it is the already achieved fullness of divinity that suggests the beneficent gratuity of what God does in sharing the good with creatures.

From the primary standpoint of emanationist imagery, Bonaventure is also able to counter the great majority of Aquinas' other worries about it. First of all, natural causes need not be limited in their effects, any more than intentional agents are. "Just as you notice that a ray of light coming in through a window is colored according to the shades of the different panes, so the divine ray shines differently in each creature."[13] Something like this argument is found as far back as Gregory of Nyssa: "The energy of fire is always one and the same; it consists in heating: but what sort of agreement do its results show? Bronze melts in it; mud hardens; wax vanishes; . . . asbestos is washed by the flames as if by water; [etc]."[14] Moreover, as Aquinas himself well knows, thinking of God in terms of a self-diffusive, perfect good is enough to make the point about the universal range of God's creative production, without any help from intentional language. The perfect good will extend its causality as much as possible to as many things as possible.[15] And the divine goodness, because it is perfect, requires an indefinitely extended multiplicity of finite goods to approximate its own goodness in finite form.[16]

---

[11] Aquinas, *Summa Theologiae*, 1a, Q19, art. 3, translated by the Fathers of the English Dominican Province, (Westminster, MD: Christian Classics, 1981), volume 1, p. 105.

[12] Aquinas, *On the Power of God*, Q3, art. 15. ad 14, translated by the English Dominican Fathers, (London: Burns, Oates, and Washbourne, 1932), volume 1, p. 204.

[13] Bonaventure, "Collations on the Six Days," Twelfth Collation, section 14, translated by Jose de Vinck, in *The Works of Bonaventure* (Paterson, NJ: St. Anthony Guild Press, 1970), volume 5, p. 179.

[14] Gregory of Nyssa, "Against Eunomius," Book I, chapter 27, translated by H. A. Wilson, in *Nicene and Post-Nicene Fathers*, Second Series (Peabody, MA: Hendrickson, 1994), volume 5, p. 71.

[15] See his *Summa Contra Gentiles*, Book 1, chapter 75, section 6.

[16] See *Summa Contra Gentiles*, Book 2, chapter 45, section 2.

In the second place, the emanationist model need not run counter to radical transcendence by suggesting that God's substance is parceled out to created things, or somehow thinned out to make them, like a trickling stream from a bubbling source of water or like a wave of heat from something much hotter. Instead (with the usual theological freedom to violate the proper boundaries of particular images/concepts), one could say that God's creation of the world is a kind of duplication of what God is in the form of something that is not God. It is not an exact duplication. There would be no point to that; creation would not be creation but God all over again. Instead, creation is a duplicate in the form of an image. God does not share God's nature or substance (since it is not a kind of thing susceptible of sharing in that sense); what God produces is an image of God. The world is the image of God (or more exactly, for Bonaventure, the image of the proper Image who perfectly shares the divine substance, Christ) that God throws off simply by being God. Like the projection of a shadow or the aura or glow of a brilliant object, like the halo surrounding the sun, this after-image that constitutes creation is not what God is, it is not part of God's own being. It is the spontaneous effect that God throws off in virtue of so intense a superabundance.

Conclusion

Talked about as *both* a natural principle and a personal agent, God must be neither in a proper sense. This is a particular version of the Dionysian principle that all things can be affirmed of God (a cataphatic version of transcendence) where this is taken to suggest, more fundamentally, that all things must be denied of God (apophasis). All theological categories become tropes; all categories taken up by theology, from out of their proper fields of application, are troped or twisted.

Therefore, only when theological use of the categories of nature and personality respects the proper senses of those categories can God be only one or the other: the God of nature (the God who is Nature) *or* a person outside the world. The charge in the modern period against pan(en)theism—that it necessarily confuses God with the world in violation of God's transcendence—suggests, then, that it is those lodging the charge who have violated God's transcendence by making categories of personal agency proper to theology and by refusing to transgress the proper boundaries that guard those categories' sense. And the reverse: the charge that talk of God as a personal agent necessarily implies God is outside the world, intervening in it from a position of otherwise sovereign isolation, suggests that those who lodge the charge violate God's transcendence by making categories of natural process proper to theology and by refusing to transgress those categories' proper boundaries. The charge against pan(en)theism is valid only where pan(en)theism develops as a strict, exclusive alternative to personalistic categories. And the reverse: the charge against a personal God is valid only where that personalism develops in rigid opposition to categories of natural process—that is, where ideas of a personal God are developed as they are in eighteenth century deism. Both these developments are unfortunately common in the modern period as theologians increasingly lose a sense of God's radical transcendence and abide by both general canons of sense making and the proper boundaries of the categories they employ.

Modern Theology 29:2 April 2013
ISSN 0266-7177 (Print)
ISSN 1468-0025 (Online)

"LOVE IS ALSO A LOVER OF LIFE": *CREATIO EX NIHILO* AND CREATURELY GOODNESS

JOHN WEBSTER

I

Christian teaching about the creation of the world out of nothing is a cardinal doctrine: on this hinge turn all the elements of the second topic of Christian theology, which treats all things with reference to God, their beginning and end, the first topic being God's immanent life. In his work of creation, God inaugurates an order of being other than himself, and this work is presupposed in all subsequent assertions about that order of being, for to create is to bring something into existence, and "God's first effect in things is existence itself, which all other effects presuppose, and on which they are founded."[1] This first effect of God is a radical beginning and precisely as such the establishment of an enduring relation. Other articles of Christian teaching about God's transitive works treat the historical course of the relation so established, but do so on the presupposition that the creaturely term of the relation has been brought into being *ex nihilo*, and that only as a reality instituted in this manner may its nature and history be understood. Teaching about creation "opens the logical and theological space for other Christian beliefs and mysteries."[2]

Because of this, Christian teaching about the creation of the world out of nothing is also a distributed doctrine, cropping up throughout theology's

John Webster
School of Divinity, History and Philosophy, King's College, University of Aberdeen, Aberdeen AB24 3UB, SCOTLAND
Email: j.webster@abdn.ac.uk

[1] Saint Thomas Aquinas, *Compendium of Theology*, translated by Richard J. Regan (Oxford: Oxford University Press, 2009), §68.

[2] Robert Sokolowski, "Creation and Christian Understanding", in *God and Creation: An Ecumenical Symposium*, edited by David Burrell and Bernard McGinn (Notre Dame, IN: University of Notre Dame Press, 1990), p. 179.

treatment of the economy with varying degrees of explicitness. Our understanding of creation is amplified and deepened by this frequent recurrence, for its full scope and meaning become apparent in relation to what is said about other divine works of nature, such as preservation and governance, and, most of all, in relation to what is said in the works of grace which culminate in the missions of the Son of God and the Holy Spirit. It is in the works of grace, in which the end of God's act of creation is secured, that the natures of God's creatures and of his own benevolence are most fully displayed. Christian beliefs about the character of the creator and of his creative act are shaped by what can be learned from considering providence and reconciliation, in which the work of creation has its *terminus ad quem* (a point given its most extensive modern exposition in Barth's ordering of creation to covenant). Equally, however, beliefs about providence and reconciliation only make full sense when we attend to their *terminus a quo*, that is, when we bear in mind that the protagonists in the economy are the creator and his creatures, and that all being and occurrence that is not God is to its very depths *ex nihilo*.

The Christian doctrine of creation treats three principal topics: the identity of the creator, the divine act of creating and the several natures and ends of created things. These topics are materially ordered: teaching about the identity of the creator governs what is said about his creative act and about what he creates. In early Christian developments of the doctrine of creation out of nothing, much turned on the perception that God's radical perfection requires extensive revisions both of how the act of creation is to be understood (it can have no material cause) and of the natures of the beings created by this act. Of course, the order of inquiry does not necessarily conform to the material order: reflection on the doctrine of creation may take its rise with any one of the topics. But reflection will not reach its term unless the entire range and the order of the matter are brought to mind.

Disarray results from the hypertrophy or atrophy of one or other element (as, for example, in theologies which reduce the doctrine of creation to teaching about created things, without adequate consideration of the creator and his work). Further, misperception or misapplication of one or other element will deform the whole, whose force depends in part upon the integrity of its constituents. It would be possible to trace how modern theologies of creation have often suffered a series of such misperceptions and misapplications, on the part of proponents as well as despisers. Here I address one such misperception: the anxiety that the pure non-reciprocal gratuity of God's creation of all things out of nothing debases the creature, for a being so radically constituted by another as to be nothing apart from that other is a being evacuated of intrinsic worth. The anxiety is misplaced, sometimes destructively so. Showing why this is the case involves dispute about the elements of the doctrine of creation, that is, exposure of points at which habits of thought are contradicted by faith in God the creator. This is not, it should be noted, a peculiarly modern task, forced upon theology by hostile circumstances. The doctrine of creation has proved a permanently contrary article of Christian teaching, requiring the release of thought from inhibiting assumptions about God and created things (Lactantius's account in the *Divine Institutes* or Thomas's in the *Summa Contra Gentiles* are classical exercises in extracting the Christian doctrine of creation from inherited misapprehensions). For all that, polemics or elenctics are subsidiary undertakings. The primary theological task in this matter is the dedication of intelligence to devout indication and description of Christian verities, whose goodness, once known and loved, dispels anxiety and draws both intellect and affections to satisfaction.

II

Before treating the matter of creaturely worth directly, we may identify in summary fashion the elements of the doctrine of creation out of nothing.

1. *Coming to understand Christian teaching about creation out of nothing is an instance of the special pedagogy by which all the elements of the Christian confession are made objects of intelligent love. The principal parts of this pedagogy are prophecy and reconciliation.*

"It is a great and very rare thing for a man, after he has contemplated the whole creation, corporeal and incorporeal, and has discerned its mutability, to pass beyond it, and, by the continued soaring of his mind, to attain to the unchangeable substance of God, and, in that height of contemplation, to learn from God himself that none but he has made all that is not of the divine essence."[3] Why is it that God must be the teacher in this matter? Partly because creation concerns an absolute "beginning", the summoning into being of what is not, and in the nature of the case such a summons cannot be an object of experience. Partly, again, because creation out of nothing is entirely *sui generis*. It is not an instance of making, nor of any causality we might know; and so we may not "inquire by what hands, by what machines, by what levers, by what contrivance [God] made this work of such magnitude".[4] Again, to think about creation out of nothing is not to ponder an event in the history of the world, but to come to see that the world, including ourselves as intelligent beings, is not the given reality which we customarily take it to be, but is something that once was not and might not have been at all. We can have this thought, however, only after a conversion of mind which is not within our capacity but rests upon divine instruction. Finally, teaching about creation is teaching about the creator, and teaching about the creator is

---

[3] Augustine, *City of God*, translated by Marcus Dodds (Peabody, MA Hendrickson Publishers, 1994), XI.2.

[4] Lactantius, *Divine Institutes*, edited by Alexander Roberts and James Donaldson (Peabody, MA: Hendrikson Publishers, 1994), II.9 (he is criticising Cicero).

delivered to creatures "under the inspiration of the Holy Spirit".[5] Not without reason, both Ambrose and Basil begin their *Hexamera* by reflecting on Moses the prophet "who imparts to us what he has learnt from God".[6]

Knowledge of God the creator and his act of creation, and of the constitutive significance of God and his act for created things, arises not by the spontaneous exercise of intelligence but by the operation of "the Holy Spirit, handing down the discipline of truth".[7] This being so, consideration of the topic of creation out of nothing carries with it the requirement that we be in the process of becoming certain kinds of persons. This is because being caught up in the Spirit's pedagogy is an aspect of sanctification. Much might be said here: of the need for cleansing prior to divine instruction; of docility and patience; of resistance to curiosity; of acceptance of limits. A good deal of what needs to be said might be gathered under the rubric of "religion" in its deep sense of being bound to God, the one "to whom we ought to be bound as to our unfailing principle".[8] We might also speak of friendship with God as a condition for knowledge of him as creator and of ourselves as his creatures. In our corrupt state, such friendship is lost to us, for we despise both our creaturely condition and our creator, and need to be reconciled. Corruption inhibits knowledge. But God the teacher is God the reconciler and overcomes our corruption, establishing the new creaturely nature objectively in the death and resurrection of Jesus Christ and applicatively in the regenerative work of the Spirit. Possessed of this new nature, creatures are being "renewed in knowledge" (Col. 3:10), including knowledge of creator and creature.

The end of consideration of this work of God is faith in God. The core of Christian teaching about creation out of nothing is not cosmology or philosophy of nature or anthropology, but the Holy Trinity's perfection and benevolence. At the beginning of his treatment of creation in the *Summa Contra Gentiles*, Aquinas takes time to spell out how meditation on the transitive works of God enables us "to admire and reflect on his wisdom",[9] "leads to admiration of God's sublime power, and consequently inspires in men's hearts reverence for God",[10] and "incites the souls of men to the love of God's goodness".[11] In such admiration, reverence and love of God, the divine pedagogy about creation reaches its term.

---

[5] Saint Ambrose, *Hexameron, Paradise, and Cain and Abel*, translated by John J. Savage (Washington, DC: Catholic University of America Press, 1977), I.1.2.

[6] Basil, *Hexameron* (Peabody, MA: Hendrickson Publishers, 1994), I.1.

[7] Peter Lombard, *The Sentences* (Toronto: Pontifical Institute of Medieval Studies, 2008), II.dist. 1, pt. 1, ch. 3.

[8] Aquinas, *Summa Theologiae* (London: Blackfriars, 1964), IIaIIae.81.1 resp.

[9] Aquinas, *Summa Contra Gentiles* (Notre Dame, IN: University of Notre Dame Press, 1975), II.2.2.

[10] Aquinas, *Summa Contra Gentiles* II.2.3.

[11] Aquinas, *Summa Contra Gentiles* II.2.4.

2. *The primary subject matter of theological treatment of creation out of nothing is God himself; it inquires first, not into the world's beginning but into "who gave it this beginning, and who was the creator".*[12]

    Here I prescind from discussing the trinitarian dimensions of creation as the work of the three persons of the godhead[13] in order to concentrate upon creation as the operation of the undivided divine essence, about which a number of lines of reflection need to be followed.

    a. Talk of God as creator of heaven and earth presupposes the distinction of God's immanent from his transitive operations, that is, the distinction of those works which remain in God and whose term is God's perfect life from those works which have an external object. The importance of this distinction is not simply that it states the difference between the inner divine processions (generation and spiration) as *actio* from the external work of creation as *factio*.[14] It is also that, by so ordering God's works, it sets before the mind the principle that because God the creator is perfect in himself, he has no need of creation, acquiring no augmentation from its existence, and being deprived of no good by its absence. The non-necessary character of God's *opera ad extra* is fundamental to understanding all the elements of the doctrine of creation out of nothing: the creator and his act of creation, the nature of creatures, and the relation which obtains between creator and created things. The careful specification of this non-necessity is, moreover, of capital importance for treating anxieties about the debasement of creatures.

    b. As creator, God is "the principle and cause of being to other beings".[15] God is perfect, and his being has no cause, because to be perfect is to be unoriginate, irreducible to some other causal reality. But as this one, God is the "first efficient cause"[16] of all things. God works transitively, and does so first by bringing all things into being as *omnibus causa essendi*. This is the first and most general statement about God as creator.

    c. To be the cause of being of all things is proper to God alone. This is so because the creator is the *first* cause who is himself without cause. "It belongs only to God to be the creator, for creating belongs to the cause that does not presuppose another, more universal, cause . . . but this belongs only to God. Therefore, only he is the creator."[17] As creator, God is not the most exalted instance of creativity; in its absolute character as that which effects existence *tout court*, his creating is

---

[12] Basil, *Hexameron* I.2.

[13] On this topic, see John Webster, "Trinity and Creation", *International Journal of Systematic Theology*, Vol.12 (2010), pp. 4–19.

[14] For the distinction of *actio* from *factio*, see Aquinas, *Summa Contra Gentiles* II.1.4.

[15] Aquinas, *Summa Contra Gentiles* II.6.1.

[16] Aquinas, Summa Contra Gentiles II.6.2.

[17] Aquinas, *Compendium of Theology* §70.

incommunicable. There can therefore be no instrumental causes in creating, for any such instrument would itself be caused and therefore incapable of being the first cause of being of other things. *Nulla creatura possit creare*;[18] God alone is creator.

d. God has power to create as "an active and a moving being".[19] Or better: God *is* this power, which is his substance and not some incidental property. Further, God is creator "through his very self":[20] his creative power is not some capacity which he has in reserve, some underlying principle of his action. The creator is not simply an immense causal agent, a capitalised Cause or Author; as "first" cause God is not merely possessed of supreme power with greater range than a finite cause. His power is not what he has but what he is.

e. God is cause of all things by his will, not by natural necessity. His work of creation is not the natural overflow of his self-diffusive being, but intentional, personal action. Creation is spontaneous divine action, not the automatic operation of a "principle of plenitude".[21] And because of this, once again, creation need not have been.

f. In creating, God acts in accordance with his goodness. Here "goodness" is meant not so much in its moral as its metaphysical sense: God's goodness is his entirely realised nature. Of this goodness of his, there can be no supplementation. In creating, therefore, God is not bringing his goodness to realisation, for this would make the creator's goodness depend upon the creature. God's goodness is not the result but the cause of his creating. But divine goodness is, indeed, the source of the being of other things. Divine goodness includes as one of its ends the existence of created goodness, of a further reality which in its own order is good. Divine goodness is creative of likenesses of itself; divine being bestows being. Here metaphysical goodness shades into moral goodness, in that God's work of creation manifests that, precisely because his perfect goodness cannot be expended, he does not begrudge other things their being, but, on the contrary, gives being to other things. "God is good—or rather the source of goodness—and the good has no envy for anything. Thus, because he envies nothing its existence, he made everything from nothing through his own Word, our Lord Jesus Christ."[22]

---

[18] Aquinas, *Summa Theologiae* (London: Blackfriars, 1967), Ia.45.5 resp.; see also Ia.65.3.

[19] Aquinas, *Summa Contra Gentiles* II.7.5.

[20] Aquinas, *Summa Contra Gentiles* II.8.6.

[21] Arthur O. Lovejoy, *The Great Chain of Being* (New York, NY: Harper and Row, 1960), p. 54; for a critique of Lovejoy, see John F. Wippel, "Thomas Aquinas on God's Freedom to Create or Not", in *Metaphysical Themes in Thomas Aquinas II* (Washington, DC: Catholic University of America Press, 2007), pp. 218–239.

[22] Athanasius, *De Incarnatione in Contra Gentes and De Incarnatione*, edited and translated by Robert W. Thomson (Oxford: Oxford University Press, 1971), III.

3. *How may the act of creation out of nothing be characterised?*

   a. The act of creation is ineffable, having no analogues in our experience
      of causation or agency. Not only does this mean that much of what is
      said about it consists of negations which draw attention to its *sui generis*
      character; it also means that, in dealing with objections to Christian
      teaching about creation, theology should not be surprised to encounter
      objections which take for granted certain simplifications which arise
      when its basic terms are assumed to be univocal. Creation out of
      nothing is ineffable, not simply because of the grandeur of the agent or
      the magnitude of the act, but because of its incommensurability as "the
      introduction of being entirely".[23]

   b. The divine act of creation is instantaneous, an operation of "incompa-
      rable swiftness" devoid of succession.[24] The words "in the beginning",
      Basil tells his readers, indicate "the rapid and imperceptible moment
      of creation" which is "indivisible and instantaneous . . . [A]t the will of
      God the world arose in less than an instant."[25] This is said partly to
      indicate that the act of creation is not an event in time but that by virtue
      of which events in time come to be; this act is not a measurable sequence
      in the world but the world's originating principle. Partly, too, it is said to
      emphasise that God's work in creation is effortless, without strenuous
      movement from intention to completion and the relief afforded by
      cessation from strain. In creating, God "both works and rests simulta-
      neously".[26] Creation is thus more like an inner act of willing than an
      external act of craftsmanship. "God made all these powers [the physical
      universe, the nations and heavenly beings] with such ease that no words
      can explain it. The mere act of God's will was enough to make them all.
      An act of the will does not make us tired. Neither did creating so many
      and such mighty powers weary God . . . Do you not see that not only for
      creating the things on earth but also for the creation of the powers in
      heaven the mere act of his will was enough?"[27]

   c. The act of creation involves no movement or change in God. Peter
      Lombard's discussion of this point shows him acutely aware that verbs
      such as "create", "make" or "do" are predicated of God according to
      a different "reckoning" from that by which they are predicated of
      creatures, for "when we say that he makes something, we do not
      understand that there is any movement in him operating, nor any

---

[23] Aquinas, *Summa Theologiae* Ia.45.1 resp.
[24] Robert Grosseteste, *On the Six Days of Creation*, a translation of the Hexaëmeron by C. F. J.
Martin (Oxford: Oxford University Press, 1996) I.xi.1.
[25] Basil, *Hexameron* I.6.
[26] Augustine, *The Literal Meaning of Genesis* in *On Genesis*, introductions, translations and
notes by Edmund Hill; edited by John E. Rotelle (Hyde Park, NY: New City Press, 2002), IV.24.
[27] Chrysostom, *On the Incomprehensible Nature of God*, translated by Paul W. Harkins
(Washington, DC: Catholic University of America Press, 1984), II.

passion in working, just as there is accustomed to befall us, but we signify that there is some new effect of his sempiternal will, that is, something newly exists by his eternal will."[28] Creatures make by moving and changing, but when God creates "in him nothing new happens, but something new . . . comes to be without any motion or mutation of his own."[29] In the same way that effort has to be stripped out of the conception of the "act" of creation, so, too, do ideas of motion.

d. The act of creation indicates the supereminence of the creator. God is not simply an immensely resourceful particular agent, but "the universal cause of being".[30] Acts of making by a particular agent presuppose something not produced by that agent upon which the agent is at work. Creation is no such act because it is the crossing of what Aquinas calls the "infinite distance" between being and non-being.[31]

e. All this leads to the principal affirmation: God's act of creating is *ex nihilo*. Creation out of nothing is an extension of teaching about divine perfection: all that is required for the act of creation is God himself, the supreme essence acting "alone and through itself".[32] Because God is such, there is no material cause of creation: no raw material, no antecedent patient entity, nothing which God presupposes, on which he is at work or which he must master. The temptation is to turn the grammatical substantive "nothing" into a metaphysical substance. But "nothing" is not some sort of inchoate stuff to which the act of creation gives form; nor is it potentiality, what Bonhoeffer in a careless thought called "obedient nothing . . . that waits on God."[33] Nothing is pure negation, *nihil negativum*. Again, like *nihil*, *ex* can also mesmerise, leading us to think that it refers to the relation of something made to that from which it was made. But *ex* "signifies a sequence not a material cause".[34] "Sequence" here does not refer to a change from non-being to being which happens to some constant; rather, the sequence is: there was nothing at all . . . now there is something. Creation *ex nihilo* is not an act of conversion or modification, but one of absolute origination. It is an act of what Kretzmann calls "doubly universal production": distributively universal (God is the cause of being for *all things*) and intrinsically universal (for all things God is out of no pre-existing

---

[28] Lombard, *Sentences* II dist. 1, Pt. 1, ch. 3.

[29] Lombard, *Sentences* II dist. 1, Pt. 1, ch. 3.

[30] Aquinas, *Summa Contra Gentiles* II.16.3.

[31] Aquinas, *Summa Theologiae* Ia.45.2 obj. 4 and ad 4.

[32] Anselm, *Monologion* in Anselm of Canterbury, *The Major Works* (Oxford: Oxford University Press, 1998), VII.

[33] Dietrich Bonhoeffer, *Creation and Fall: A Theological Exposition of Genesis 1–3* (Minneapolis, MN: Fortress Press, 1997), p. 34.

[34] Aquinas, *Summa Theologiae* Ia.45.1 ad 3.

subject the cause of *being*).[35] God is utter plenitude and sufficiency and so the cause of the entire substance of all things.

4. *What does creation out of nothing indicate about the nature of created things?* Initially, it proposes a negative: the totality of created things is not eternal, necessary or underived. But this initial negative is preparatory for a positive theological statement that created things have their being in relation to God. Created things do indeed have being. They are not nothing, but participate in the good of being. There is that which is not God, and that which is not God *is*. But the being of created things is had by the divine gift, or *per participationem*.[36] The viability of the idea of "participation" depends upon its not being deployed in such a way as to threaten the distinction between uncreated and created being which is basic to the concept of creation.[37] Participation does not imply, for example, that the act of creation is simply a natural process of emanation, diffusion or dispersal of divine substance. "Creatures . . . are not born of God [*non de Deo nata*] but made by God out of nothing."[38] Rather, participation is theologically to be understood in terms of the operation of creative benevolence, and so in terms of the *differentiated* sharing of creator and creature in the good of being, each in their proper order and mode. By the work of divine love, finite things come to share in the universal good of being, but only in a finite manner, and only as they stand in relation to the creator God, the source of being. This relation *constitutes* creatures. Every element of creaturely being and action is what it is in "the very dependency of the created act of being upon the principle from which it is produced."[39] There is, therefore, a *depth* to created things. To consider them, we have to understand not only their finite causes but the first cause, tracing them back to their source, which is God. Creatures have being as *principiata*, as effects of God, their *principium*. The movement by which we understand how creatures participate in being is this: "we trace everything that possesses something by sharing, as to its source and cause, to what possesses that thing essentially . . . But . . . God is his very existing. And so existing belongs to him by his essence, and existing belongs to other things by participation. For the essence of everything else is not its existing, since there can be only one existing that is absolutely and intrinsically subsisting . . . Therefore, God necessarily causes existing in everything that exists."[40]

---

[35] Norman Kretzmann, *The Metaphysics of Creation: Aquinas's Natural Theology in* Summa Contra Gentiles II (Oxford: Clarendon Press, 1999), pp. 70–100.

[36] Aquinas, *Summa Theologiae* (London: Blackfriars, 1975), Ia.104.1 ad 1.

[37] On this, see Rudi te Velde, *Participation and Substantiality in Thomas Aquinas* (Leiden: E. J. Brill, 1995); idem., *Aquinas on God: The "Divine Science" of the* Summa Theologiae (Aldershot: Ashgate, 2006), pp. 123–146.

[38] Augustine, *Unfinished Literal Commentary on Genesis* in *On Genesis*, I.

[39] Aquinas, *Summa Contra Gentiles* II.18.2.

[40] Aquinas, *Compendium of Theology*, §68.

5. *What does creation out of nothing indicate about the relation of God and creatures?* Creation is an operation of generosity on the part of one who in his inner trinitarian life is wholly realised, satisfied and at rest. God gains nothing and loses nothing by the existence or non-existence of creatures, having "no need for the things he created" since he is "perfectly happy within himself."[41] Without this—seemingly austere but in reality entirely delightful—affirmation, the entire conceptual and spiritual structure of teaching about creation out of nothing collapses. It may be explicated by speaking of the relation of creator and creature as a mixed relation, real (constitutive) on the side of the creature but not on the side of the creator. Such entire inequality ought not to be considered a denial of the creator's relation to created things: God loves, and in providence and reconciliation acts towards, that which he causes to be. Rather, a double assertion is being made. First, the creator is radically incomposite. As the cause of finite being, God is not one term or agent in a set of interactions, not a "coeval, co-finite being",[42] but unqualifiedly simple and in himself replete. Second, to deny that God bears a "real" relation to created things is to characterise the *kind* of relation which he has to creatures, one in which God is "in himself his own beatitude . . . all-sufficient to himself and needing not the things he made."[43]

With this, we begin to touch on the anxiety that the relation of created things to the creator is such that they have no honour.

III

Classical Christian doctrines of creation out of nothing furnished the theological and metaphysical principles for a positive evaluation of created things, an evaluation given material intensification by faith's contemplation of the mysteries of providence and redemption. That absolute creatureliness should be such a good is no longer self-evident to us. In his *System of Christian Doctrine*—which contains what is surely one of the most discerning treatments of the Christian doctrine of creation of the last two centuries—the great mediating dogmatician, Izaak Dorner, set out an account of God the triune creator as "the fount of all existence and life", one having "power, in unison with his love which ever tends towards reality, to impart to his ideal creations substantive existence, and make them stand forth in independent being."[44] But the

---

[41] Aquinas, *Summa Theologiae* Ia.73.2 resp.

[42] David Braine, *The Reality of Time and the Existence of God: The Project of Proving God's Existence* (Oxford: Clarendon Press, 1988), p. 352.

[43] Aquinas, *On the Power of God*, translated by the English Dominican fathers (London: Burns, Oates and Washbourne, 1932), IV.2 ad 5.

[44] Izaak A. Dorner, *A System of Christian Doctrine*, translated by Rev. Prof. Alfred Cave and Rev. Prof. J.S. Banks (Edinburgh: T&T Clark, 1881), vol. 2, p. 39.

tradition from which Dorner spoke was already well in retreat, its terms having largely lost their suppleness and explanatory power, and its spiritual appeal having waned. What has happened?

In the preface to the *Proslogion*, Anselm spoke of God as *summum bonum nullo alio indigens*, the one whom *omnia indigent ut sint et ut bene sint*, (supreme good requiring nothing else, which all other things require for their existence and well-being). Such an understanding of the divine nature, extended by teaching about *creatio ex nihilo*, seems to drain created things of value. It does so, first, because it appears to consign creatures to a state of permanent indigence, wholly contingent upon God for origination and continuance; second, because the creator's perfection is entirely untouched by their existence or non-existence; third, because no relation exists between creator and creature save one of radical inequality in which the creature gives, and the creator receives, nothing. In effect, *creatio ex nihilo* brings with it a metaphysic of privation: to be a creature is to be humiliated, devoid of integrity or power of self-movement or self-subsistence, and so lacking intrinsic worth. To be *ex nihilo* is to be (almost, apart from the gratuitous act of divine causation) *nihil*.

The objection is at once speculative and practical. In attempting to unravel it, theology has both dogmatic-historical and spiritual-ascetic tasks. The requisite dogmatic-historical work consists in making Christian specifications of the identity of God the creator, his creative act and his creatures, deploying these to shed light on the historical course of the objection. Theology asks: at what points in the history of theological, metaphysical and moral-political thought have exponents or critics of Christian doctrine in some measure missed the rhythm of teaching about creation out of nothing, lost heart about its fruitfulness or wholesomeness, and felt themselves therefore at liberty or obliged to compromise the matter of Christian doctrine? In what ways and with what results has an evangelical metaphysics of creation been harassed or replaced by one owing no allegiance to the gospel? More particularly: in what ways do mutations in ways in which the natural and human orders are understood, and in which human life is enacted, derive from and reinforce distorted understandings of the creator? "[E]rrors about creatures", Aquinas remarks, "sometimes lead one astray from the truth of faith, so far as the errors are inconsistent with true knowledge of God."[45] Illuminating such "errors" is the dogmatic-historical task of theology.

The second, spiritual-ascetic, task consists in theology's occupancy and promotion of a spiritual climate in which the force of the objection can be diminished and the persuasiveness of gospel teaching commended. Intelligence follows love, and love is nourished by habits of life by which goods are sought out and made matters of delight. When love is faint, it must be kindled, and one of the tasks of theology—not its only task, but by no means

---

[45] Aquinas, *Summa Contra Gentiles* II.3.1.

its least—is to assist in the kindling of love and love's intelligence. It can only do this, however, when it is itself a work of religion, of faith instructed by and adhering to *this* God who works *thus*. In a theological culture in which such instruction and adherence are lived realities, anxiety or resentment about the creaturely condition may find relief.

Apprehensiveness that creation *ex nihilo* entails creaturely ignominy is both a cultural-historical condition and a spiritual malaise; theology cannot separate these. The cultural-historical factors demand exquisite inquiry, examining, for example, shifts in conceptions of motion inaugurated in the early modern period, initially in the philosophy of nature and derivatively in conceptions of human being and action. The shifts would include a narrowing of divine causality to efficient causality; decline of appeal to final causality in the explanation of nature, or the reorientation of final causality to human, not divine, purposes; a sense that natural motion is self-contained, not requiring talk of God's creative and providential operations to render it intelligible; in short, the retraction of the concept of a divine *source* for natural and human movement.[46] Alongside this, attention would need to be directed to loss of confidence in the explanatory power and innocence of appeal to first principles in making the natural and human world intelligible.[47] Appeal to *principia* rests in part upon a sense that the world is a *principiatum*—not just a given state of affairs but that which is what it is by virtue of its relation to its source—and in part upon trust that this source is benign plenitude. When this double assent is absent, the *principium* becomes that to which the *principiatum* can be reduced, broken down and so evacuated of substance. Of such destructive reduction, *creatio ex nihilo* may be judged the primary instance. Corresponding to shifts in causality and in the explanatory value of first principles is a loss of a sense of the interiority of things, that is, of the need for intelligence to penetrate through the surfaces of things in order to perceive that by which they are constituted. In the case of human creatures, interiority—a basic concomitant of creatureliness—is edged out by reflexivity in which human consciousness is, as Michael Buckley puts it, both its own source and its own term.[48]

These are crude characterisations, no more than an agenda for analytical work. The analysis would try to discover how there has arisen a condition in which the axiom *aut gloria Dei aut gloria homini* has gathered such cultural

---

[46] See here James A. Weisheipl, *Nature and Motion in the Middle Ages* (Washington, DC: Catholic University Press of America, 1985); Richard Sorabji, *Matter, Space, and Motion: Theories in Antiquity and their Sequel* (London: Duckworth, 1988); Simon Oliver, *Philosophy, God and Motion* (London: Routledge, 2005).

[47] On this, see Alasdair C. MacIntyre, *First Principles, Final Ends and Contemporary Philosophical Issues* (Milwaukee, WI: Marquette University Press, 1990), and especially the remarkable set of analytical exercises in Kenneth L. Schmitz, *The Texture of Being: Essays in First Philosophy*, edited by Paul O'Herron, (Washington, DC: Catholic University Press of America, 2007), esp. pp. 21–73.

[48] Michael J. Buckley, *Denying and Disclosing God: The Ambiguous Progress of Modern Atheism* (New Haven, CT: Yale University Press, 2004), p. 84.

authority, one in which God and creatures are natural antagonists, "two units in a symmetrical or asymmetrical relationship, each poised in such contradiction that one must sink if the other is to rise."[49] Theology will, however, go further. Errors about creatures are symptomatic of spiritual disorder, the entry of some evil into the creature's relation to God. Thinking about the world and ourselves in relation to God as source and sustainer is always a way of disposing ourselves in relation to God; *nolens volens* it always takes up an attitude. This is not to reduce thought to passion (a vulgar polemical trick), but rather to say that thought may not be detached from religion and religious failure manifest as mistrust, resentment, impatience, pride, love of some untruth. We may not exclude the possibility of *caecitas mentis*; we may need the healing and illumination of intelligence if we are to know and love our created condition.

As theology displays how it can be that creation out of nothing is not a matter of the creature's dispossession but rather the conferral of good, it begins from its principal part, the doctrine of God, determinations of the creator's identity and act constituting the ground on which all else rests.

Creation is a work of wholly adequate love. Part of this love's adequacy is its voluntary character: it is fully spontaneous and self-original, nothing more than God's will being required for creatures to come to be. But creative divine volition is not caprice but purpose, direction of entire capacity to another's good; and it is purposive *love*, most of all because this other does not antecede the gift of its own being but receives the gift of life from God. Love *gives* life, and love gives *life*. In willing to create, God wills the realisation of life which is not his own: "Love is also a lover of life".[50] Only God can do this; only God can bring about a life which is derived yet possessed of intrinsic substance and worth. Because God is not one being and agent alongside others, and because he is in himself entirely realised and possesses perfect bliss, he has nothing to gain from creating. Precisely in the absence of divine self-interest, the creature gains everything; *because of* (not *in spite of*) the non-reciprocal character of the relation of creator and creature, the creature has integrity. "[T]he creatureliness of the creature (the received condition) is not a nullity, but is rather the ingress of the creature into being, so that, on the basis of that ingress, can be seen the absolute *nihil* that was the creature's nonontological predecessor. The creature is *ex nihilo*, that is, it stands *outside of* absolute privation by virtue of the creative generosity. The creative generosity is the ground of the absolute inequality between creator and creature, that very inequality that has raised the threat to the creature's integrity. But that very creative generosity is also the ground for the very being of the creature."[51] Benevolent love establishes and safeguards the integrity of the beings which it creates.

---

[49] Buckley, *Denying and Disclosing God*, p. 94.
[50] Dorner, *A System of Christian Doctrine*, vol. 2, p. 15.
[51] Schmitz, *The Gift: Creation* (Milwaukee, WI: Marquette University Press, 1982), p. 74.

Created integrity includes created act. God creates *agentia ordinem habentia*, "subordinated active things".[52] How do we free ourselves of the habit—spiritual as much as intellectual—of opposing (at least in our own case) subordination and proper agency? By reflecting on the character of God's creative action. In establishing another thing in being, God bestows finality, a tendency or active bent and movement towards the completion of that thing's nature. This bent and movement is an effect of God's initial donation of being, and is held and stirred by God's maintaining and governing presence to the creature. God is "in all things in the manner of an agent cause."[53] It is just at this point that scrupulous consideration (contemplation) of the divine creative action may not be relaxed. There is an over-extension of the concept of God as cause of being and action (and a consequent over-extension of the creature's causal dependence upon God) according to which "no creature has an active role in the production of natural effects".[54] To this, Aquinas advances four objections, each arising from attentiveness to the divine attributes, and, in particular, from a belief that anxieties about debasement of creatures may stem from insufficient consideration of what might be called the perfecting effect of God's perfection.

First, such is the divine wisdom that in its products there is nothing useless, no sheerly passive and redundant creature. "[I]t is contrary to the rational character of wisdom for there to be any thing useless in the activities of the possessor of wisdom. But, if created things could in no way operate to produce their effects, and if God alone worked all operations immediately, these other things would be employed in a useless way by him, for the production of these effects."[55] Second, in communicating his likeness to creatures, the creator communicates not only being but a proportionate agency: "if [God] has communicated his likeness, as far as actual being is concerned, to other things, by virtue of the fact that he has brought things into being, it follows that he has communicated his likeness, as far as acting is concerned, so that created things may also have their own actions."[56] Third—this is the most telling argument—perfect power communicates perfection, including perfection of action: "the perfection of the effect demonstrates the perfection of the cause, for a greater power brings about a more perfect effect. But God is the most perfect agent. Therefore, things created by him obtain perfection from him. So, to detract from the perfection of the creature is to detract from the perfection of divine power. But, if no creature has any active role in the production of any effect, much is detracted from the perfection of the creature. Indeed, it is part of the fullness of perfection to be able to communicate

---

[52] Aquinas, *Compendium of Theology*, §103.
[53] Aquinas, *Summa Contra Gentiles* III.68.12.
[54] Aquinas, *Summa Contra Gentiles* III.69.1.
[55] Aquinas, *Summa Contra Gentiles* III.69.13.
[56] Aquinas, *Summa Contra Gentiles* III.69.14.

to another being the perfection one possesses. Therefore, this position detracts from the divine power."[57] Perfect power does not absorb, exclude or overwhelm and dispossess other dependent powers and agents, but precisely the opposite: omnipotent power creates and perfects creaturely capacity and movement. Exclusive power is less than perfect, and falls short of divinity. Fourth, as the highest good God makes "what is best";[58] the creatures of such a God therefore share in the self-communicative, active goodness of their creator. "God so communicates his goodness to created beings that one thing which receives it can transfer it to another. Therefore, to take away their proper action from things is to disparage the divine goodness."[59]

In short, to attribute all created effects to God as omnicausal is not to rob creatures of their proper action, because what God in his perfect wisdom, power and goodness causes is creatures who are themselves causes. The idea whose spell must be broken is that God is a supremely forceful agent in the same order of being as creatures, acting upon them and so depriving them of movement. What Aquinas commends here—something which Barth also reached towards in his theology of covenant and of God's evocation of active human partners—is that the plenitude of God apart from creatures does not entail the thought of God's segregation as sole cause, but rather the opposite: God's perfection is seen also in bringing into being other agents. God bestows being and activity; this is part of the special sense of creation out of nothing in the Christian confession.

Such specifications in theology proper show that affirmation of the world's integrity of being and movement does not require denial of creatureliness. All that is not God is out of nothing, and its existence is sheerly gratuitous, non-necessary. From God's creative act there arises a condition of "absolute unconditioned inequality" in which God the donor of being is "the founder of the entire order within which the giver gives and the recipient receives".[60] Such inequality—so runs our anxious argumentation—humiliates the creature, because without genuine diversity of being and capacity for action there can be no relations of dignity. In the absence of Christian characterisations of the creator, this would be so—if, for example, divine creative action were reduced to continuous retrieval of creatures from nothingness and not understood as bestowal of being, or if absolute contingency were all that needed to be said about creatureliness. But the creator, once again, is benevolent and gives *being*: to be from nothing is not to be nothing but to *be*, instituted as an integral order of reality and given the capacity for operation.

From this may be drawn a double assertion about created acts. First, no created thing is the principle of its own action; the creature is a *moved* mover.

---

[57] Aquinas, *Summa Contra Gentiles* III.69.15.
[58] Aquinas, *Summa Contra Gentiles* III.69.16.
[59] Aquinas, *Summa Contra Gentiles* III.69.16.
[60] Schmitz, *The Gift: Creation*, pp. 62f.

In the order of operation no less than in the order of being, the creature possesses no capability for pure self-origination. "Created act is a received act."[61] This is so because created substance is "determined in and through its radical participation in and relation to the Source of its existence. The supposit of the creature does not stand in any way 'outside' of or 'prior' to the ontological relation, not even as a possibility, but is brought into being within that relation."[62] *Sicut ars praesupponit naturam, ita natura praesupponit Deum . . . Ergo et Deus in operatione naturae operator.*[63] Second, the creature is a moved *mover*. God who is the creature's principle is the creature's source; not an abyss into which the creature tumbles, but one who in conferring being also bequeaths act. The relation of creatureliness includes "nonpassive receptivity",[64] a given capacity for becoming through the enactment of created life.

The reality and dignity of created act does not eradicate the non-reciprocal character of the creator-creature relation, but rather indicates that that relation is not malign. That which is *ex nihilo* and has being by divine gift adds nothing to what is uncreated; even after it has come into being, the creature is not a reality to which God is "other", some correlate in a common order. Just because this is so, the creator does not displace the creature. To be created out of nothing is not to suffer deprivation but to be given a nature whose performance will certainly involve acts of courage and may include—for example—magnanimity and magnificence, the extension of spirit to great things, the performance of some great work.

---

[61] Schmitz, *The Texture of Being*, p. 125.
[62] Schmitz, *The Texture of Being*, p. 128.
[63] Aquinas, *De potentia* in *Quaestiones Disputatae* II, edited by P. Bazzi, (Turin: Marietti, 1965), III.7 s.c. 2. "Just as art presupposes nature, so does nature presuppose God. . . . Therefore God also operates in the operation of nature."
[64] Schmitz, *The Texture of Being*, p. 196.

Modern Theology 29:2 April 2013
ISSN 0266-7177 (Print)
ISSN 1468-0025 (Online)

CREATION AND THE GLORY OF CREATURES

JANET MARTIN SOSKICE

Near the Coliseum in Rome stands the Basilica of San Clemente, a medieval church built upon the ruins of a fourth century basilica. It is the apse of the medieval church that concerns us here for it contains a Byzantine mosaic, dating from between 1110–1130 CE, depicting the Tree of Life or (it is the same thing to the mosaic artist) the cross of Christ. The crucified Christ rests peacefully on a dark cross, eyes shut, flanked by Mary the Mother of God and St. John. Standard so far but less so are the twelve doves which adorn the cross: these are the Apostles, also represented as rams flanking the Lamb of God in the border below. But the real energy of the image of the cross springs, literally and figuratively, from the side of Christ. A stream of blood falls down his pierced side to fill a fountain that overflows into four streams which are the rivers of paradise. From these deer are drinking (Psalm 42.1 "As a deer longs for flowing streams so my soul longs for you, O God."). The cross seems to stand planted in the fountain but, while it is a cross, it is also a great tree. From the living water at its base grows a vine, an acanthus, which fills the golden space of the apse. The tendrils of the vine unfold in voluptuous array, each coiling around a mosaic vignette—in one a man tends cattle, in another a woman feeds chickens. The vines embrace wild nesting birds (many of these) who feed their young, and also a cleric (supposedly St. Augustine) who writes in a book.

It is an image of the new creation, not of heaven so much as this world made harmonious and whole. The Byzantine artist has provided a vision of salvation construed, as etymologically it should be, as *salus*: health, flourishing and well-being. The space of the apse is finite but these tendrils could

Janet Martin Soskice
Jesus College, Cambridge CB5 8BL, UK
Email: jcs16@cam.ac.uk

extend without limit, making nests for all of life, each in its particularity. I would like to keep this image in mind as I turn to the topic of *creatio ex nihilo*.

In an essay on creation in the Psalms, James Mays writes, somewhat acerbically, that "creation" in the sense as commonly used today is not a notion that appears in the Psalms:

> the term has come to mean no more than the natural world in the vocabulary of New Age religion, nature romanticism, environmental enthusiasm, artistic aestheticism, and even in unselfconscious traditional religion and liberal piety. There is no term or text in the Psalms, or indeed in the entire Bible, for creation in this sense.[1]

If slightly overdrawn his point is well taken—creation in the Bible is about an activity and the outcome of the activity, and the "actor who creates is always Yahweh."[2] The doctrine of creation as found in the writings of the early Christians is also not about animals and birds. It is not about "nature", at least not primarily, but about God. As in the Psalms "creation" is both the activity of God and the outcome of God's activity. We need as modern readers to avoid an easy equivalence of "nature" and "creation", not least because modern secular writers readily speak of "creation" when they have no intent of implying the existence of a Creator. Conceptually "creation" implies a "Creator", whereas "nature" does not. Indeed some early modern writers preferred to use the term "nature" (suggesting a free-standing, autonomous whole) to get away from the idea of a Creator. By contrast and in reaction the seventeenth-century Rabbi David Nieto, leader of London's Sephardic community, insisted that Jews believed in divine creation and not in a "Universal Nature".[3]

It should be added that the developed theology of creation does not come from the Book of Genesis, or not from Genesis alone. Despite their reference to the biblical texts, the Rabbis and the theologians of the early Church seemed uninterested about any story of cosmic origins involving a literal six days (most in fact rejected this since the sun and the moon were only created on the fourth day so, they reckoned, the "days" could not be days in our sense.) The guiding citations are more frequently from the Psalms and the Book of Isaiah, writings which repeatedly link God's power to create with his power to save. Here are some examples:

> "Our help is in the name of the LORD, who made heaven and earth" (Ps. 124.8)

---

[1] James L. Mays, "'Maker of Heaven and Earth': Creation in the Psalms" in William P. Brown and S. Dean McBride (eds.), *God Who Creates* (Grand Rapids, MI: Wm. B. Eerdmans Publishing Company, 2000), p. 75.

[2] Loc. cit.

[3] See José Faur, *Golden Doves with Silver Dots: Semiotics and Textuality in Rabbinic Tradition* (Bloomington, IN: Indiana University Press, 1986), pp. 18ff.

"By the word of the LORD the heavens were made.
And all their host by the breath of his mouth . . .
Let all the earth fear the Lord;
   let all the inhabitants of the world stand in awe of him.
For he spoke, and it come to be;
   he commanded, and it stood firm. (Ps. 33.6–9)

Praise him, sun and moon;
   Praise him, all you shining stars!
Praise him, you highest heavens and you waters above the heavens!
Let them praise the name of the LORD
   for he commanded and they were created. (Ps. 148.3–5)

Shower, O heavens, from above,
   and let the skies rain down righteousness;
Let the earth open, that salvation may spring up,
and let it cause righteousness to sprout up also:
I the LORD have created it. (Is. 45.8)

It is worth noting that the Psalms and Isaiah are the biblical texts most frequently cited by both Qumran and by the New Testament writings.

We know that the period of Second Temple Judaism was a time of upheaval and distress for the Jews. Foreign domination coincided with a foment of Messianic expectation. There were debates about the coming of the Messiah and the faithfulness of God to creation and here the Psalms were perceived to be to the point. It is not surprising that texts from inter-testamental literature contain what seems to be the first clear expression of the doctrine of *creatio ex nihilo* which I will define, for present purposes, as the teaching that God has created all that is, including matter, space and time, and has done so freely out of love.

In II Maccabees (a text hostile to Hellenism but written in excellent Greek) the mother of the seven martyred sons encourages them to lay down their lives saying,

I do not know how you came into being in my womb. It was not I who gave you life and breath, nor I who set in order the elements within each of you. Therefore the Creator of the world, who shaped the beginning of humankind and devised the origin of all things, will in his mercy give life and breath back to you again, since you now forget yourselves for the sake of his laws. (2 Macc. 7.22–23)

From a people in tribulation come texts that speak of deliverance, of a God who created and who can re-create, a God who gave life and who can restore life. These are also the first of the Jewish writings where we see consideration of the resurrection of the dead, a question still debated by the Sadducees and the Pharisees in the time of Jesus. In the same story from 2 Maccabees the mother of the youngest brother, last to go to his death, leans towards him and says in their native language (presumably Aramaic),

> I beg you, my child, to look at the heaven and the earth, consider and see everything that is in them, and recognize that God did not make them out of things that existed. And in the same way the human race came into being. Do not fear this butcher, but prove worthy of your brothers. Accept death, so that in God's mercy I may get you back again along with your brothers. (2 Macc.7.28–29)

The implication is that the God who made "all that is" can surely raise the dead, an argument found later in Islam. Resurrection involves the power to give life, to restore. In the books of the New Testament resurrection is linked to the promise of a new creation that, like the first, is made by God's Word.

We have, then, in II Maccabees, and in the Psalms and Isaiah, powerful reflections on creation. Whether, however, this is *creatio ex nihilo* will depend on how that teaching is defined. A good deal of the debate on "how early?" and "how Jewish?" is *creatio ex nihilo* has revolved around the question of matter— did God create it? when was it insisted that God created matter?, and how much did the ancient sages really worry about the question? The first chapters of Genesis could be read, and were read, by some Jewish and Christian writers in antiquity as suggesting God created out of "something" that already existed—some primordial element—or out of matter (*ex hyles*). Interpretation of the Hebrew *tohu wa-bohu* of Genesis 1–2 was, and remains, contested.[4]

Another inter-testamental text, the Wisdom of Solomon, speaks of God's "all powerful hand, which created the world out of formless matter" (Wis.11.17). Does this suggest *creatio ex hyles* or, alternatively, since it was written in Greek, might it be a gloss on the Septuagint's rendering of *tohu wa bohu* with two Greek alpha-privatives, "And the earth was invisible and unstructured"? It certainly seemed open to Jews reading Hebrew scriptures, and to Jews and Christians reading the Greek of the Septuagint, to see Genesis describing God as creating from "something", a view especially congenial for readers versed in Plato's *Timaeus* where the demiurge moulds a pre-existing matter. Enough early Christian thinkers may have been drawn to the platonic notion that God moulds creation out of pre-existing elements for Origen (c. 185–284) to have expressed himself with exasperation against this view in his *First Principles*.[5] However the most reasonable conclusion to

---

[4] See Menahem Kister, *"Tohu wa-Bohu,* Primordial Elements and *Creatio ex Nihilo"*, *Jewish Studies Quarterly*, Vol. 14 (2007), pp. 229–256.

[5] "In regard then to this matter, which is so great and wonderful as to be sufficient for all the bodies in the world, which God willed to exist ... I cannot understand how so many distinguished men have supposed it to be uncreated, that is, not made by God himself the Creator of all things, but in its nature and power the result of chance." *Origen on First Principles*, trans. G.W.

draw about the ambiguity of *from nothing/from something* in Greek Jewish texts of this period is that this was just not something that had begun to trouble them.[6] It will become a point of pain for Christians in the second century, as Paul Gavrilyuk discusses in his article in this issue, when countering Gnostic suggestions that matter was evil, recalcitrant or outside the purposes of God.

What we can say with certainty is that from early on the Jews believed in a God who was a free and loving Creator, and that this distinguished their accounts of origin from those of Plato and Aristotle.[7] The earliest theology of creation seems to be, like the language of the Psalms, confessional and doxological, underscoring the freedom, power and goodness of God. Such is still the tone of the New Testament and of the first- and second-century Christian fathers for whom belief in God, Creator of heaven and earth, is a *central confession*, as it would be in the Creeds.[8]

The striking and distinctive teaching we call *creatio ex nihilo* has many strands and was subject to many developments from the inter-testamental period through to the middle ages and the decisive writings of Moses Maimonides and Thomas Aquinas. It is not a teaching of Greek philosophy. Aristotle thought it absurd: from nothing, nothing can come. God and the universe were both everlasting in Aristotle's scheme, and corollaries of each other. There could not be the universe without God, nor could there be God without the universe. In Jewish and Christian teaching, by contrast, God need not have created at all. Aristotle's God is the cause of motion, but not the cause of beings. Plato's demiurge moulds a pre-existing matter. That God made "all that is" and did so from no compulsion but freely out of love seems to emerge distinctly from Judaism and early Christianity in defence of a conception of God who has made and cares for all things. It is a rupture in ancient cosmology. The Creator, moreover, is called upon as Saviour in time of distress.

Butterworth, (London: S.P.C.K., 1936), p. 79. Origen may just be addressing pagan philosophical opponents, of course.

[6] This is the view of Gerhard May who writes that Hellenistic-Jewish philosophy expressed the omnipotence of God and his role as creator, but "did not engage in a fundamental debate with the Platonic and Stoic doctrine of principles. And so it could not develop a doctrine of *creatio ex nihilo*. The statements about creation of non-being or from non-being . . . are not to be understood as antitheses to an eternal matter and to the principle of 'ex nihil nihil fit' but to be considered as an unreflective, everyday way of saying that through the act of creation something arose which did not previously exist. As soon as it was freely recognised that creation by the biblical God was more than the forming of matter, that he brought forth the world in sovereign freedom and without any external conditions, the expression 'Creation out of nothing' offered itself as a formula pregnant to describe the particular character of the biblical concept of creation." Gerhard May, *Creatio ex Nihilo*, trans. A.S. Worrall, (Edinburgh: T&T Clark, 1994), p. 21.

[7] I would say, too, from later "middle" and "neoplatonists". See below.

[8] On this see Gavrilyuk, op. cit., and also the excellent article on "Doctrine of Creation" by Paul M. Blowers in *The Oxford Handbook of Early Christian Studies*, eds. Susan Ashbrook Harvey and David G. Hunter (Oxford: Oxford University Press, 2008).

Happy are those whose help is in the God of Jacob,
whose hope is in the LORD their God,
who made heaven and earth,
the sea, and all that is in them;
who keeps faith forever;
who executes justice for the oppressed;
who gives food to the hungry. (Psalm 146.5–7)

The One who creates can redeem. The Psalms repeatedly link God's creative and saving power to the story of the Exodus and the crossing of the Red Sea.

Gerhard May, the doyenne of students of *creatio ex nihilo*, insists that this teaching is really only fully established in Christian writings of the second century, driven by controversies with Gnosticism. May's analysis, however, revolves around the question of the creation of matter, only one of the aspects of *creatio ex nihilo*.[9] If, as it seems on May's own analysis, the question of where matter came from didn't much concern earlier thinkers, it might be better to look to alternatives. If we make our focus the sovereignty and freedom of God in creating, and the idea that all creatures have their being by God, we might find clues to another pre-history for the teaching. And here Philo makes an interesting study.

Philo is a Greek-speaking Jew of first-century Alexandria, a contemporary of Jesus and Paul but with no apparent knowledge of them or the infant Christian movement. There had been significant Jewish populations in Alexandria, probably since its foundation as a "new town" by Alexander the Great in 331 BC, and they were (like all the city's inhabitants) Greek-speaking. It is thought that the books of the Hebrew scriptures were translated into Greek (becoming what we call the Septuagint) for the needs of this Alexandrian Jewish population. Philo was wealthy and well educated in Greek philosophy and, like some of the earliest Christian writers, feels little tension between his Jewish faith and the Greek philosophical writings he has been brought up in. In fact he thinks Plato is correct on many points not least because Plato has, through some obscure means, learned from Moses.[10] He knows Plato's *Timaeus* and invokes it in his own commentary on the book of *Genesis*.

However Philo is not in his own terms a philosopher. He writes as an exegete of the Jewish scriptures that he, like St. Paul, reads in Greek. His writings are all extended commentaries on Scripture, heavily informed by

---

[9] May speaks of the "decisive basis of the doctrine of *creatio ex nihilo*, that the biblical conception of God demands that matter also be created." *Op.*cit., p. 15.

[10] Some pagan philosophers of this period also believed Plato had learned from Moses. John Dillon writes, "Philo may well have been acquainted with that part of the Pythagoras legend that we find evidence of much later in Iamblichus," *Life of Pythagoras* (14), according to which Pythagoras spends a while in Palestine "consorting with the descendants of *Mochos* the prophet and philosopher". John Dillon, *The Middle Platonists* (London: Duckworth, 1977), p. 143.

Hellenistic thought.[11] Philo is interesting to us because we see in play in his writings all the principles central to the doctrine of divine transcendence that is enshrined by *creatio ex nihilo*.

Philo is widely held either not to hold to *creatio ex nihilo* or to be inconsistent on it, especially when it comes to the status of matter. Gerhard May thinks Philo "postulates a pre-existent matter alongside God", moulding a matter which verges on the malign.[12] On May's reading Philo, though not a dualist who posits matter as "an ontologically equal principle alongside God", nonetheless "took over the Greek teaching about pre-existent matter, without thinking it through independently".[13] The picture is of someone who has not yet absorbed the implications of a particular received (Platonic) belief for the teaching about the sovereignty of God to which he is committed.

But if the doctrine of creation was in flux in this time, then so too was Greek philosophy. As already mentioned neither Plato nor Aristotle conceived of a Creator God. For instance, in Aristotle's scheme there could be no world without God, but equally no God without the world. This changed in the period we know as "middle" or "eclectic" Platonism, the period during which Philo and the New Testament authors wrote. A varied mixture of Stoic, Aristotelian and neo-Pythagorean ideas, led Platonists of this period to posit a belief in a One who was the source of the many, a position much more amenable to Jews and Christians, and most fully worked out by the third century Neo-Platonist, Plotinus.

Philo can be called a Middle-Platonist, for such is his philosophical formation, but only at the risk of thinking of him principally as a philosopher. In his own terms Philo was an exegete of Scriptures. It was always Scripture that were his primary authority, and he was jealous for what he believed those Scriptures told him of God. So when John Dillon writes that all Philo brings to the Middle Platonic mix "is a distinctive streak of Jewish piety, a greater personal reverence for God than one would expect to find in a Greek philosopher" . . . (which) "also leads on occasion to a downgrading of the ability of the human intellect (unaided by God's grace) to comprehend truth" our ears should prick up for, as I shall argue, it is this "greater reverence for God", which we might understand as a greatly enhanced sense of divine transcendence, which will prove so important.[14]

---

[11] In this Philo and the Jews of Alexandria were by no means alone. In Philo's time Greek was the working language of the eastern Roman Empire. Paul's native language was Greek and there were Greek-speaking cities in Judaea and Galilee. By the time of Philo, Paul and the New Testament writings, "Greek rhetoric, philosophy and literature were the stable of elite education", including that of elite Jews. See Tessa Rajak, *Translation and Survival: The Greek Bible of the Ancient Jewish Diaspora* (Oxford: Oxford University Press, 2009), pp. 94–95.

[12] Op.cit., p. 10.

[13] Ibid., p. 15, p 12.

[14] Dillon, *The Middle Platonists*, p. 155.

Philo wrote a commentary, known to us as *de Opficio Mundi* (On the Creation of the Cosmos), on the first books of Genesis. In this he posits, as do other Middle-Platonists, a double creation in which God creates an "intelligible" cosmos which is the model for the "sense perceptible" cosmos. Things are further complicated by his insistence that the "intelligible" cosmos is not chronologically prior to the "sense-perceptible" one, since God does not create in time. Philo believes creation is instantaneous and the "days" of creation are a figurative way in which Moses, whom he takes to be the author of Genesis, speaks.[15] Even in this work Philo seems not so much interested in physical cosmogony (far less in anything approaching modern cosmology) than in laying down a picture of God as Creator of the world and its order. The ordering of the "days" of Genesis he understands as a figurative means (since creation is "simultaneous") by which Moses anticipates the "ordering" given by the Law at Sinai. In this work Philo persistently stresses that God as Creator is one, and that God alone creates.[16]

The expressions that border on *creatio ex nihilo* are voiced in Philo, more often than not, when his topic is the sovereignty of God and thus often in contrast to the philosophers: "God, being One, is alone and unique, and like God there is nothing" (*Leg.II.1*). Here are just a few more of Philo's views: God has created the world out of non-existence. All things are dependent on God, but God is sufficient to himself and was so before the creation of the world.[17] He creates from his goodness and governs what he creates. He does not change or alter. God, says Philo, "created space and place coincidentally with the material world" (*Conf.* 136). God created time itself, "For there was no time before the cosmos, but rather it either came into existence together with the cosmos or after it (*de Opficio Mundi* §26).[18] In concluding *On the Creation of the Cosmos according to Moses* he attacks Aristotle, saying that one of the beautiful lessons taught us by Moses is that "the cosmos has come into existence", a teaching especially important "on account of those who think it is ungenerated and eternal, attributing no superiority to God" (*de Opfic.* §171; see also §7).

---

[15] See Runia's commentary to Philo's *On the Creation of the Cosmos according to Moses*, pp. 132–133.

[16] See David Runia, "Plato's *Timaeus*, First Principle(s), and Creation" in ed. Gretchen J. Reydams-Schils, *Plato's Timaeus as Cultural Icon* (Notre Dame, IN: University of Notre Dame Press, 2003), p. 137.

[17] "How must it not be impossible to recompense or to praise as He deserves Him who brought the universe out of non-existence?" (L.A.III.10). "He is full of Himself and sufficient for Himself. It was so before the creation of the world, and is equally so after the creation of all that is. He cannot change nor alter and needs nothing else at all, so that all things are His but He Himself in the proper sense belongs to no one" (de Mut. IV.27). "Through His goodness He begat all that is, through His sovereignty He rules what he has begotten" (de Cher. 27–28). See also Fug 46, Moses II.267.

[18] Philo, *On the Creation of the Cosmos according to Moses*, introduction, translation and commentary by David T. Runia (Atlanta, GA: Society of Biblical Literature, 2001). See Runia's comment on this on p. 157.

My own interest in Philo came first not from what he had to say about God as Creator but what he had to say about naming God. This turned out to revolve entirely around his elevated ideas of divine transcendence. For Philo, God is strictly speaking "unnameable" and indeed Philo is our earliest source for a number of divine epithets that relate to this. John Dillon says "At *Somn.* 1 67, for example, God is described as 'unnameable' (*akatanomastos*) and 'unutterable' (*arrhetos*) and incomprehensible under any form (*kata pasas ideas akataleptos*), none of which terms are applied to God before his time by any surviving source."[19]

Since God is Creator and not a creature, God cannot strictly *be like* any created being. It follows that we cannot *class* God or insert God into any category appropriate to our created kind. On the other hand, and equally from his Jewish faith, Philo knows that God must not be left in the realms of abstraction. The God of the Pentateuch is personal and providential. In attempting to bridge this gap between the God who is totally *unlike* all created, finite beings and yet who is nonetheless present to us in the intimacy of disclosure, Philo anticipates a problem central to what is sometimes called mystical or negative theology but which I prefer to call the theology of the divine names. For if we say that God is "wholly Other", we must explain what justifies our language of praise and adoration. Jews (and Christians) do not characteristically want to say nothing at all about God. The God of the Pentateuch is personal and providential. How can such a way of speaking be justified?

Whenever, in his commentaries, questions about knowing and naming God arise, Philo turns to the example of Moses. He returns again and again to Exodus 3, the burning bush, to Exodus 20 where Moses ascends the mountain of Sinai and "approaches the dark cloud where God was", and to Exodus 33 where Moses asks to see God's glory, all texts of epistemological salience for Philo. Indeed Exodus 3 and Exodus 33 receive prominence not just in Philo but amongst the Rabbis and early Christian theologians as instances of divine self-naming.

Philo, writing in Greek, routinely understands the "I Am Who I Am" of Exodus 3 metaphysically—God, for Philo, is the Existent (*to on*). It is not, says Philo in an important expansion on the text, "the nature of Him that IS to be spoken of, but simply to be". We need to remember that Philo's exegesis—even when, as here, it sounds most metaphysical—is driven by his understanding of who God is in his Scriptures, the Creator of all that is. Here is another of his comments on Exodus 3:

> . . . . "I am He that IS" (Ex. 3.14), which is equivalent to "My nature is to be, not to be spoken." Yet that the human race should not totally lack a title to give to the supreme goodness He allows them to use by

---

[19] Dillon, *The Middle Platonists*, p. 155.

licence of language, as though it were His proper name, the title of Lord God of the three natural orders, teaching, perfection, practice, which are symbolised in the records as Abraham, Isaac and Jacob. (*de. Mut..* II.12–13)

A God who creates heaven and earth cannot properly be named in earthly words; however, "by licence of language" that same God has given names to us by which God may be named. The name Philo believes is given to Moses in Exodus 3 is, curiously, "the Lord, the God of Abraham, and Isaac and Jacob". This, Philo believes, is the name that is the name for all generations, which indeed incorporates the "generations" of the people Israel.[20]

To recap, the doctrine of creation *ex nihilo* is a biblically-inspired piece of metaphysics—not a teaching of hellenistic philosophy pure and simple, but something that arises from what Greek-speaking Jews found in their scriptures. Because God is "creator of all that is" and not a creature, the divine essence is strictly speaking unknowable to us. It follows that God is unnameable in any way that might suggest a delineation of the divine essence. This philosophical and rational constraint paradoxically means that primacy in matters of naming God must be given to revelation and to scripture. Indeed apparent philosophical inconsistency on the question of the pre-existence of matter in Philo and the early fathers may arise because they are driven not by philosophical premises and concern for cosmological consistency but by the scriptures that they are exegeting. So for instance Clement of Alexandria (late second century) will mix Hosea with Isaiah, Psalms, and Jeremiah to extol the God who is not far off and who fills heaven and earth (Jer. 23.23). How this "filling" might be parsed philosophically is not his primary concern. But it becomes a concern for Christian writers who must explain how their God is not an adjunct of the natural world, but the one from whom all things have their being and on whom every thing in its creaturely reality entirely depends.

I have avoided thus far such terms as "negative theology", or "cataphatic" and "apophatic," as anachronistic to this early stage and also because I am puzzled over who is and who is not considered to be a practitioner of "negative theology"—usually not Augustine, for instance. But here is Augustine in the *de Trinitate*:

we should understand God, if we can and as far as we can, to be good without quality, great without quantity, creative without need or necessity, presiding without position, holding all things together without

---

[20] Hebrew scholars take Exodus 3.15 to be saying that the Tetragrammaton is the name "for all generations". Elsewhere Philo, like Aquinas, identifies "He that Is" (*ho on*) as serving as God's proper name (Cher. 27 ff). There is no reason, of course, why more than one "licensed" name could not serve in this way. None of them, from Philo's point of view, is adequate.

possession, wholly everywhere without place, everlasting without time, without any change in himself making changeable things, and undergoing nothing. Whoever thinks of God like that may not yet be able to discover altogether what he is, but is at least piously be on his guard against thinking about him anything that he is not. (*de Trinitate*, Book V, Prologue)[21]

Augustine never tires of saying that what God "is" we shall never know, at least not in this life. These negations are not the collapse of reason in despair but rather its proper deployment in the face of the One who is the source and cause that all that is. By Augustine's time this is firmly linked in Christian thought to *creatio ex nihilo*.

As with Philo, it is the doctrine of *creatio ex nihilo* that lies behind this crisis in speech. Indeed, as Carol Harrison has persuasively argued, it is this teaching and not random sampling of Plotinus that delivered Augustine from the materialism which still held sway in his thought when he was a follower of the Manicheans.[22] It is this developed sense of divine transcendence that enables him to see that God is at once entirely beyond our understanding and yet most intimately present—closer to me than I am to myself. It is this that enables him to affirm that "all that is" is Good, and that God can never be thought of as a spiritual overlord of a debased material realm. God, for Augustine, is Being Itself and the source of all being. In this teaching "souls" and "angels" are just as much creatures as dung beetles and dinosaurs. This point is expressed in the Nicene Creed by confessing God to be "Maker of heaven and earth, and of all things visible and invisible."[23]

If Augustine's *Confessions* show the same dynamic with regard to knowing and naming God as Philo then one would expect soon to find Moses and the "I AM WHO I AM" of Exodus 3—and we do. Shortly after his conversion, and while with his friends at Cassiciacum, Augustine reads the Psalms. The final version of Psalm 4, he tells us, wrung a cry from the very depths of his heart. Here is his full comment in the translation of Maria Boulding:

> *In peace! Oh. In Being itself!* What did it say? *I will rest and fall asleep.* Yes, who shall make war against us when that promise of scripture is fulfilled, *Death is swallowed up in victory?* In truth you are Being itself,

---

[21] St. Augustine, *de Trinitate*, Book V, Prologue The Trinity, trans. Edmund Hill. OP (Brooklyn, NY: New City Press, 1991), p. 190.

[22] See Carol Harrison, *Rethinking Augustine's Early Theology* (Oxford: Oxford University Press, 2006), Chapter 4.

[23] On this see Rowan Williams, "God for Nothing: Augustine on Creation", *Augustinian Studies*, Vol. 25 (1994), pp. 9–24.

unchangeable, and in you is found the rest that is mindful no more of its labours (*Conf. IX.11*).[24]

For many modern theologians to answer the question "Who are you, God?" with "Being itself" is worse than no answer at all—the Christian theologian trading divine insight for dubious Greek metaphysics. But this is to misunderstand Augustine for, as Maria Boulding has pointed out, *idipsum*, "the Selfsame", is linked by Augustine here and throughout his works with the mysterious name for God as given to Moses from the burning bush—the "I AM WHO I AM". Augustine may well have found the notion that God is "being itself" in Porphyry, the student of Plotinus, some of whose works he read in Milan, but he need not have done. The idea was freely available in the works of earlier, Christian Middle-Platonists, and embryonically at least in Philo, whose work was well known to Augustine's mentor St. Ambrose.[25]

As mentioned, we do not find a creator God in either Plato or Aristotle. We do find a One which is the source of the Many in Eudorus, an Alexandrian philosopher of the first century BCE, but why should we not think Eudorus already influenced by Hellenistic Judaism, given the large and literate Jewish population of his Alexandria? Certainly by the time we get to Porphyry and Plotinus in the late third century, we must take into account Numenius of Apamea, a second century "middle" Platonist and an acknowledged influence on Plotinus. Numenius has a Platonic scheme with a First God and a Demiurge—the First God he calls "Being Itself" (*ho on*). This goes far beyond Plato who makes no such claim for God. What is remarkable is that Numenius was self-confessedly interested in and impressed by the Jewish writings, and it is these, and especially the Septuagint of Exodus 3.15, that seem the likely source of his name for the First God ("Being Itself"—*ho on*). Numenius credits Moses with receiving the "revelation" that the First God is "Being".[26] Even were we to leave Numenius out of the picture it is now widely accepted that Plotinus knew the works of Philo who, as we have already seen, already in the first century spoke of God as "the Existent" and did so on the basis of Exodus 3 and the request of Moses for a name.

---

[24] Augustine, *Confessions*, trans. Maria Boulding, OSB (London: Hodder & Stoughton, 1997). Henry Chadwick translates "in peace . . . the selfsame. . . ." as "I will go to sleep and have my dreams".

[25] I have written about Augustine on these matters in more detail in "Augustine on Knowing God and Knowing the Self" in *Faithful Reading: New Essays in Theology and Philosophy in Honour of Fergus Kerr O.P.*, ed. Simon Oliver, Karen Kilby, Tom O'Loughlin (London: T&T Clark, 2012), pp. 61–74.

[26] This is suggested by Miles Burnyeat in his "Platonism in the Bible: Numenius of Apamea on *Exodus* and Eternity" in *The Revelation of the Name YHWH to Moses: Perspectives from Judaism, the Pagan Graeco-Roman World, and Early Christianity*, ed. George H. van Kooten (Leiden: Brill, 2006), see especially pp. 158–160.

Nor can this identification be simply attributed to Philo's Hellenism. The Palestinian Targums Pseudo-Jonathan (14a), written in Aramaic, glosses the *"ehyeh esher ehyeh"* (I Am Who I Am) of Exodus 3.15: "He who spoke and the world came into being, spoke, and everything came into being."[27] This linking of the "I AM WHO I AM" of Exodus to the Creator of the book of Genesis is the more interesting since the Targumist is likely to have realised, as Philo and most of the Christian fathers did not, that the Hebrew "I AM WHO I AM" ("ehyeh esher ehyeh") is a pun or play on words on the Tetragrammaton (*YHWH*), which gives the appearance of a form of the verb *"to be"*.

I do not think we should complain that the wholesome streams of Judaism and Christianity are here contaminated by Hellenistic philosophy. This is a discredited exercise and Robert Wilken is surely right in saying that we should speak now not about the hellenization of Christianity but the Christianization of Hellenism.[28] And nowhere more so than in the distinctively Jewish and Christian teaching of *creatio ex nihilo* and the reflection on Being and participation attendant on it.

Judaism and Christianity precipitated a revolution in western metaphysics. *Creatio ex nihilo* excludes both an Aristotelian cosmology in which the world and God necessarily co-exist and imply one another, and Neo-Platonic emanationism in which the world flows unconsciously and ineluctably from the Godhead like rays of light from the sun. Creation for Jews, Christians and (when they appeared on the scene) for Muslims is intentional. God wills to create. It is a gift. Also ruled out is the notion of a "descending hierarchy of existence" in which the more "material" a being is, the further it is from God. The distinction, as David Burrell often reminds us, is between the Creator and Everything Else.

It may appear that these metaphysical reflections are remote from the array of living creatures that unfold in all their mosaic "this-ness", their place and particularity, in the San Clemente apse, but I would suggest, quite the contrary.

In the Septuagint version of the famous "fiery furnace" story of the Book of Daniel (purged from modern Protestant translations but still to be found in Catholic bibles) the three servants of God—Shadrach, Meschach and Abednego, thrown into the flames by King Nebuchadnezzar—begin to sing, glorifying and blessing God and invite "all things the LORD has made" to bless the LORD: "Angels of the Lord! all bless the Lord", heavens, waters, sun and moon, showers and dews, fire and heat, night and day, frost and cold, lightening and clouds, mountains and hills, springs of water, seas and rivers, sea beasts, birds of heaven, animals wild and tame, sons of men, servants of the

---

[27] Similar glosses are found in other Targumim.

[28] Robert Louis Wilken, *The Spirit of Early Christian Thought* (New Haven, CT; Yale University Press, 2003), p. xvi.

Lord, all are enjoined to bless the Lord for "he has snatched us from the underworld, saved us from the hand of death . . . for his love is everlasting" (Dan. 3.51–90). This is a God of creation, salvation and justice, and with the Christian conversion of the "Lord who saves" into Jesus Christ, it is the God of the new creation captured on the San Clemente apse.

Creation is not something that happened to the universe long ago. It is not the distant accomplishment of a distant God. *Creatio ex nihilo* underscores the belief that God imparts the being of all created things, visible and invisible. The world is graced in its createdness which is happening all the time. In Christian understanding it is the Word through whom all things are made who redeems and renews all things—hinds and stags drinking from the waters of life—the new creation that embraces in its tendrils the nesting birds, the sheep and the shepherd, the sober bishop at his writings.

INDEX

Modern Theology 29:2 April 2013
ISSN 0266-7177 (Print)
ISSN 1468-0025 (Online)

CONTRIBUTORS BIOS

David Burrell, C.S.C., Theodore Hesburgh Professor emeritus in Philosophy and Theology at the University of Notre Dame (IN, USA), served as rector of the Tantur Ecumenical Institute in Jerusalem (1980), spurring sustained inquiry into comparative theology: *Knowing the Unknowable God: Ibn-Sina, Maimonides, Aquinas* (1986), *Freedom and Creation in Three Traditions* (1993), *Original Peace* (with Elena Malits,1998), *Friendship and Ways to Truth* (2000), as well as translations of Al-Ghazali: *Ninety-Nine Beautiful Names of God* (1993) and *Faith in Divine Unity and Trust in Divine* Providence (2001), followed by essays exploring *Faith and Freedom* (2004) and *Learning to Trust in Freedom* (2010), as well as a theological reflection on Job: *Deconstructing Theodicy* (2008), and recently, *Towards a Jewish-Christian-Muslim Theology* (2011).

Virginia Burrus has taught in Drew University's Theological School and Graduate Division of Religion since 1991. Her publications include: *The Making of a Heretic: Gender and Authority in the Priscillianist Controversy* (1995); *"Begotten, Not Made": Conceiving Manhood in Late Antiquity* (2000); *The Sex Lives of Saints: An Erotics of Ancient Hagiography* (2004); *Saving Shame: Martyrs, Saints, and Other Abject Subjects* (2007); and, co-authored with Mark Jordan and Karmen MacKendrick, *Seducing Augustine: Bodies, Desires, Confessions* (2010). She is past President of the North American Patristics Society, Associate Editor of the *Journal of Early Christian Studies*, and co-editor of the University of Pennsylvania Press series "Divinations: Rereading Late Ancient Religion."

Paul Gavrilyuk is Associate Professor of Historical Theology at the University of St Thomas, Saint Paul, Minnesota. He is the author of *The Suffering of the Impassible God: The Dialectics of Patristic Thought* (Oxford, 2004; Spanish edn. 2012; Romanian edn. forthcoming) and *Histoire du catéchuménat dans l'église ancienne* (Le Cerf, 2007; Russian edn. 2001). He also co-edited with Sarah Coakley, *The Spiritual Senses: Perceiving God in Western Christianity* (Cambridge, 2012; Polish edn. forthcoming).

John Hughes is the Dean of Chapel and a Fellow of Jesus College Cambridge, where he teaches philosophy, doctrine and ethics for the Faculty of Divinity. His book, *The End of Work: Theological Critiques of Capitalism* (Wiley-Blackwell, 2007) explored the relationship between theologies of labour, Marxism, and British Romanticism. He has recently contributed chapters to collections on Apologetics and Anglican and Catholic Social Teaching, and is working on a project on Creation and the Divine Ideas.

Jon Mackenzie is a PhD candidate at the University of Cambridge. His thesis explores the concept of human subjectivity as it arises within the theology of Martin Luther. By locating Luther's account of the human subject within the framework of a theology of place, the standard critiques of solipsism and individualism can be obviated, offering Luther as a valuable resource for a contemporary rendering of human subjectivity.

Vittorio Montemaggi is Assistant Professor of Religion and Literature in the Department of Romance Languages and Literatures at the University of Notre Dame, where he is also Concurrent Assistant Professor in the Department of Theology and Fellow of the Nanovic Institue for European Studies. Following degrees in theology and European literature, his research has centred on the relationship between language, truth and love. To date, his publications have focused primarily on Dante's *Commedia*, and he is co-editor with Matthew Treherne of *Dante's "Commedia": Theology as Poetry* (University of Notre Dame Press, 2010). His current research also explores the work Primo Levi, Roberto Benigni, Shakespeare, Dostoevsky and Gregory the Great.

Andreas Nordlander teaches philosophy of religion at the Centre for Theology and Religious Studies at Lund University, Sweden. Holding degrees in philosophy, theology and religious studies, his recent doctoral dissertation focused on nature and human subjectivity in phenomenology and Christian theology. In his current research he continues to explore the interface between theology and philosophy with regard to nature, life and mind; he is also editing a collection of original articles in philosophical theology to appear in Swedish.

Janet Martin Soskice is Professor of Philosophical Theology at the University of Cambridge and a Fellow of Jesus College. She is the author of *Metaphor and Religious Language* (O.U.P. 1984); *The Kindness of God* (OUP, 2008), *Sisters of Sinai* (Chatto and Knopf, 2009) and editor of *Feminism and Theology*, with Diana Lipton (OUP, 2003 and *Creation and the God of Abraham*, with David Burrell, Carlo Cogliati and Bill Stoeger (CUP, 2009).

Kathryn Tanner is Frederick Marquand Professor of Systematic Theology at Yale Divinity School. Her publications include: *God and Creation in Christian Theology: Tyranny or Empowerment?* (Blackwell, 1988); *The Politics of God:*

Christian Theologies and Social Justice (Fortress, 1992); *Theories of Culture: A New Agenda for Theology* (Fortress, 1997); *Jesus, Humanity, and the Trinity: A Brief Systematic Theology* (Continuum/Fortress, 2001); *Economy of Grace* (Fortress, 2005); and *Christ the Key* (Cambridge, 2010).

Rudi te Velde is Lecturer in Philosophy at the Faculty of Catholic Theology at Tilburg University; he also holds the Catholic Thomas More Foundation Chair of Philosophy and Christianity in the Department of Philosophy of the University of Amsterdam. His publications include: *Participation and Substantiality in Thomas Aquinas* (Brill 1995); *Aquinas on God* (Ashgate 2006); "Natural Reason in the Summa contra Gentiles", in Brian Davies (ed.), Thomas Aquinas. Contemporary Philosophical Perspectives (Oxford University Press, 2002); "Evil, Sin, and Death: Thomas Aquinas on Original Sin", in Rik van Nieuwenhove and Joseph Wawrykow, The Theology of Thomas Aquinas (University of Notre Dame Press, 2005). He is member of the Thomas Institute at Utrecht.

John Webster is Professor of Systematic Theology at the University of Aberdeen, and a Fellow of the Royal Society of Edinburgh. His recent publications include *The Domain of the Word. Scripture and Theological Reason* (T&T Clark, 2012) and *God Without Measure. Working Papers in Christian Dogmatics* (T&T Clark, 2012); his book On *Creation and Providence* will be published by Baker Academic in 2013.